The Indian Legal System

The Research Group

Zainab Lokhandwala
Raikamal Roy
Saika Sabir
Akhilendra Pratap Singh

The Indian Legal System

An Enquiry

Mahendra Pal Singh
Niraj Kumar

OXFORD
UNIVERSITY PRESS

OXFORD
UNIVERSITY PRESS

Oxford University Press is a department of the University of Oxford.
It furthers the University's objective of excellence in research, scholarship,
and education by publishing worldwide. Oxford is a registered trademark of
Oxford University Press in the UK and in certain other countries.

Published in India by
Oxford University Press
2/11 Ground Floor, Ansari Road, Daryaganj, New Delhi 110 002, India

ISBN-13: 978-0-19-948987-9
ISBN-10: 0-19-948987-4

Typeset in Adobe Garamond Pro 11/13
by The Graphics Solution, New Delhi 110 092
Printed in India by Nutech Print Services India

Contents

Tables

Figures

Statutes

1. Permanent Settlement Act, 1793
2. Charter Act, 1833 (3 and 4 Will. E. 85)
3. Caste Disabilities Removal Act, 1850 (Act no. 21 of 1850)
4. Charter Act, 1853
5. Government of India Act, 1858 (21 and 22 Vict. c. 106)
6. Indian Penal Code, 1860 (Act no. 45 of 1860)
7. High Courts Act, 1861 (24 and 25 Vict. c. 104)
8. Native Converts' Marriage Dissolution Act, 1866 (Act no. 21 of 1866)
9. Special Marriage Act, 1866
10. Societies Registration Act, 1869/Societies Registration Act, 1860 (Act no. 21 of 1860)
11. Indian Evidence Act, 1872 (Act no. 1 of 1872)
12. Indian Christian Marriage Act, 1872 (Act no. 15 of 1872)
13. Indian Contract Act, 1872 (Act no. 9 of 1872)
14. Brahmo Marriage Act, 1872
15. Scheduled Districts Act, 1874 (Act no. 14 of 1874)
16. Specific Relief Act, 1877 (Act no. 1 of 1877)
17. Negotiable Instruments Act, 1881 (Act no. 26 of 1881)
18. Easement Act, 1882 (Act no. 5 of 1882).

Cases*

* These have been arranged in the order in which they appear in the book.

Foreword

Professor (Dr) Mahendra Pal Singh, Dr Niraj Kumar, and their learned associates have done well in introducing problems of identity of the Indian common law jurisdictions in the studies of comparative law and jurisprudence. Professor Singh is one of the few law teachers to have successfully pioneered the traditions of learning, teaching, and research in comparative law in India, and in this work, he (and his colleagues) has preciously turned India itself into a comparative law terrain.

The Indian Legal System: An Enquiry puts me in the mind of the great little work of Shri Motilal C. Setalvad, which I studied as a budding law scholar. But Setalvad's Hamlyn lectures (Setalvad, 1969)[1] decidedly characterized Indian legal system as a common law culture and mainly traced continuities between the English common and Indian law. He expanded what might be termed 'constitutional common law'.[2]

---

[1] But see also, K.M. Sharma, 'Civil Law in India', *Wash. ULQ* 1 (1969): 1–39.

[2] This expression is a favourite one in American constitutional studies: see, for example, Henry P. Monaghan, 'The Foreword: Constitutional Common Law', *Harvard Law Review* 89, 1 (1975): 1–45; Abigail R. Moncrieff, 'Common-Law Constitutionalism, The Constitutional Common Law, and

This work, in contrast, wonders whether Indian legal system can be characterized as such. Its general, and welcome, conclusion is that 'the state legal system is a vibrant mix of several parallel operations, influences, importations, and mutations of features that originate in non–common law jurisdictions', and that it, in several cases, 'accounts for the operation of other legal systems, and as a result … may be termed as a mixed legal system'.

Indeed, it insistently asks whether a 'comprehensive regrouping of the Indian legal system is the need of the hour—one which will explore India's colonial legacy, the compendium of Western knowledge, as well as indigenous Indian legal practices to recast the Indian legal system'. The work in your hands thus poses a decisive and formidable question: decisive because it would explore both the hybridity and liminality of some non-state legal systems and formidable because it invites both historical and empirical research.[3]

The grievance that the pre-contact law and jurisprudence is much ignored is accentuated by this work. And it is useful to know (Chapter II is a significant curtain raiser) that the Indian legal culture remains hospitable to 'multiple legal systems'. This is equally true of the state as well as non-state legal systems.

The book valuably reminds us that very long before legal pluralism was discovered as theory, it was practised vigorously in the precolonial law in India. How far constitutional law and jurisprudence may have affected the practices of diversity and plurality remains an open question but certainly the demosprudential leadership of the Supreme Court (Baxi, 2016; 2017) insists upon the constitutional

---

the Validity of the Individual Mandate', *Boston University Law Review*, 92, 1245 (2012).

[3] Conceptually if all legal systems display a hybrid character, comparison always involves a study of the origins, types, and diversity of hybrid systems. Thus, the tasks of comparative law and jurisprudence are aggravated by the hybrid nature of concepts used in all legal systems. See, for a most recent demonstration, Paul T. Babbe, Hon T Orth, and Charlie Wong, 'The Honoré-Waldron Thesis: A Comparison of the Blend of Ideal-Typic Categories of Property in American, Chinese and Australian Land Law', *Tulane Law Review*, 91:740–88 (2016–17).

virtue of attaining the unity and integrity of India through plurality and not by perversity.

The main valuable message of the book is: 'Religion-based, caste-based, village-based, tribe-based, and trade/profession-based legal orders are not operative in India only at the periphery of the state legal system, but evidence clearly shows that they exist on the very centre stage of Indian society.' And 'these informal community-based systems are the first resort for most Indians who attach more legitimacy to these systems rather than the state system'; there are ample indications that 'the state legal system itself may sometimes be at the periphery of Indian society'.

While too much has been written about classical Hindu law and jurisprudence, not much is known to students, researchers, and learners about the law and jurisprudence of the Mughal period and the princely kingdoms, which have been left largely to historians of medieval period. And much of First Nations law and jurisprudence is left to the craft of ethnography and vocation of anthropology, with the unfortunate result that lawpersons remain parties to epistemicide (killing of native knowledges). The book does well at least to direct legal consciousness and conscience to importance of these formations. What also needs to be recalled is that the British administrators (the mercenaries and missionaries) knew far more intimately the situation of pre-contact law and jurisprudence than do present-day 'Macaulay's bastards'!

How to recover that knowledge is a main problem; and one needs, in teaching, research, and learning Indian law, to go beyond the accumulation of jurisdictions first by the Company Bahadur and then by the Raj. A real task of comparison begins not by a reverse epistemicide but by knowing how the British rule understood law–society interaction to the benefit of the empire and what role the common law principles may have played in the 'long walk to freedom'.[4] I refer here to the work on subaltern resistances and the doctrine of rule of law (Baxi, 1993; Thomson, 1975) (as a set of normative expectations) (Luhmann, 2014).

---

[4] I borrow here the title of Nelson Mandela's great autobiography (published by Little, Brown Book Group; New edition, 1995).

At this point, one must draw a distinction (implicit in this project) between the theory of common law, mostly residing in values and principles, and doctrines (Hamburger, 2008)[5] from the administration of justice in the formative contexts of 'imperial legality' (Benton and Lisa Ford, 2016; Baxi, 2017). The latter in administering justice according to the law did not respect what has been called the 'spirit of the common law' (Pound, 1921). If that spirit accentuated principles of fairness, equality, limited government, and justice (at least as implying the doctrine of rule of law), one does not find much of this spirit in the imposed domination of the British Empire. At best, the empire approximated benevolent despotism (Rawls, 2002).[6] How far the common law tradition was a benevolent despotism in United Kingdom and whether the common law as transplanted to the colonies, particularly to India, was an articulation of the common law's despotism remain crucial questions concerning the imposition of law (Baxi, 1985; Singha, 1998).[7]

Also at stake is the question both of identification of the common law and the task of drawing of limits of the common law, or the dialectic between judicial review and Parliamentary sovereignty. Perhaps, Lord Chief Justice Bridge put the matter well when His Lordship said: 'Now, for the court to revive or reimport a power within the sphere of the common law, the boundaries of which it is for the court itself to draw, is one thing. But to apply the newly rediscovered common law power to extend a purely statutory field of authority is quite another.'[8] It has also been suggested that the courts must recede when Parliament is shown to be attentive/responsive to a problem. Lord Reid famously said: 'Where Parliament fears to tread it is not for the courts to rush in.'[9]

---

[5] This is a stunning historical study of the evolution of principles animating the developments in the common law.

[6] See also Upendra Baxi, 'Global Justice and Deliberative Democracy', in *Democracy Realized, Documenta* 11, ed. Okuwi Enwezor et al., 113 (Osfildren-Raut, 2002)

[7] See also Benton (2016) and Baxi (2017).

[8] See *Siskina (Owners of Cargo Lately Laden on Board)* v. *Distos Compania Naviera SA* [1979] AC 210 (CA) 241 (Bridge LJ).

[9] *Shaw* v. *Director of Public Prosecutions* [1962] AC 220 (HL) 275.

Respecting both these views, James Goudkamp (2017) has recently examined a wave of enactments seeking to 'restate' the common law but has found, in effect, seeking (if not accomplishing) changes in it. His focus is on the Social Action, Responsibility and Heroism Act, 2015 (SARAH). Although the Bill was not much amended, it was abundantly critiqued in the House of Lords:

> SARAH was trenchantly criticised during the debates, especially in the Lords. Lord Pannick remarked said [*sic*] that he could not 'remember a legislative proposal that has been the subject of more sustained ridicule and derision'.... Neither, he said, could he 'remember a more pointless, indeed fatuous, piece of legislation'.... Numerous retired Law Lords launched withering attacks on SARAH. Lord Walker of Gestingthorpe remarked that he was 'genuinely shocked by the low standard of draftsmanship in the Bill—presumably it was prepared by government lawyers'.... Lord Hope of Craighead derided SARAH as 'half-baked'... Lord Brown of Eaton-under-Heywood described SARAH as being 'objectionable'... 'absurd'... and its enactment 'a waste of legislative time'... Lord Woolf referred to certain provisions of SARAH as 'very worrying'... Lord Lloyd of Berwick was most scathing of all. He said that SARAH 'was never properly thought out in the first place' and that one of its provisions 'looked like a clause drafted on the back of an envelope'... His overall assessment was that SARAH was 'inherently ridiculous' ... and 'so defective ... that the only feasible amendment is to take each of [its operative] clauses in turn and remove [them]'.... SARAH, he predicted, '[would] be treated with derision when it comes before the courts.' (Goudkamp 2017)

Few enactments, in Britain or in India, have received such withering criticism! But they demonstrate how difficult remains the enterprise of restating the common law, even as an act of pure legislative power or political expediency.

It is true of all countries born out of the modern self-determination principle that the law is more often imposed than received. Law is both historically and sociologically alien to most people in developing regions. While this work addresses some aspects of the alienation (and indeed some steps taken to mitigate this) the larger concern remains: *How to decolonize legal consciousness?* This already presupposes two things: (*i*) that this feat is doable and (*ii*) it is altogether desirable.

On both these questions, opinions may significantly vary among the constitutional elites, on the one hand, and, on the other, among the dispossessed, disadvantaged, and the disenfranchized classes of Indian citizens. Charting out a middle path, this work invites attention to the contours of what a truly decolonized legal consciousness may look like. This is a huge and worthwhile challenge, and I hope is further engaged by an anguished constitutional conversation.

Upendra Baxi
Emeritus Professor of Law
University of Warwick, UK, and University of Delhi, India
September 2018

Preface

The book is part of a larger project undertaken to understand the nature of the Indian legal system in a comparative perspective. The Indian legal system is generally taken to be an extension of the common law system of England. Apparently, it may be justified because in the broader classification of modern legal systems most of the former colonized countries are classified as either common law or civil law systems, based on the system of the colonizing country, irrespective of their diverse backgrounds and even current realities.

In the course of learning and teaching law for nearly six decades, and particularly teaching the course on the Indian legal system at the University of Delhi, India, for over three decades, the history of our legal system was traced only from the creation of the East India Company in England and its entry in India in early seventeenth century. I was always hounded by the question whether we did not have any indigenously created and evolved law and its administration in India, despite having an unbroken history of over 4,000 years during which the country was governed by several empires, some of which had massive geographical boundaries and existed for centuries. Did they not have any legal systems that left behind any trace or impact in the psyche and social and political lives of the people who lived by or under them, while the British, who subject to several exceptions, ruled India effectively for less than a century? Later, Professor Baxi introduced the idea of state and non-state legal systems in a course at the University of Delhi, which primarily emphasized on the extant tribal and other community legal systems within the country.

Although in the course of teaching and learning historical and sociological jurisprudence, discussions related to the more funda-mental issues pertaining to the relationship between the law and tra-ditions of the people came up, it was hardly explained with reference to or in the context of our own legal system. Later, some exposure to Western societies both in the common law and civil law systems, and experience with the efficiency and efficacy of laws and the legal system in normal course without apparent use of force or its instru-ments, led to my connecting the observance of law to internalized processes, which results not so much from force as from the social and political background of a society in which a legal system evolves. Does the common law system, which is assumed to have constituted our current legal system, have a similar background in India as it had in England, or where it was taken by the British to be applied primar-ily to British or European people as in the United States, Canada, or Australia? If this query is answered in the negative, naturally we cannot establish that the degree of bond between the people of India and their law and the legal system will be the same as that of people in England or in the West with their legal systems. Consequently, the borrowed or imposed legal system cannot work or operate as effectively and efficiently as it works in the country of its origin. In that situation, the question arises whether we should return to pre-modern Indian system of laws or we should bring greater harmony between people's behaviour and the laws by which they are governed. It may be a difficult process, but relying on our Constitution as our indigenous product, we may in the course of time establish greater harmony between the habits and behaviour of the people and their laws and legal system.

These issues have been quite prominent in my mind for some time, which I have been raising with my academic colleagues and students from time to time in the hope that they will be taken up for investigation by someone, if not by me. They have engaged me not because of any nationalistic ideology or the desire to return to our precolonial past but with a view to examine and promote the efficiency and effectiveness of our current legal system in the light of what the historical and sociological jurists and legal thinkers as well as the anthropologists, sociologists, and others engaged in establishing the relationship between the society and its law have propounded.

I am glad that Professor Ranbir Singh, vice chancellor, National Law University, Delhi, India, has given me the opportunity to run the university's Centre for Comparative Law equipped with excellent infrastructure and assistance of a researcher of my choice, where besides running the two courses on comparative law, I could have the opportunity of making a beginning on this long-standing project on the nature of the Indian legal system. I express my sincere thanks to him. I also acknowledge my sincere gratitude to Professors Werner Menski and B.B. Pande for their valuable suggestions for improving the initial draft. Dr Niraj Kumar, my colleague at the university, by his association with the centre has been a big support in running the courses as well as this project. I am not sure whether the project would have ever taken off if he were not associated with the centre. I am grateful to him for his association with the centre and hope that he would take project to its logical conclusion even in my absence. Initially, Dinesh Singh followed by Kanika Gauba and finally Akhilendra Pratap Singh were of great assistance in running the courses as well as pursuing this project. I am very thankful to them too. Finally, Professor Helmuth Schultze-Fielitz triggered the project by successive grants for two years from Schultze-Fielitz-Stiftung, Berlin, Germany. He has helped me by way of similar grants in the past also. I shall always remain grateful to him. The grant was almost exclusively utilized for payment to researchers employed for executing the project. Among them I express my sincere thanks to Raikamal Roy, Saika Sabir, and Zainab Lokhandwala, who by their imaginative planning and distribution of work have brought the project to the stage of production of this book. Pasquale Viola, a PhD scholar from Italy, has also taken keen interest in the progress of the project. I sincerely thank him and all others who have directly or indirectly associated themselves with this project.

I hope the concerned persons will read the book with interest and make their suggestions and critical comments for giving the project a direction that helps in making our legal system efficient and effective.

Mahendra Pal Singh
National Law University, Delhi
September 2018

Acknowledgements

The initiation of this project and the production of this book have been possible because of an unconditional financial grant by Schulze-Fielitz-Stiftung, Berlin, Germany, presided over by Professor Helmuth Schulze-Fielitz, to whom I was introduced by my long-standing friend Professor Helmut Goerlich. But for this grant, the project would have never taken off. On behalf of the Centre for Comparative Law, my colleagues at the centre, and researchers engaged in the project, and my own, I express my sincere thanks to Schulze-Fielitz-Stiftung and its president, Professor Schulze-Fielitz, and also to Professor Goerlich. I am also equally thankful to National Law University, Delhi, India, and its vice chancellor, Professor Ranbir Singh, for facilitating the execution of the project in every possible manner. I hope the two institutions and their chiefs will continue to support the project in future too.

Mahendra Pal Singh
National Law University, Delhi

Summary of Arguments

Legal, anthropological, and historical literature acknowledges the undisputed presence of multiple legal traditions in India, but the existence of uniform laws applicable to all citizens questions plurality at some levels. The existence of multiple non-state legal traditions alongside a proclaimed formal state legal system certainly poses a challenge to the common law identity of the Indian legal system. This also necessitates extensive research on a diverse set of legal traditions in India. Hence, the Centre for Comparative Law, National Law University, Delhi, India, has conducted research on exploring the nature of the Indian legal system. Schulze-Fielitz Stiftung, Berlin, Germany has sponsored this study to conduct research on the following broad areas:

1. Understanding the nature of the Indian legal system outside its definition as a singular system, and include non-state legal systems (such as tribal and customary laws).
2. Identifying alignments between Indian legal practices and those other legal orders that have emerged from the process of unification of several legal systems.
3. Creating a theoretical knowledge base (from an interdisciplinary perspective) on the prevalence of non-state legal systems notwithstanding the promise of uniform state law.

4. Understanding the relevance and role of non-state legal systems in pluralist societies such as India.

Through this book we present our research and findings on some of the aforementioned issues. These four broad areas of research presuppose that the identification of Indian legal system with the English common law system uncritically accepted colonial practices of British India. It is historically acknowledged that colonialism and law share a reciprocal relationship, where law was used for the expansion of colonial rule and was not an accurate reflection of the needs of the society. When common law was introduced in India by the British colonizers to better integrate the Indian legal system, they did not refer to the prevailing legal practices of the time. Neither was it an exact appropriation of common law as understood in England. We argue that this is an underlying cause for the gap between state legal system and the practices of the people. This is arguably the reason behind preference for non-state legal practices among several communities in India, despite there being a formal state legal system in existence.

A brief history of the legal universe in India prior to British incursion shows the diversity of legal practice in precolonial India. While we acknowledge that the legal system in precolonial India was diverse, we primarily focus on some prominent legal systems, particularly, the legal systems of the Mughals, the Marathas, and some southern Indian kingdoms. A brief history of legal systems under these dynasties contributes to the understanding that Indian legality was well established before the advent and the attempted transformation by the British. The existence of sophisticated precolonial legal systems shows that the lack of reference to these structures while transplanting common law into India by the British and its continuation after Independence was an oversight, which has had significant impact on contemporary India. This impact is manifested in the incongruency between the state legal structures and the social reality of the people, who continue to favour traditional, non-state legal practices over approaching state legal apparatuses such as the hierarchical courts of law to settle their disputes.

When British colonizers took over the Indian polity, there was a certain degree of legal consciousness in the society, if not in the form recognized by the British. Hence, the establishment and growth of common law in India was only a gradual process that was further strengthened by establishment of certain kind of dominant legal apparatus over the eighteenth, nineteenth, and early twentieth centuries. In post-Independence India, the Congress leadership and other stakeholders decided to continue with the common law system, with no empirical support or verification of the hypothesis that the common law system was best suited to Indian conditions. This decision was driven by a specific state ideology of being modern, which, among other things, could be achieved through a uniform legal system. Events and developments in the transitional phase, 'from colonial to postcolonial', strengthened the foundation of the common law system in India. These explorations lend significant insight into the normative basis for the acceptance of common law in India. Hence, we argue that no empirical study was conducted that proves that the common law model would fit India best. This, according to our research, gives scope for certain exceptions and contradictions in the operation of the Indian legal system. What we see today is a continued reliance on both state and non-state legal systems and a hybrid muddle of state-sanctioned exceptions to uniform law and unrecognized, yet socially legitimate, traditional legal practices based on customary law of communities and tribes.

We then move from generals to specifics in making an assertion about the limitations of the state legal system in India. Personal laws, tribal laws, and informal community practices are three broad areas that provide evidence to the claim that non-state legal systems in India prevail despite the promise of a uniform state law. We further strengthen our arguments by including examples of such alternative legal traditions and practices that function in independent India.

Although an absolute picture of the Indian legal scenario would call for a more detailed empirical analysis, through this research we identify the problematics of positioning the Indian legal system under the common law family. Marking allegiance to the common law family not only gives a decidedly singular identity to the plural legal universe in India, it also ignores and excludes legal practices outside the common law system. It is argued that legal systems cannot be seen in isolation from the cultures of groups whose affairs they regulate. Excluding non–common law understandings of legal practices in India leads to a selective and partial understanding of how the Indian legal system operates in its totality. This can, in turn, repeat several historical wrongs.

Sociologists of law repeatedly draw attention to the relationship between law and society. While some argue that society cannot exist without legal order, others claim a fundamental, defining characteristic of being human is to be lawful. And extension of these claims, made by sociologists such as Émile Durkheim (*The Division of Labour in Society*, 1933) and Eugen Ehrlich (*Fundamental Principles of the Sociology of Law*, 2001) and historians such as Henry Maine (*Ancient Law: Its Connection with the Early History of Society, and Its Relation to Modern Ideas*, 1861), is that specific social structures must have specific legal orders. For example, for Durkheim, pre-industrial society had legal orders with severe physical penalties for offences, while industrial society had legal orders with less severe penal sanctions. For Maine, traditional society was characterized by legal system governed by status, and modern society was characterized by legal systems governed by contract. In fact, for Maine, transition to contract was the key feature of arriving into modernity.

While all these claims have been critiqued in some measure or other, what they demonstrate is that through the history of knowledge and that of the social lives of people, law and society have an unmistakable and tenable relationship. This leads us to examine those societies where law seems to be divorced from social reality. As we will demonstrate through the course of the book, the people of India either ignore or are oblivious to state law in favour of informal and traditional legal practices, which they find to be more synonymous with their cultures and their everyday lives, or practice a mix of state and non-state law in the management of their disputes. It is in a small and select percentage of the Indian population that state law is the first and the primary system for maintaining social order.

Such situations are not as unique as one would imagine. Even in sixteenth-century Europe, unofficial, and by that definition, non-state legal systems vied for representation and recognition. The people, confronted with alien rule, saw themselves fighting to retain their legal cultures amidst sudden and large-scale social transformation that threatened to bring to an end to their customary practices. However, such situations *are* unique to those nations where foreign systems of rule, with no reference to local realities, have threatened to displace indigenous structures, as was arguably, albeit partially, the case in India. The reasons for the acceptance of transposition of foreign systems into indigenous territory are many and diverse. In India, the elite who colluded with colonial powers, an English-educated middle class, and an internalization of criticisms of tradition and pre-industrial modes are some of the factors that contributed to the acceptance of the 'modern' legal system introduced by the British. However, underlying this superficial acceptance was a significant section of the population that did not agree to the supremacy of the common law system. This was also due, in part, to the exceptions that the British themselves made in India, and the deviations they themselves followed from the common law system as it emerged in Britain.

Our hypothesis of why the state legal system in India is at a distance from the people's preferences can then be presented as such:

1. Legal systems emerge from the societies which they regulate. Keeping this in mind, the common law system is distant from the people's preferences in India since it was a colonial introduction and no indigenous systems or practices were referred to while it was being consolidated in nineteenth-century India. Independent India uncritically accepted the common law system on practical considerations, without conducting empirical research into the Indian legal reality of the time, continuing the errors of the colonial government.
2. If the Indian legal system is identified as predominantly a common law system, the history and the formation of the common law system in England too must be taken into consideration. On closer examination, we can see that the common law system in India did not much resemble the common law system in England, raising questions about the Indian legal system's identification with the common law family.

It is, at the same time, important to note that India *does* have several features of the common law tradition. However, it also has several major features that closely resemble other legal families, such as the codes and a general impetus to codify (as is the case in the civil law system), customary legal systems based on Hindu and Islamic law, and the presence of state-acknowledged systems of tribal law. Furthermore, the creation and exposition of law through juristic and interpretative exercises carried out by scholars, jurists, and philosophers is a feature in the civil law, Hindu, and Islamic legal families, which has found its way into the Indian legal system through routes other than the common law system.

Questioning India's common law allegiance need not entail its radical distance from *all* Euro-centric legal classifications. As Baxi (*Towards an 'Indian Legal Theory'?* 2016) argues, it is not fruitful to dismiss the West entirely, since 'progressive Eurocentrism' is inclusive of the 'non-European others'. For Baxi, a combination of Indian legal realities *before* colonialism, along with inclusive Western practices, are essential for arriving at an 'alternate Indian jurisprudence'—one which will be an epistemologically inclusive and empirically sound practice, keeping in mind indigenous developments as well as European learning. It is with this last objective in mind that we move to the third and final hypothesis of our research: A comprehensive regrouping of the Indian legal system is the need of the hour—one which will consider India's colonial legacy, the compendium of Western knowledge, as well as indigenous Indian legal practices to recast the Indian legal system.

Introduction

The common law system was introduced in India through British colonization. This legal system, which was primarily developed during mid-nineteenth-century colonial administration, has been accepted as something which is fully Indian, both intellectually and institutionally (Galanter, 1966). Ever since British colonization, an 'expropriation of law' has been claimed to take place, where the state through mid- and end-colonial era', and after Independence, became the *sole* architect of law, rendering other ordering systems secondary or obsolete (Galanter, 1968). Even after Independence, we continue to work with the basic laws given to us by the British, and the tools they used for making the law.

While it is often argued that common law in India, having developed on Indian soil, has incorporated certain Indian characteristics as well, it is still widely accepted that it formally belongs to the common law family. The development of the Indian common law system has also been compared to the import, use, and subsequent transformation of the English language. After 300 years of continuous flux, the spoken and written English language in India became different from its original form. In the same way, the legal system also considerably received an Indian touch; it was not a simple transposition of the common law model, but developed through admixture with an autochthonous background (Nariman, 2006).

However, both Nariman and Galanter identify the Indian legal system as primarily a common law system. Additionally, indigenous Indian law too transformed significantly at the hands of the British when it was being incorporated within the common law system, and the Indian 'touches' may not have been very Indian after all (Mani, 1989; Agarwal, 1994; Cohn, 1996). Even though common law in India might have acquired an Indian imprint after significant period of time, its imposition and implementation in colonial India led to long-lasting repercussions due to its significant incompatibility with existing Indian traditions. Nariman himself goes on to argue that '*Dharmasastras* [a primary precolonial legal-philosophical referent] did not visualise an ordered legal system, but they did conceptualise an aspiration—*nyaya*—which we now call justice' (Nariman, 2006, p. 2). Arguing on similar lines and specifically about the Hindu law, Menski says: 'While there is no such thing as one codified Hindu law embodied in the ancient texts, the idea of common sociocultural and ultimately legal tradition cannot be denied' (Menski, 2003, p. 163).

British legal mechanisms developed in their own historical contexts, and their institutions have their own, unique history of evolution in England, with little or no relation to India and its conditions. The colonizers imposed these very tools and institutions on India, with rudimentary reference to Indian traditional laws—Hindu and Muslim—and customary practices. In the aftermath of the Indian Rebellion (also known as the Sepoy Mutiny) of 1857, the British rulers engaged in the expansion of the imperialist project through law. They justified their more or less permanent rule by creating consensus that Indian natives were incapable of governing themselves (Mantena, 2010). It was under these circumstances that the British Empire came to invent the twin discourses of justice as equity, and justice as liberty. What is distinctive about the notion of equity as it historically developed in Britain is that, as opposed to the concept of justice under the law-natural (on which the Burkean discourse of imperial justice was based), the principle of justice as equity is grounded in the 'conscience' of the monarch (Mukherjee, 2012). This was hugely similar to the notion of justice as rendered via the common law tradition through the king in the medieval ages, and this was how it started to gain ground in the legal system of India.

In the early seventeenth century, the Crown, through a series of charters, introduced the judicial system functioning under its authority in the three Presidency towns (Bombay, Calcutta, and Madras). In the eighteenth century, with the strengthening of the British rule in India, a more uniform pattern emerged. A uniform judicial system called the Mayor's Court was introduced in all Presidency towns. Soon thereafter, by Royal Charter, the courts derived their authority directly from the Crown. Later in 1773, a system of appeals to the Privy Council was initiated, and this was also a historic landmark in the development of the Indian judicial system, because the Privy Council continued to function as the last court of appeal in India till 1949 (Misra, 1964). The principles of English law infiltrated the jurisprudence administered by the courts in the guise of rules of 'justice, equity and good conscience'. These principles were applied whenever there was an ambiguity about the application of existing customary or religious laws (Derrett, 1961; Jain, 2007).

Common law garnered its roots in India in numerous other ways, which include, first, support from the legal professionals. The common law–trained judges, lawyers of the Privy Council, and the higher judiciary in India were brought to bear the imprint of the English outlook and techniques upon the judicial administration of India. They were naturally disposed first to look to the legal tradition to which they had been 'accustomed for a lifetime' and only *secondly* to turn to continental tradition (Galanter, 1989). This factor, though perhaps imperceptible, was in no way insignificant in the reception of English law in India. Second, the doctrine of stare decisis, firmly entrenched in India after the passing of the High Courts Act of 1861, can be said to have precluded reference to other judicial systems (K. Sharma, 1969).

The Privy Council in *Waghela Rajsanji* v. *Shekh Masuldin* [1887] 14 IA. 89 held that 'justice, equity and good conscience' meant the application of the rules of English law if found suitable to Indian conditions. In a rigidly precedent-oriented judiciary, as India's, the effect of this decision, it is fair to assume, was to implicitly discourage reliance on principles of other judicial thinking, especially when the Privy Council itself did not commend such a practice.

In addition to these factors, a planned effort was made, beginning in 1833, to introduce English law through codification. The law commissions of 1833, 1861, and 1879 were directed to frame for India 'a body of substantive law, in preparing which the law of England was used as a basis' (Acharyya, 1914). Much of the common law introduced in India has been codified particularly on the suggestions and the recommendations of those law commissions. As Rankin observes: 'The influence of the common law in India is due not so much to a "reception," though that has played no inconsiderable part, as to a process of codification carried out on the grand scale' (G. Rankin, 1946, pp. 19–20). The basic statutes governing civil and criminal justice that have been codified are the Indian Penal Code 1860, Indian Evidence Act, 1872, the Code of Criminal Procedure, 1973, and the Code of Civil Procedure, 1908. The Indian Contract Act, 1872, the Negotiable Instruments Act, 1881, and the Transfer of Property Act, 1882 are also a few other legislations among a large number which have been codified based on the English common law system, and still continue to be applicable in postcolonial India. Through these developments, common law was incorporated into the Indian legal system.

Acceptance and Post-Independence Continuation of Common Law in India

Although much has been spoken by the postcolonial critics about the unsuitability of the British-style law in India, in practice it seems almost impossible to take an absolute departure from the English legal system. In the early phase of Indian Independence there were open discussions about the need for large-scale reforms of the existing official legal system (Galanter, 1972). However, these discussions had very little impact on the framing of the Indian Constitution. During both the Non-Cooperation Movement of 1920–2 and the Civil Disobedience Movement of 1931, attempts were made to boycott the official courts (seen as agents of British subjugation) and replace them with truly Indian tribunals that would be conciliatory in nature. The Gandhian publicists and scholars also criticized the existing law as 'complex system that promotes criminal mentality and crime' (Galanter, 1972).

It should be noted that Gandhi and his proponents were not entirely dismissive of the functioning of the Constituent Assembly; they, in fact, appreciated it as a logical outcome of the parliamentary programme that the Congress had pursued under Gandhi's leadership. Nevertheless, Gandhi believed that achieving parliamentary democracy was not a sufficient condition for attaining true swaraj. As opposed to a state-centred, top-down model, he proposed a 'concentric circles of individual swaraj, village swaraj, and parliamentary swaraj' (Pantham, 2008, p. 69). This, according to him, could be achieved through an absolute departure from the Western model of democracy and by its replacement with a panchayat-based or 'village-minded' constitutional framework (Pantham, 2008).

However, Gandhi's critique of Western modernity could hardly have an impact on the Congress leadership, who were in charge of the new nation (Dasgupta, 2014). In the Constituent Assembly, there were no proponents speaking for the restoration of Dharmashastra or other customary laws. All attempts made by the Gandhian traditionalists to reform polity based on village autonomy were also rejected by the Constituent Assembly with the only exception being the inclusion of a directive principle in favour of village panchayats under the Constitution (Galanter, 1972). By and large, the Constitution endorsed the existing colonial legal system.

'The reform of our legal profession and legal system does not lie in the way of "Village Panchayat Revival". It is a suicidal policy that will lead only to factions and anarchy' (Galanter, 1972, p. 41).

It would be wrong to argue that the Congress leadership and legal professionals of India were entirely against any kind of legal reform. The law professionals and the judges agreed that the existing legal system had several flaws, such as delays, complexities, and expenses, yet they believed that these flaws had nothing to do with the foreignness of the legal system. In response to the proposal of restoring panchayats as an indigenous legal system, they argued that restoration of indigenous or traditional systems was not a remedy to these problems.

When in 1958 the proposal for an indigenous system was forwarded to the First Law Commission of independent India, the commission had rejected the idea of making any fundamental change to the existing legal system. It recommended that at the most it would be possible to utilize some of the features of the judicial administration that were practised in the past in the form of judicial panchayats. In fact, the commission was critical of the assertion that 'the present legal system is alien to our genius' and argued to the contrary that there were commonalities between the present legal system and the traditional Hindu system, stating that 'even the ancient Hindu system comprised those features which every reasonable minded person would acknowledge as essential features of judicial administration, whether British or other...' (First Law Commission of India, 1958, Volume 1, p. 631). Later in 1979, the Eightieth Law Commission report, which discussed several aspects of judicial administration with specific reference to appointment of judges, reiterated that India was indeed a common law country (Eighth Law Commission of India, 1979).

Hence, the commission concluded that our legal institutions and most of our laws were similar to the common law of England in terms of universal governing principles. Common law in India developed simultaneously with its own discipline and practice (Khare, 1972), and since Indian lawyers were trained in the same system, the commission decided that the most convenient solution for us was to continue with that system; 'for over a century Indian courts have functioned like the British and the American courts, relying on precedents and treating them as authoritative' (First Law Commission of India, 1958, Volume 1, pp. 628–9).

It would not be very far-fetched to argue that the decision of continuing with a modern legal system based on common law was taken consciously, because the vision of achieving a modern, progressive society was closely tied to the idea of a society governed by law. Nehru and other elite nationalists claimed that it was not the modern institutions themselves but the compromised form in which these institutions came to India which was a problem. Hence, the solution according to them was to remove the impediments of colonial domination rather than rejecting the path of modernity (Dasgupta, 2014). Since the liberal conception of English common law is an intrinsic feature of modernity, it provided a significant base to the postcolonial nation state for establishing a universal modern regime of power. Despite the constant attempt at superseding the colonial rule, there is not much negotiation that took place here.

Some scholars such as Marc Galanter also supported India's common law identity on similar and a few additional grounds. Galanter argues that even the common consensus for the reform of the existing legal system did not imply a complete departure from the official law, but rather reshaping the indigenous laws in line with the official laws (Galanter, 1966). Moreover, it was also widely believed that common law principles have led to the development of fundamental human rights, and in *all* the countries that 'inherited the English legal system, the Common Law is the foundation of all laws and legal systems' (Venkatachaliah, 2013, p. 57). Adoption of these views, nevertheless, was based on feasibility and convenience and not on any sound scientific reason. Empirical research into the current state of legal affairs in India was not conducted, and the British system was perpetuated. Common law was accepted as *the* foundation of the Indian legal order, not considering the impress of several centuries of non-English developments in philosophy and law.

Implications of Identifying India as a Common Law System

While the state legal system confers itself the highest legitimacy, it is often superseded in practice by alternate systems of traditional and customary law (Department-Related Parliamentary Standing Committee on Personnel, Public Grievances, Law, and Justice, March 2016). Characterized by such non-observance of formal law, coupled with delays and deferrals in the state system, India's common law system is conventionally seen as falling short compared to its Western counterparts—the accepted notion being that law and society in certain communities in the West share greater congruency with each other than in India. In contrast to England and some of its former colonies, law in the European continent had developed under a different tradition traceable to Roman law, known as civil law, which has its own history and tradition of growth.

British introduction of common law in India could have potentially stunted India's own, socially conscious, and organic legal development. India's plural legal reality immediately questions its self-identification as solely a common law nation, raising related questions of research that can probe its resemblance to civil law systems instead. Menski argues that interpreting the Indian legal system as closer to a common law system was a misrepresentation, and clearly political (Menski, 2006). In this context, classifying India as a common law system potentially ignored certain characteristics Indian legal traditions could share with civil law systems.

India is often mistakenly portrayed as a common law country (de Cruz, 1999, pp. 125–6); hardly an adequate description of Indian law, because this ignores the complex mixture of various legal systems that constitute Indian law. This is, first of all, 'a political message, to the effect that India was, and continues to be, under British influence, rather than the French colonial model. Further, it flatters the élite perceptions of the colonial past as well as those sections of the present Indian élite who have imbibed the message that anything South Asian is intrinsically inferior' (Menski, 2006, p. 203).

It is also said that in view of India's peculiar history and demography, British rulers also introduced or received the civil law system in India in the form of codes as well as legal propositions such as justice, equity, and good conscience (Derrett, 1968, pp. 305–7). However, *no* existing Indian legal systems were referred to for making some of the Indian codes such as the Indian Penal Code. Macaulay even went as far as to say that the code could not be considered a 'digest of any existing system, and ... no existing system has furnished us even with a groundwork' (Sullivan, 2010, p. 147) for establishing and implementing the Indian Penal Code. Later chapters of the book deal with the nature and the intent of the Indian Penal Code in greater detail.

The Government of India has attempted to account for diverse legal practices to bring the state and the non-state legal systems more in consonance with one another. However, uncovering the nature of the Indian legal system becomes a necessary first step in informing such decisions. Upendra Baxi (2016) in one of his works on the possibilities of an Indian legal theory recalls a phase in 1970s–80s India when an attempt was made to develop an Indian legal theory. Professor G.S. Sharma and members of what Baxi calls the 'Jaipur School of Law' started thinking about 'an alternate jurisprudence for

India' (Baxi, 2016, p. 74), one which took 'universal' philosophies of law as well as India's particular legal thoughts into consideration.

> Regressive Eurocentrism stood for colonialism and imperialism and somewhat fake European Enlightenment values, which claimed all human rights and rule of law to be its sole products. In contrast, progressive Eurocentric thinkers ... eschew these Westphalian virtues and remain inclusive of the non-European others, and the contribution they have made (and continue to make) to spotlight, when not to resolve, some antinomies among law, power, and justice (Baxi, 2016, p. 79).

For Sharma, accepting Eurocentric ideas uncritically in postcolonial nations was not *really* postcolonial, rather, it led to neo-colonialism. To achieve an idea of alternate jurisprudence in India, it was not enough to simply continue what British colonialism gave to us, it was necessary to look at precolonial legal developments as well. However, Sharma acknowledged that Western legal theory and practice had much to teach us as well. He made a distinction between 'progressive Eurocentrism' and 'regressive Eurocentrism'. Sharma, by taking into consideration both Indian precolonial aspects and pertinent Western ideas, attempted to 'build a bridge between progressive Eurocentrism and "Eastern thought" in legal theory and social sciences' (Baxi, 2016, p. 79).

The affirmation of the British rule of law tradition in postcolonial understanding of Indian legal system and its gradual entrenchment into the Constitution tells us about the working of the postcolonial Indian state and government. There exists simultaneously in India one formal state legal system and an agglomeration of informal systems, which can be called non-state legal systems (Baxi, 1986). Studies as recent as the mid-1980s, such as the People of India project, find that the people of India often prefer to follow informal, non-state legal systems over the state legal system, creating a significant gap between law and society. If rule of law is to be understood as mutual adherence by actors of the state and its subjects to a common reference point of law (The World Bank, 2017), state law in India and the people's preferences are often inconsistent.

It is useful here to also note that several attempts (the latest being in March 2016) have been conducted by the Indian state to incorporate, integrate, and even occasionally subsume customary law within the fold of state law.

The March 2016 report on the findings of a parliamentary committee set up to inquire into possible avenues of synergy between the state and the tribal legal systems in India established the following:

1. It is officially acknowledged that the state legal system views tribal legal systems as competing systems of law, and attempts to mitigate this incompatibility.
2. Attempts at codification have been conducted within the rubric of state enforced Common Law to arrive at general principles of law across disparate tribal systems.

(Department-Related Parliamentary Standing Committee on Personnel, Public Grievances, Law, and Justice, 2016)

Existence and recognition of these parallel legal systems has also led scholars to argue the application of Common Law in India was historically, at best, partial. Newer avenues of imagining those parts of the Indian legal system that do not adhere to common law definitions need to be explored and a comprehensive regrouping along the lines of Örücü's description needs to be done. Other scholars are even critical of the term 'legal system', preferring the term 'legal tradition' instead to show that national legal systems are often a miscellany of different legal traditions that have historically influenced and continue to influence each other (Glenn, 2004).

Örücü says, 'It is essential to look at the constituent elements in each legal system and to regroup legal systems on a much larger scale according to the predominance of the ingredient sources from whence each system is formed' (Örücü, 2004, p. 363).

Hence, both the conceptions of 'law' and the 'Indian legal system' can be broadened by incorporating customary laws at the local level and tribal laws, as well as conceptions of *dharma*, *nyaya* (justice), and *niti* (ethics) in Hindu practice (Sen, 2009), and *din*, *siyasat* (politics), and *sharia* in Islamic practice (Alam, 2004), which may continue to influence praxis.

Chapter Overview

In this backdrop, we have conducted this research to (*i*) understand the nature of the Indian legal system outside its definition as a singular system, and include non-state legal systems, such as tribal and customary law, and (*ii*) provide theoretical arguments from an interdisciplinary perspective on the prevalence of non-state legal systems despite the promise of state law. We present the findings of our research through this book, divided into following parts.

In Chapter I, we briefly trace the history of legal systems in India, starting from the ancient period, not oblivious to the proposition that the broad divisions of ancient, medieval, and modern were colonial categories, with the main intention of dividing Indian history into distinctly communal phases. However, as phases of time in the chronology of Indian history, these divisions can be considered as basic organizing categories. We primarily focus on the Mughal polity to give a glimpse of what legality in precolonial India looked like. On examination, we see that the social bases for law and the state were acknowledged and embedded in the legal cultures of ancient India. It has also been noted that while being the dominant tradition, the Hindu legal tradition was in no way the *only* one, and institutions and systems which formed through this period reflected this plurality. Secular systems of law existed alongside those with religious bases.

Allowing for local customs to persevere and operate independent of larger systems was allowed both in ancient and medieval periods. Moreover, several characteristics of decidedly 'modern' legal orders, such as a body of professional legal practitioners, the notion of evidence, and the need for independent judges, among others, were present in India before the medieval period itself. British intervention attempted to give to the Indians again their law in taxonomies, organizational schemes, and interpretations more suited to their systems of knowledge. Under Mughal rule, both territorial integrity for law and order (such as in the case of the Rajputs) and the operation of traditional village panchayats were allowed without significant intervention. The immediate and sweeping changes the colonial administration envisioned were a far cry from the centuries of syncretic and slow social transformation precolonial India had been accustomed to.

The establishment and growth of common law in India introduced a certain kind of dominant legal apparatus over the eighteenth, nineteenth, and early twentieth centuries, with partially and significantly transformed understandings of India's legal plurality. While initial British attitudes in India may have been closer to that of a temporary trusteeship, after the revolt of 1857, a concentrated effort was made to revisit history and pinpoint instances of India's distance from modernity and inherent barbarism, ignoring centuries of pluralism. The conscious rewriting of Indian politico-legal history served as an ideological justification of the British Raj and contributed to reforming and reorganizing the Indian legal system, leading to newly fashioned Anglo-Muhammadan and Hindu laws. Customary and indigenous laws, while being partially accounted for, were also being refashioned and reorganized according to a new British hierarchy. In an ironic move, India's plural reality itself was leveraged as a necessary condition for the implementation of dominant and uniform law. Since a singular law of the land could not be identified, as Hindus and Muslims were governed by different sets of laws, common law was introduced as the law of the land. Post-Independence India continued the common law system without much change, keeping in mind the promise of uniformity and equality before law that a monolithic legal system would give to India.

In Chapter II, we explore the events and developments both in colonial and newly independent India that created India's contemporary identity as a nation relying in significant measure on both state and non-state law. We look at what can be considered the first pan-Indian drive to consolidate one, uniform legal system, which was continued in the years after Independence. However, this was rife with exceptions and contradictions, setting in place the conditions for the continued reliance on informal systems of law. What the exceptions and contradictions demonstrate is that despite colonial attempts at implementing uniformity, discriminatory processes ensured that separate standards of justice were practised not just for white people, but also several groups of Indians, contrary to the promise of equality before the law.

Ideological justifications centred on the *need* for British rule in India continued in the domains of education, culture, and religion. British rule in India was now a full-fledged enlightenment project—a mission to educate and to civilize. But the 1858 proclamation that formally declared British rule in India made several promises. It promised equal protection of law to all. It also promised the retention and respect of tradition and custom. The two, however, would be difficult to balance, and the British in India demonstrated great inequality in practice of law, contrary to their stated promise. The Indian Penal Code was one such 'gift' the British 'gave' to India, promising equality before law, notwithstanding that it has been argued that the Penal Code was implemented more to curb 'white violence' (racial violence targeted towards Indian servants and plantation workers) against Indian natives than to achieve pan-Indian utopias of uniform law and governance. British planters and other unofficial classes in India treated their Indian helpers with extreme cruelty. Despite the implementation of the Indian Penal Code, and other promises of formal equality which promised *all* individuals equality before the law, white offenders got away with minor fines. A proliferation of medico-legal literature systematically designed to prove the weakness of the Indian Constitution supported court proceedings in favour of the British offenders.

Several colonial statutes consistently upended the notion of 'rule of law', which British legal transformations in India promised. Classifications of communities into criminal tribes, special laws for backward areas, the semi-autonomous operations of panchayats, and state distance from personal law were all demonstrated instances of colonial *contradictions* to uniform law. The rhetorical stance of uniform and equal law was often made murky in its actual operation through the multiplicity of exceptions and contradictions. Moreover, early-Independence moves towards maintaining gender equity and equal rights to all were often selectively so, and demonstrated implicit biases in operation. Special constitutional privileges in India continued this general ambiguity between the claims of uniform law and the differential processes embedded in its details. While maintaining plural ethos was the purported claim of every one of these processes, they often displayed implicit discriminatory biases as well. It is not remiss to argue that postIndependence, several British colonial law and governance errors have been replicated.

In Chapter III, we attempt to look at broad themes or subject areas in which the state legal system does not operate at all or does not operate to the exclusion of other systems, such as personal law, tribal law, or other informal, community-based mechanisms, in addition to examining how the state itself often devolves some of its responsibilities to non-state instruments. In this chapter, we cite specific examples from case law and survey findings that help prove the fact that India is far from being only one state legal system, which is the common law system. Published survey findings and constitutional and legislative (ergo judicial) references to other systems shall be included in this chapter. These examples have been explored with the intention of showcasing that, unlike Western positivistic thinking, the state is not always the only legitimate source of law. Neither are state mechanisms the only authentic givers of justice, and the state's verdict is often not binding. While the previous section highlights several of such exceptions both in colonial and independent India, this section deals with examples and descriptions of alternate legal traditions and practices in India.

While so far it has been fairly clear that through history, state law has been at the top of the hierarchy of legal provisions, local-level functioning of law and order has largely been left untouched. While enforcing Islamic law in criminal matters, Mughal administration allowed regions and subsidiary kingships to retain their traditional systems in all other legal practices. Colonial India, too, accepted local, traditional, and customary practices in some version at the lower levels (not to mention considerable number of states in India did *not* adopt common law during the colonial period). Pan-Indian state laws perform a similar function of practising general statewide control while making a proliferation of exceptions at what it considers hierarchically lower levels, as well as different demographic categories. However, personal laws often escape even the general legal scrutinies laid down by the state legal system, as do several customary community practices. In the domain of tribal and other community customary traditions and mechanisms of law, on the one hand, the state has continued to attempt to widen its scope and incorporate more traditional practices under its sway, while, on the other hand, practices which are outside even of the accommodations and recognitions of the state have persisted in governing the lives of the people well after Independence.

Based on our findings so far, in the concluding chapter we present our analysis and arguments. Having successfully refuted the common claims about the singularity of the Indian legal system, in this section we further present our interpretations and clarifications on the legal scenario in India. We conclude with preliminary hypotheses on how and why there exists a wide gap between the state law and people's perception and observance of it. Arguably, in countries with colonial past, identification with one, unique, Western family of law is problematic. More so when the legal system occupies a hybrid position regarding its own genesis, its precolonial past, and its postcolonial continuities. Law and society largely believed to be or idealized to be in consonance with each other do not reflect any congruency. The book, in its attempt to sketch India's legal trajectory and the formation of its current legal situation, hopes to highlight the tensions between singular and plural, traditional and modern, and general and specific. It leads us to the future of uniform state systems, especially given the ideal of a uniform civil code stated in the Constitution. It raises important questions about the extent of state control into the lives of the people and the formation of international standards and their applicability to the Global South. It enables us to re-examine colonial 'gifts' and reconsider their present-day applicability.

Research Design

This book is the first of a series on aspects of what can loosely be called the Indian legal system. By this we mean the formal, state, common law system, as well as the informal, community-based, and non-state methods of social order and dispute settlement. It is within this universe that we have tried to locate the formation of the state legal system—the common law system—as the dominant legal system in India and its impact. Through this book we present our understanding of why the Indian legal universe cannot be classified under a singular common law identity. To arrive at this understanding, we began with the following normative premises:

1. India is primarily considered to be a common law country. Order and cohesion in India is maintained through one, formal system of law.

2. India's common law heritage was historically established and consciously continued after Independence, despite discrepancies on ground.
3. The Indian legal universe continues to be a hybrid of several (often conflicting) legal traditions, which constantly pose challenges to the common law state legal system to attain primacy.
4. There is a 'gap' between the law in statute and the law in practice. The law of the formal state legal system is often ignored, and local customary practices and traditions are used to reach binding settlements pertaining to resolution of disputes. In certain cases, informal adjudication systems are ignored too and offences escape register altogether.
5. India's Common Law heritage cannot be uncritically accepted.

We then tested these normative premises within the framework of interdisciplinary research, borrowing insights from law, legal history, sociology and social anthropology, and cultural theory. We approached these questions through a qualitative analysis of literature, data, and cases and historical records from both primary and secondary sources. Figure I.1 highlights main stages of research.

I
• Development of theoretical and logical framework to achieve research objectives

II
• Review of research design and expert consultations

III
• Qualitative ananlysis of data from the People of India project

IV
• Review of secondary literature
• Research on primary sources

V
• Reporting and disseminating research findings

Figure I.1   Stages of Research
Source: Authors.

We started with developing a logical framework by first, identifying the objectives of this research and then listing out possible verifiable concepts to be examined further. The next step was to identify the means through which such verifications could be possibly conducted to finally analyse how they contribute to the purpose of this study. Figure I.2 presents our logical framework. To create a preliminary theoretical base for this research, we began with building a comprehensive bibliography of all relevant books, journals, articles, and institutional reports that provide information on various aspects of Indian legal system—nature of Indian law, impact of colonialism, postcolonial development of Indian legal system, communities in India and their practices, and the functioning of the non-state legal system. We also collected relevant literature on broad theoretical understandings of legal systems in other jurisdictions as well as literature on the commonality between the postcolonial legal developments between these jurisdictions and India.

We understand that this project can be accomplished only through an interdisciplinary study of law and other social sciences. Hence, we have also included anthropological work on villages in India, tribes in

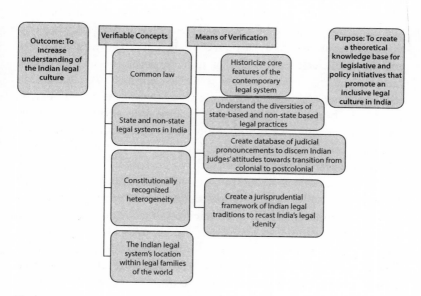

Figure I.2. Logical Framework of the Study
Source: Authors.

India, and other studies that document the practices both legal and customary of specific communities in India. The team then reviewed and documented the relevant literature, which was later used to substantiate the findings of this book.

After the initial phase of designing a framework for this research we had intensive review consultation. The first review meeting was held with our expert consultant, K.S. James, professor at the Centre for the Study of Regional Development, School of Social Sciences, Jawaharlal Nehru University. In this meeting, the team presented the preliminary design of the research and the parameters that we had set to accomplish the objectives of this study. Important suggestions were given on research methods, including specific advice on the limitations of conducting this study through empirical research. Given the constraint of time and resources, we were advised to approach the analytical question of 'why' there is a preference for other indigenous legal systems among communities through qualitative analysis. We intended to further strengthen our findings by analysis of secondary data available from the People of India project.

We had our second round of review meeting with Rukmini Sen at Ambedkar University, New Delhi. We received significant suggestions from her on our research design and the scope of the project. Sen confirmed that the best way to approach this research would be through qualitative analysis of secondary data. The team was also advised to include an analysis of judicial pronouncements—those cases where the customary law stands in conflict or side by side with the state law, organized phase wise, that is, select number of cases from both colonial and postcolonial time periods. Based on our expert reviews, we modified our research design and included examples from findings of *People of India* and relevant judicial pronouncements to support our research.

The team also took networking initiatives with stakeholders, such as civil society advocates for tribal rights, which were conducted to arrive at recommendations for reconciling the state and the non-state legal systems in India. P. Sivaramakrishna of SAKTI, who advocates for the greater rights of the Chenchu tribe in Andhra Pradesh and Telangana, over a one-day session, gave key insights into possible means to integrate informal tribal knowledge systems with state practices.

Initially, we began with survey data, that is, the published findings of the Anthropological Survey of India's People of India project. This was the preliminary testing ground to see how much, as per latest readily available and most comprehensive data, do communities in India rely on their traditional, informal, customary, and non-state practices to maintain social order. We conducted a review of survey findings to extract from the large universe of the survey (the survey claims to cover over 4,000 communities in India), those samples that could be studied in relation to their reliance on non-state legal practices in modern India. Five regions—Andhra Pradesh, Assam, Delhi, Himachal Pradesh, and Gujarat—were reviewed to find the prevalence of informal legal redressal mechanisms (community and caste panchayats or other informal organizations or institutions that work to settle disputes). These contributed to establish how historically there have been significant deviations from uniform law in India. Empirical research on the kind of legal practices that proliferate in India is crucial since no such research was conducted at the time of Independence and the consolidation of the new nation.

The regions were selected in accordance with four general territorial divisions of the country—north, south, east, and west. In addition to this, Delhi served as an urban foil to the predominantly rural data gleaned from the other areas. While these samples are selective, they provide glimpses into regionally and socially diverse communities, and their negotiations with state and non-state law. It is important to note that nearly every state reviewed, including predominantly urban Delhi, reported some degree of reliance on non-state law in matters of social order till as late as the 1980s (when this survey was conducted).

To form analyses and address research already conducted on related topics, we conducted a comprehensive review of secondary literature, focusing on literature from the disciplines of law and legal theory, history, sociology, and social anthropology. These formed the bases of our arguments and enabled us to determine the scope and the outcomes of the research.

We also conducted research on primary historical sources such as debates of the Constituent Assembly of India, state manuals, and district gazetteers to sketch a picture of state and law-making in colonial and modern Indian history. Secondary literature on precolonial legal systems also demonstrated that some such practices continue to influence legal reality in contemporary India. To effectively chart the official, attempted co-option, transformation, and even erasure of these practices under colonial introduction of the common legal system was a necessary component of our research. To form an understanding of state negotiation and formal (albeit selective) *acceptance* of legal diversity in India, we conducted research on primary legal sources. This involved research into legal documents such as the Law Commission reports, Constitution of India, statutory law, and specific cases dealing with legal pluralism in many forms. Qualitative content analysis on sources such as medieval narratives, Mughal and colonial administrative documents, Government of India documents, and case law was conducted to build a narrative on official discourse regarding law and order in India.

We present the preliminary analysis and findings of our research through this book. This book will serve as a knowledge base for both legislative and policy initiatives in India and other postcolonial nations with common legal and historical backgrounds. This book also lays down a roadmap for future research on the Indian legal system.

Explanatory Note on Terminology

In this book, we have used few key concepts in a very specific sense. We define the scope of this research by limiting our understanding and usage of these underlying concepts. The following terms have been used in the book, and require greater clarification for their use.

Adivasi

Adivasis in India represent those tribes that claim 'indigenous' Indian origin. Their 'original' status, however, is one that has been contested. Hardiman (1987) notes that according indigenous status only to tribes, and extending originary rights to land, excludes several historical realities. He argues many tribal populations too had a history of movement and migration and different economies of cultivation and sustenance, indicating that they too had perhaps, at one point of time, displaced other populations which inhabited the areas before them. However, Baviskar (2006) argues that despite contestations such as Hardiman's (and perhaps the members of the Constituent Assembly opposed to Jaipal Singh's claims of Adivasis being the original inhabitants of India), the word 'Adivasi' has not been dismissed in everyday language and usage, and that gives it a certain legitimacy of use. For Baviskar, 'The accretions of political and administrative usage over time have rendered the term a "social fact".… The combined weight of international and national law, administrative practice, and political internalisation by the people has imparted to the term a legitimacy that is hard to ignore' (Baviskar, 2006, p. 36).

For this book, the words 'Adivasi' and 'tribes' have been sometimes used interchangeably as there is significant overlap between the terms. However, when using Adivasi, it has been done largely in the context of those mainland Indian tribal communities who either claim to be Adivasis or have been called so in official state discourse.

Community

'Community', in sociological terms, broadly and generally means a small or large group of people associated with one another either on terms of kin–clan relations, space and region, religion, linguistic affiliation or other such markers of identity. In the People of India project, the editor K.S. Singh identifies a community as one that is described by a sense of 'we-feeling' (K.S. Singh, 2002), and it is this broad definition that we approach our understanding of community by.

Chatterjee (1993) argues that communities cannot be identified on the basis of 'determinate social institutions such as totemism or caste, or religious denomination' (p. 164), among others, rather they can also refer to symbolic cultural categories, such as language, the nation, and so on. Keeping in mind these understandings, our use of the term 'community' ranges across these meanings—sometimes regional, sometimes national, and sometimes based on kin–clan relations.

Legal System

A legal system may be defined as the legal rules and how they operate procedurally in the legal institutions of any country (Raz, 2012).

Contemporary comparatists have moved away from this narrow definition, stating that legal systems are the general 'juristic philosophy and techniques shared by a number of nations with broadly similar legal systems' (Winterton, 1975, pp. 69–70). This broad understanding really describes the notion of *parent legal families*, such as the civil law and common law families (David and Brierley, 1985). For purposes of identification, analysis, and/or comparison, categorizing jurisdictions into parent legal families (or the 'major' legal systems) means their classification under a *generic heading* by virtue of having similar characteristics (de Cruz, 2008, p. 3). These characteristics range from historical background and development, distinctive institutions, and ideology to predominant and characteristic mode of thought and its sources of law (Zweigert and Kötz, 1992).

There is hence an implicit acknowledgement of the inherent differences between legal systems within the same parent legal family, that is, *each legal system is unique* (Lundmark, 2012, p. 33). In the Indian context, legal systems are understood as any set of laws that apply over a given jurisdiction and the ways in which they are interpreted and enforced. For the purpose of this study we shall employ this term in its widest connotation, such that we do not exclude different varieties of legal systems owing to their mere non-resemblance to the state legal system; for instance, those systems that are more than just a means of adjudication of claims, dispute resolution and maintenance of social order, but also a way of expression and enforcement of a 'culture' (tribal legal systems and other traditional legal systems). This means that though the attributes that any state legal system possesses, such as, its rules, procedures, institutions, modalities, intents, purposes, and so on, might not be satisfied in the strict sense by a traditional legal system, yet this should not be a reason to rob it of its status as such.

Legal Tradition

A legal tradition is a legal system in its cultural context. Merryman (2007) writes that a legal tradition is a set of:

> deeply rooted, historically conditioned attitudes about the nature of law, about the role of law in the society and the polity, about the

proper organisation and operation of a legal system, and about the way law is, or should be made, applied, studied, perfected, and taught. The legal tradition relates the legal system to the culture of which it is a partial expression. It puts the legal system into cultural perspective. (Merryman, 2007, p. 2)

Any legal system will hence comprise many legal traditions and sub-traditions (Merryman, 2007) that have acuminated historically to contribute to the richness of any particular jurisdiction's legal heritage. These traditions provide an insight into the evolution of the legal system that exists. Notwithstanding that some scholars do not see a difference between 'legal system' and 'legal tradition' (Razi, 1959), it is still very useful to maintain that difference for better understanding of highly complex, pluralistic, or hybrid/mixed legal systems. Yet, in spite of such complexity, there seems to exist a broad generalization that most legal systems in the world exhibit traits and characteristics that are predominantly identified with any one or more parent legal families; whether or not this is true is sometimes irrelevant, as it is only a means of identification for commensurability with other jurisdictions (Glenn, 2014). Thus, multiplicity of legal traditions within any legal system, say, one that is identified as a common law system in a country such as India, should cause no confusion as such: as it only conveys the fact that this legal system is most closely associated with the common law parent family, and that the common law tradition is the most dominant one among other traditions that pervade its legal landscape (de Cruz, 2008, p. 5).

However, all this is in the context of the state legal system. The Indian state legal system is composed of several traditions, such as the common law tradition, Hindu tradition, Muslim tradition, indigenous legal traditions, and so on. However, aside from the state legal system, when we look at other legal systems, for instance, a tribal legal system, in that too we can see the influence, co-existence, and evolution of several legal traditions. Today, when the state's courts are to apply customary indigenous law, then, on the one hand, one can notice the percolation of the customary indigenous legal tradition into the state legal system, but, on the other hand, one can also notice the state legal tradition's percolation in the indigenous system.

Mixed Legal Systems

The concept of 'mixed legal systems' is closely associated with the 'parent legal family' scheme. However, it is a product of a slightly different approach to classification of legal systems. Contrary to the parent legal family approach, Örücü has proposed a reclassification of legal systems under 'family trees'. This approach starts with the assumption that all legal systems are mixed, either covertly or overtly, and they are grouped into respective legal families according to the proportionate mixture of the ingredients (Örücü, 2004). Today, each jurisdiction contains several overlaps, legal transplants, and mutations from other jurisdictions (Malmstrom, 1969). Having said that, 'mixed legal systems' or 'hybrids' refer to those systems whose constitutive elements bear no clear resemblance to any *one* major legal family. This is so because there is no predominance of ingredient sources within that system that can be traced to any one family tree (Palmer, 2001, pp. 2–9). In the context of the study, we refer to mixed legal system in the national context.

In the postcolonial context, the idea of 'mixed legal systems' becomes increasingly pronounced as there is always evidence of existence legal orders prior to the colonial period, along with drastic changes and customization of major legal systems in order to fit the requirements of the postcolonial nation state. India has, thus, been aptly classified as a mixed legal system by some comparativists owing to its common law, religious law, and customary law traditions (du Plessis, 2006). Hybridity, 'the co-existence of diverse and discrete legal traditions within a single jurisdiction' (Donlan, 2015, p. 157), is evinced through the fact that there exists, in a broad sense, not only a plurality of law and legal traditions but also, in the more narrower sense, an adherence to more than one parent legal system (or family tree as per Örücü's approach).

State and Non-state Legal Systems

The categories of state and non-state legal systems are one of the ways to organize diverse legal practices and traditions within a region into broad, indicative groups. This arises from the recognition in sociology and in jurisprudence of how most societies in the world refer to more than one legal order. These societies, 'in addition to the state law display kindred regulatory systems of norms, institutions and culture performing functions similar for social groups that the state law aspires to perform for the entire country' (Baxi, 1986, p. 66).

The national legal system, or state law, is categorized as the state legal system, while the amalgamation of local group regulatory systems, those which regulate the affairs at the level of the community, the village, or other such groups, are categorized by Baxi as the non-state legal system. Together, the state and non-state legal systems contribute to the understanding of the Indian legal system in its entirety. Examples of the non-state legal systems range from the erstwhile heterogeneous village panchayats to community and caste councils. Baxi's focus is to understand how formal and informal domains of law and order interact with one another to give possible answers to the persistence of legal plurality despite the uniformist tendencies of nations and their mechanisms of law and governance.

We too, through this book, intend to illustrate the various ways in which the formal and informal domains of law work within the territorial bounds of India, and why people's preferences do not always match with what is given to them in the form of state law. Without venturing into the veracity of calling the group regulatory systems as 'law', like Baxi, we intend to use the two terms as broad complexes of norms, and study the relationship between the two. This is not to say that there exist only two categories that neatly bifurcate the Indian legal system and that constituent systems must fall into one of the two categories alone. These are guiding definitions to look broadly at how formal and non-formal legal mechanisms interact with one another to create a plural legal culture in India.

Tribe

Tribes in India are classified based on grounds such as 'geographical isolation, simple technology and condition of living, general backwardness, to the practice of animism, tribal language, physical features' (Xaxa, 1999). However, not all tribes in India satisfy *all* these definitions. While tribes of peninsular India often show lower levels of technology, being relatively less isolated, tribes of north-east India, though considered to be inaccessible and isolated, are thought to have demonstrated greater technological self-sufficiency. This also led to the separation of mainland and frontier tribes into two separate schedules as per the Constitution of India (Statutory Commission Report, 1930; Kurup, 2008–2009).

Additionally, 'tribe' as a general concept has a different history than its application in India. The concept of 'tribe' as introduced in India was derived mostly from colonial ethnographers' accounts based on their encounters with various communities in India. Béteille (1986) argues that anthropological definitions of tribes were arrived at by looking mostly at 'simple, pre-literate, small-scale, and isolated societies in Australia, Melanesia, the Pacific Islands, North and South America, and Sub-Saharan Africa' (Béteille, 1986, p. 297) with little or no ethnographic input from India.

In this book, 'tribes' has been used as a term referring to those groups listed under the Fifth and the Sixth Schedules of the Indian Constitution. In addition to 'tribes' as an administrative category as listed in the Constitution, this book also refers to tribes that come under the definitive characteristics noted by Xaxa, although all the characteristics may not be simultaneously present in all the groups identified as tribes.

I

Tracing the History of the Legal System in India

When we speak of the legal system in India, there exists an amalgamation of different understandings of the legalities that have existed in the subcontinent over the years, introduced in several phases by different political structures and regimes. Looking at the relevance of this project, it is imperative to trace the dominant legal systems that existed prior to the East India Company, majorly within the expanse of northern India, and the kingdoms to the west, along with few overlapping examples of parallel legal systems existing in southern India.

We then focus on prominent examples of colonial legal change—largely the transformation that took place in Indian legal and political orders with the advent of the British. Indian legal orders gradually changed from a plural system with a protected place for indigenous legal authorities to one dominated by a type of state law that relied heavily and increasingly on English legal texts, sources, and procedures. The common view of many legal historians is that India represents an example of nearly complete displacement of an indigenous legal system by a European legal order. The long historical process is described by Galanter as the absorption of indigenous law into modern British law, and as Cohn states, a transition from an Indian status to a British contract (Cohn, 1996). Hence, it would be significant to explore the British engagement with existing legal practices in India and subsequent transformation of law of the empire and that of the Indian communities.

Historical Context

India's colonial period has generated an enormous body of scholarship whose underlying theme has chiefly been about how colonial ideals, values, knowledge, and power led to the 'transformation' of Indian society (Cohn, 1996). Implicit in the term 'transformation' lies the idea of what lay *before* and what resulted *after*. In this context, Indian legal history has traversed through several phases, where each period influenced the one that followed in terms of laws, legal methods, judicial processes, legal philosophy, and, more generally, the sociological, economic, and political up the corpus of a legal system in the societal context (Deshpande, 2006).

The beginning of India's recorded legal history can be traced to the ancient Vedic period, where some sort of formal legal system operated over the northern plains of the Indian subcontinent (Havell, 1918). This period is also referred to as the Bronze Age, which saw the rise of the Indus Valley Civilization in ideas that made the northwestern region of the subcontinent. Law was closely associated with philosophical discourse for the learned elite, on the one hand, and a matter of religious prescriptions for the masses, on the other. The Vedas, Upanishads, and other religious texts of this period are examples of these two facets of legal thought coalescing together to create a legal order for society (Davis, 2010). Ancient Indian philosophy includes six systems or schools: Samkhya, Yoga, Nyaya, Vaisheshika, Mimamsa, and Vedanta. These texts comprise the basis of Hindu law, later enriched over the course of time by different Hindu philosophical schools and also greatly influenced by the Jain and Buddhist traditions.

Classical Hindu law is founded on the concept of 'dharma', which means righteousness or duty, and also connotes 'law' (Menski, 2003). It broadly covers the domains of legal as well as religious duties. Literary elucidations of dharma can be sourced from the Vedas (*shruti*: divine or sacred law owing to its divine authorship), Smritis (based on the concepts elucidated in the shrutis, but authored by smritikars, and *ergo* retaining only some aspects of divinity), and *achara* (practices and customs of the people). First, all four Vedas (Rig, Yajur, Sama, and Atharva) contain references of different dimensions of dharma. These can be better understood with the help of the Smritis, which contain a retelling of traditions and customs that include duties and obligations that find mention in the Vedas themselves. The Smritis are thus highly authoritative texts, as they are received and passed on by those who trained in Vedic discipline. Third, achara comprise those norms of a community or group that are relied upon to ascertain dharma on particular matters upon which the Vedas and the Smritis are both silent. In this way, there is a deep connection between these three sources in terms of their authoritative value (Davis, 2010). This arrangement also reflects the extant plurality of law even in the ancient period, where customs of a given community or group were attributed to immense legitimacy.

The king himself had to remain in conformity with dharma, that is, he could not digress from his kingly duties as per these dharmic sources (Maine, 1890). In ancient India, kingly duties were based primarily on the attainment of dharma, and closely related to these, the attainment of *artha* and *kama*. The term 'artha' can be taken to mean the enjoyment of property, and 'kama', the maintenance of law and order and the legal system. In this context, dharma, artha, and kama make up the *trivarga* ideal that conceptualizes the dominance of the role of the state (king) in matters of property, family, and caste (R.S. Sharma, 2015). According to Maine (1861), the first concept of 'state' in ancient India not only embodied a spirit of legal pluralism, but was also subservient to *society*. The state was not elevated to a higher pedestal than society itself; rather, the former existed in service of the latter (Maine, 1861).

The Dharmashastra is a voluminous compilation of texts that contain rules any individual ought to follow as an ideal human being; it is an example of Smriti. Topics covered in the Dharmashastra can be divided into three broad categories. The first expounds the duties of an ideal householder, this includes rules on four castes (*varnas*), daily rituals, food, sacrifices, life-cycle rites, and so on. The second category deals with laws and legal procedures. This is *rajadharma*, that is, the duties (and functions) of a king in matters of state administration, promulgation of court, observing legal processes, and matters of evidence. The third category deals with the law of punishment that should be imposed after any sin is committed (Davis, 2010). Some of the most prominent Dharmashastra texts are the Manusmriti (200 BCE–200 CE), Naradasmriti (100 BCE–400 CE), Yajnavalkya Smriti (200 CE–500 CE), Brihaspati Smriti (200 CE–400 CE), Vishnu Smriti (700 CE–1000 CE), and Katyayana Smriti (300 CE–600 CE). Along with these original texts, the body of Dharmashastras also comprises interpretative texts, digests and commentaries, legal opinions based on the shastras, and so on. These texts were often used for legal judgments and opinion. It is not clear if single or multiple authors wrote these texts (U.C. Sarkar, 1958).

Hindu law in the period immediately preceding the colonial era had evolved a great deal since the ancient period. However, the *degree* and *extent* of transformation that it underwent in the colonial period at the hands of the colonial administrators and historians is unparalleled in any other phase of Indian legal history (Galanter, 1968; Jaffe, 2014; Menski, 2003). The classical Hindu legal tradition underwent a metamorphosis starting from 1772, when the British adopted a new set of rules for justice dispensation in India, all the way up to 1864, when British translators and self-proclaimed Gentoo scholars took it upon themselves to regive Indians their own law; what emerged as a result from this ancient Hindu legal tradition was its Anglo-Hindu legal hybrid (Menski, 2003). In the forthcoming sections, we shall explore how the departure from the Dharmashastra tradition transformed and diluted the very essence of 'Hindu' law that pervaded different parts of India in different forms and versions in the ancient period.

A detailed study in ancient legal systems will show that Indians in that period possessed a high sense of justice. This is evident from not only the systematic apparatuses of law (sources of law, means of interpretation, and justice systems) in different kingdoms and under the administration of different kings in ancient India, but also the *graduation* and *evolution* of these systems (Murthy, 2010). Hence, Indian society gradually adapted and transformed legal and judicial rules, procedures, and institutions to cope with the growing socio-political and economic complexities of society. The classification of law and disputes into civil and criminal, the rise of professional legal practitioners, existence of a system of pleading and production of evidence in court, including concepts of burden of proof, the necessity of independence of judges, development of theories of punishments, and so on were features that existed even before the onset of the medieval era. Two hundred years of 'colonial legal repression' wrought significant change in the way these concepts are understood today; so much so, that their efficacy faded all the while British common law ideals asserted themselves as a means of self-realization of British imperial purpose (Tharoor, 2016).

Before exploring this chapter, it is important to note that the periodization of history into ancient, medieval, and colonial was introduced by British authors and historians with a latent intent to divide India (and by extension its history) into communal phases (Thapar, 2000, citing James Mill's *The History of British India*, 1848). The beginning of this historical period is marked by the rule of the Turko-Afghans (Muslim Sultanate) that preceded the Mughal dynastic rule. Muslim rulers attached immense importance and legitimacy to the sacred scriptures (much like the Hindus in the ancient historical period). Their faith served as a guide to the way they organized themselves politically and regulated social relations among their subjects (Murthy, 2010), However, legal pluralism, owing to the heterogeneity of society, was recognized throughout this span of time (Menski, 2003). In order to understand this further, it is imperative to look into the *general* administrative set-up under the Turko-Afghan rulers and then later under the Mughals. This set-up was closely linked to the *judicial* set-up that made up much of the oeuvre of the legal system prevalent at the time.

The administrative scheme of the Muslim Sultanate was broadly as follows: executive and judicial powers were vested in the sultan (king) (Murthy, 2010); he was the supreme commander of the armed forces and appointed persons to high military and civil positions in his administration. The sultan, in order to be recognized as the king, sought a certificate of recognition from the caliph. The sultan could have a *naib sultan* (deputy) in case he was a minor. Under the sultan lay his council of ministers, Diwan-i-Wazarat, which comprised wazirs, who held different portfolios of state administration. There were other important officers that were not part of the Diwan-i-Wazarat such as the *aziz-i-mumalik* (military chief), *dabir-i-khas* (head of departments of records), *sadar-us-sudur* (the Islamic ecclesiastical head), *barid-ul-mumalik* (chief of intelligence), and the *qazi-ul-quzat* (chief justice and highest judicial officer) (Jackson, 1999).

This system of state administration was carried forward and only slightly modified by the Mughals. The significant change, aside from a similar council of ministers and chiefs of different spheres of state activity, was a different categorization of administrative divisions (due to the large size of the Mughal Empire compared to that of its predecessor). At the centre, the Mughal emperor (who enjoyed a more glorious position compared to that of the sultan, where he was omnipotent and the sole director and authority of the state machinery) had a council of ministers, or wazirs, inferior to him (J. Sarkar, 1935). Apart from the military chief, treasurer, head of state records, and so on, the Mughal Empire comprised a host of other positions such as *khan-i-saman* (high steward), *daroga* (head of the mint), *nazir burjutat* (chief engineer), and *muhtasib* (in-charge of maintenance of public morals). However, the true administrative prowess of the Mughals can be gauged by their hierarchical system, where the entire empire was divided into provinces (*subas*), each headed by a *subadar* (also designated as *nizam* or *sipahsalar*). These subas were further divided into districts (*sarkars*). Every sarkar was further divided into *paraganas*, where a single village stood at the very last rung of administration. The Mughals allowed for territorial rulers such as the Rajputs to continue with their system of administration in their respective subas or sarkars. This meant that at the regional level, local customs, traditions, and systems of administration that included judicial administration were not overhauled by the Mughal rulers, rather, they were allowed to operate with certain modifications regarding higher appeals and applicability of Islamic laws (J. Sarkar, 1935).

The judicial administration under the Muslim Sultanate and the Mughals brought into India models of judicial administration from Persia, Arabia, Egypt, and Syria, and effected necessary changes in order to fit Indian needs. At the helm of the judicial system stood the royal court, or the emperor's court, which mainly exercised appellate jurisdiction and very limited original jurisdiction (related to offences against the state) in both civil and criminal matters. The emperor was assisted by the *darogah-e-adalat* (*munsarim* of the Court), a *mufti* and a *mir adl*, and even the *mohtasib* (M.P. Singh, 1968). The next highest court of judicature was the chief court of the empire (or the court of the Qazi-ul-Quzat). The chief justice was the highest judicial officer of the empire who performed civil, clerical, and even religious duties. He had the authority to try civil and criminal, original and appellate cases and supervise the work of the provincial courts. He also collected the *jizya* and his office acted as the state registry for deeds and conveyances (M.P. Singh, 1968). Aside from the royal court and the court of the Qazi-ul-Quzat there were many other courts that exercised limited jurisdiction based either on territory or on subject matter. These included the chief revenue court, presided over by the diwan-e-ala, which decided cases on revenue, finance, and agricultural matters. An appeal from this court (as was the case in the chief court of the empire) lay in the Royal Court before the emperor himself (M.P. Singh, 1968).

At the provincial level, similar courts with limited territorial jurisdiction prevailed—the Court of the Governor (presided over by the *subadar*), the chief appellate court (the court of the *Qazi-e-Suba*), and the revenue court of the province dispensed justice for civil and criminal matters. At the district level, the qazi-e-sarkar presided over the chief criminal and civil courts of each district. Under these courts stood the Faujdari Adalat, which tried cases pertaining to riots and breach of security, the Kotwali Adalat, which tried specific criminal matters, such as disruption of law and order, and the Amalguzari Adalat, which served as the revenue court of the district. Subedars, faujdars, shiqdars, amils, and kotwals were administrative officers who were involved in justice delivery based on common law and equity (M.P. Singh, 1968).

It is to be noted that panchayats, or village councils, were allowed to operate with immense legitimacy in terms of the local laws and customs they applied, the way they tried matters placed before them, and the decisions delivered by them to maintain social control at the village level. Furthermore, the Mughals applied Islamic law (sourced from the Quran, Sharia, as interpreted through Ijma and Qiyas, and Urfi law, or Islamic jurisprudence as per Sunnism as broadly understood by the Hanafiyah school of law) to only criminal matters. Non-Muslims were exempted from following the Muslim personal law and all accruing rights and obligations (Jois, 2010). This was a result of the Mughals realizing the extent of pluralistic political, social, and legal disciplines in India's vast expanse.

The empires of the Marathas and the Vijayanagara kingdom also provide excellent examples of highly sophisticated and crystallized state legal systems in the southern parts of India. The judicial system established by Shivaji, which was followed by his successors, can best be termed as a system of feudalization of justice (J. Sarkar, 1935). The Maratha king was supported by the *nyayadhish* (judge), *panditrav* (Brahmin advisor), and the *dharmasabha* (dharma assembly) at the central level. Under this, justice was delivered by those comprising the *rajmandal* (feudal lords) and the sardars in charge of Maratha provinces. Here, a system of trial by majlis at the local level faded away and in its place the system of trial by panchayat originated (Gune, 1953).

The Wodeyar and the Travancore kingdoms developed unique systems of judicial administration. The state was divided into village-level *taluk*s (geographical administrative division), almost each having a taluk court under the charge of the amildar. He was accountable to the *hoblidar*, who was the caretaker of a *hobli* (a small group of villages). The judiciary was hierarchical, with the Commissioner's Court at the apex; this was followed by the Huzur Adalat and Sadar Munsiff courts that dealt with both criminal and civil matters (Bhatia, 2001). In Travancore, a similar system of hierarchy existed, starting from the court of the diwan at the centre all the way down to the village-level, where councils enjoyed an autonomous identity to manage legal affairs of the people. It is interesting to note that the British did not alter much of the judicial structure in this region except for minor interventions. The imposition of the common law system to these parts of India is thus questionable in principle, as it arguably resulted in an overnight switch from a system that had evolved over hundreds of years to a British legal system that was imposed in the northern parts of India, not even in Travancore itself (Supreme Court of India, 2007).

Scholars of ancient and medieval Indian history have mixed opinions about the role of religion in ancient Indian polity. Some argue that ancient and medieval states of India were theocratic in nature (Deshpande, 2006). It was Kautilya (371–273 BCE) who endeavoured to separate the state from religion, a movement that found resonance in Western jurisdictions much later in the day. As opposed to this view, others have argued that religious dogmas and philosophical views had a very limited role in running the state institutions (R.S. Sharma, 2015). In different epochs, the state meant different things for Indian society; yet India's diversity and plurality has been evinced time and again not only through judicial administrations and systems of the past, but also through the accounts of foreign observers such as Fa Hein and Alexander the Great (Murthy, 2010).

Many interesting features of Indian legal history up to the beginning of the colonial era can be observed. On the one hand, plurality is palpable with the contrasting sets of people that made up the Indian state; people differed on the basis of varnas, religion, tribe, trade or occupational group, and so on, and, accordingly, judicial administration responded to such differences. The prevalence of customary informal bodies at the village and tribal levels co-existed harmoniously with the operation of royal, state-instituted, formal courts at the district, province, and central levels of the state (Menski, 2003). Thus, the legal 'chaos' and 'vacuum' often cited by Britishers in the early colonial era, who credit themselves with *giving* Indians the common law system, was in actuality a highly evolved and complex legal system, perhaps so deeply connected with the socio-cultural needs and aspirations of the Indian populace that it could be easily mistaken to be a set of mere social norms enforced by an informal traditional court rather than dispassionate formal adjudication through the normative letter of the law in the Western construct.

The present-day conception of the Indian legal system as a common law system is one among many ideas about India that have been inherited postcolonially from the British. The way law was perceived and wielded as a tool for the preservation and advancement of society changed with the advent of colonialism, where Indians saw their own history from the eyes of the British, and diverse and variant versions of India's past succumbed to the British popular narrative (Mukherjee, 2012). Immediately preceding the consolidation of British power in India, India's legal landscape was highly pluralistic and diverse not only at the subsidiary level (customary legal orders in villages or among communities) but also at the state level (the way kingdoms managed their legal affairs at the level of their respective governments).

India comprised over 500 political dominions (kingdoms, states, and so on) that had their own systems of adjudication of disputes, maintenance of law and order, and methods of creating and recognizing law. In this sense, the aforementioned descriptions of the Mughal, Maratha, and southern Indian kingdoms are only illustrative of *some* of the most powerful and influential kingdoms in Indian medieval history. They, however, comprised several other smaller sub-kingdoms and dominions. For instance, the Mughals ruled over most of north India at the acme of their reign, and even though several Rajput kingdoms were under the suzerainty of the Mughals, they still operated autonomously with respect to their respective legal systems. Within a span of only a few decades under the British rule, one system attempted to superimpose itself upon hundreds of such systems and traditions; it would be hence illogical to assume that such a legal system with alien legal procedures, laws based on alien ideas and values, and institutions that emulated alien courts could have penetrated deeply or profoundly into Indian society. The system, however, was implemented with British colonial force and power; yet the real question is whether it was received with volition or not. Today, whether this system has been internalized in the true sense is dependent on the idea of whether the means employed in the colonial period for superimposition warranted any means of internalization at all.

British Scheme of Administration of Justice

The Company after becoming the de facto territorial rulers of India might have been content to carry on the system of government they had inherited from their Mughal predecessors, but it soon became apparent that this course was not open to them (Lindsay, 1936). In the report of 1773, Warren Hastings declared that the judicial system of the Mughals was neither efficient nor could it provide any security for its subjects and because of this the entire province had fallen into disorder (Lindsay, 1936). 'The Mohammedan courts, such as they were, were established only at the chief seat of government and were nothing more than engines of oppression under the control of corrupt judges, subject to the influence of the Nawab. At the capital, justice was perverted; in the districts, away from the capital it was denied. All judicial authority in those parts had been usurped and was being exercised by the revenue officials for their private profit' (Lindsay, 1936, p. 343).

The 1773 report also justified the need for British administration on grounds of universal application of Muslim law, notwithstanding the multiplicity of religious and customary practices among Indians. The report states that India has a mixed population, comprising largely of the Hindus and Mohammedans, and each of these bodies were subject to their own customary legal tradition. However, the Muslim courts in matters pertaining to civil disputes could not dispense any law but their own; hence, these courts were closed to Hindus. With respect to criminal matters, Muslim criminal law was applied universally but it excluded the testimony of all witnesses not of the faith of Islam (Smith, 1906).

With these justifications, Warren Hastings drew a scheme of administration of justice that essentially had two features: first, the decentralization of judicial administration through introduction of subordinate courts, and second, the protection of personal laws and usages of Hindus and Muslims. Both civil and criminal courts were introduced in each of the provincial divisions under the control and supervision of the European servants of the company. These district courts were under the hierarchies of two principal courts of appeal at the capital with respective civil and criminal jurisdiction (Lindsay, 1936; Moncrieff-Smith, 1927). The British courts engaged with customary laws in their unique ways, but at the same time ensured that where applicable the cases should be decided broadly on the principles of religious laws applicable to the parties (Lindsay, 1936; Menski, 2003; Moncrieff-Smith, 1927). The uniqueness of the British courts' engagement with the religious and customary practices has been discussed later in detail.

This scheme of judicial administration introduced by Warren Hastings also laid the foundation for the modern judicial set-up in India, though during Cornwallis's regime it was modified to a great extent (Lindsay, 1936). In the initial stages, the judiciary only comprised of Company's servants. Since they were mostly traders they had no legal training to deal in native laws; therefore, both Hindu and Mohammedan laws were not easily comprehensible to them. Through later reforms, professionals trained in law were appointed as judges. However, these professionals acting as judges also had very little knowledge of local customs and law, and were assisted by Oriental scholars in translation and interpretation of local customs and laws (Fuber, 1935).

The judicial set-up at the Presidency town of Calcutta was different from the one at the *moffusil*, or interiors. The Royal Charter of 1774 replaced the Mayor's Court with the first Supreme Court at Calcutta (Fuber, 1935). Besides, there were other subordinate courts in Calcutta that had very limited and loosely defined jurisdictional powers. The Supreme Court was established primarily with the intention to control the Company and its servants; however, later its powers were extended to decide other disputes only within the settlements of Calcutta (Fuber, 1935). Courts' jurisdiction over the Company's servants often led to friction between the Court and the governor and his council; this also stalled, to a great extent, the attempt of the company to set up their own courts in the territories outside the Presidency. The conflict generally ensued from the fact that the judges in these courts were trained in English law, and, therefore, had contempt for all other systems of law but their own and disregarded the amateur courts of the company comprising of non-law professionals. Later, it also turned out that their own procedures were unsuitable to the conditions in India, and it led to frequent confusions and alarm among the subjects to whom it was to be applied (Fuber, 1935; Smith, 1906). In the long run, however, it seemed less viable to continue with this dual system, and later in 1861 it came to an end with the amalgamation of the Supreme Courts and the company's court into the high court (Setalvad, 1960).

During the early nineteenth century, a series of liberal imperial administrators such as Elphinstone, Bentick, Macaulay, and others had envisioned the British Raj as a temporary trusteeship. Without any elaborate theory of development, they hoped to train Indians to become capable of self-government, finally eliminating the need for imperial control (Singha, 1998). Some of the official records, however, indicate that this attitude of the British rulers had begun to erode after 1857. In *Alibis of the Empire*, Mantena argues that it was the outbreak of the Indian Rebellion of 1857, or the Sepoy Mutiny, that finally destroyed the foundations of liberal imperialism and opened the way for a new paradigm articulated by Henry Maine

(Mantena, 2010). After the event of the revolt, the British rulers were successful in creating a consensus that Indians are incapable of modernity and self-government, which became an 'alibi of empire' that justified a more or less permanent British presence and led to the gradual decline of the liberal imperial ideal of trusteeship (Mantena, 2010).

For this reason, some of the early British historians such as Alexander Dow were entrusted with the task of revisiting the despotic nature of various ruling paradigms in India. Their work emphasized upon the Mughal–Indian political model to show the arbitrary and despotic nature of the rule, unchecked by any institution (social or political) and primarily resting in one person. Under this regime, there was complete absence of rule of law and matters such as inheritance and primogeniture were based on the inevitable struggle of the progeny of the ruler. Moreover, justice was solely dependent on the person acting as a judge, who could be easily influenced by money, status, and other advantages connected to the office (Cohn, 1996). These historians had, therefore, laid down the ideological infrastructure for British rule in India. In Cohn's words:

> In its cleaned-up version it was expressed thus: Indians are best ruled by a 'strong hand', who could administer justice in a rough-and-ready fashion unfettered by rules and regulations. The courts, their procedures, their regulations, and the propensity of Indians to perjury and to the suborning of witnesses only served to delay justice and made the simple peasant folk of India the prey of the urban-based lawyers, merchants, and agitators. This would lead to the alienation of the 'natural' loyalty the masses always felt for the strong, benevolent despot. As benevolent despots, the British were to appear in several forms—as 'platonic guardians', as patriarchs habitually addressed by the simple folk as ma-bap (mother and father), as authoritarian rationalist utilitarian, and in times of crisis as the not-so-benevolent Old Testament avengers. (Cohn, 1996, p. 65)

Thus, the revisionist British historians tried to rewrite history to show the benevolence of the colonial ruler. Through these narratives, they tried to completely camouflage the dark and violent side of the empire. There are few early works of the British historians in India that have reported on the implicit violence of imperial rule, deciphering the benevolent and bloodless myth of Pax Britannica, by revealing its sometimes-brutal core (Kolsky, 2010). And only by the close of the nineteenth century did some of the Indian scholars write about the 'white violence' and about the mischievous acquittal of the British men accused of brutalizing Indians (Kolsky, 2010).

> [In 1885], Mr. Glover was charged with killing his coolie in Dacca. The European doctor who examined the corpse testified that the coolie's death was caused by the rupture of his spleen following heavy fall. Several eye-witnesses testified that the dead man fell on a piece of iron only after Glover repeatedly kicked him in the back. Glover was acquitted of murder and fined 200 rupees in connection with the man's death. (Kolsky, 2010, p. 137)

In this regard, Spivak argues that British created a justification for the 'Raj' not only on ideological and scientific grounds, but also by the institution of law—both through creation and obliteration of certain textual ingredients (Spivak, 1988). Hence, the colonizers created a need for bringing about law and order through an organized legal system. At this stage, the task at hand for them was to come up with a codified rule of law that was designed to provide the colonial state a mechanism to discipline a growing population of white settlers, capitalist, and planters in India, who otherwise were immune from local criminal jurisdiction and therefore outside the bounds of law. Henry Maine emerged as a pivotal character in this regard. He was one of the first imperial administrators to engage with the prevalent customary and religious practices and to transform them into legal form.

Driven by the desire to construct a definitive knowledge of their subjects, the British rulers involved themselves with the task of grasping the religious scriptures of the different communities, as they were seen to be a significant and legitimate source of information (Menski, 2003). Hence, they invested in the task of discovering Indian traditions through these scripturesand recorded them under different categories of Hindu and Muslim practices (Cohn, 1996). Arguably, the colonizers 'protected' the customary rights of the subjects in a way that would organize these practices into schemes that often benefited the colonizers in the power relationship between the colonizer and the colonized. Thus, by codifying the religious laws, the British in colonial India reduced a polymorphous legal structure to a far more clearly organized system—which was essentially comprehensible only to the colonizer (Spivak, 1988). In his discussion on Islamic law and English texts with respect to the organization of various Islamic religious practices, John Strawson argues that British created 'legal orientalism', the overriding aim of which was to make Islamic law understandable to the English lawyer or official (Strawson, 1995). Customs and practices of the indigenous communities in India were protected with an objective to rigidify them for the convenience of the colonial ruler.

Scholars of Muslim law in British India argue that British engagement with the Muslim law had led to the birth of 'Anglo-Mohammedan' law—a new independent legal system that was substantially different from both the British or Islamic law practices in India prior to 1864 (Powers, 1989). Until 1864, muftis, who had the primary responsibility of correcting and interpreting the Islamic doctrine on a given subject, assisted the British magistrates. Later when this practice was abandoned, the magistrates predominantly relied upon textbooks on Islamic law, translated legal text, and personal experience for deciding cases. As the entire judicial system comprised of jurists trained in English law, they continuously integrated the notions of English law with the indigenous customary practices (Powers, 1989).

Thus, in outlining the system of Muslim law, the British jurist predominantly relied upon the religious scriptures. Even the colonial courts generally decided in favour of customs driven from the religious scriptures and would exempt Muslim families in some parts of the country from a strict application of Islamic law where it stood in conflict with any existing customary practices (Jalal, 2001). In courts, the British jurist referred to religious scriptures for interpreting the rights (at times also in favour of women) with respect to marriage, property, *mehr* (dower), and other such civil issues.

To grasp the religious text of the Muslims in India, the British administrators took note of the differences between all the major schools of legal scholarship that had evolved during the Mughal rule in India, including the Sunni and the Shi'a. For the interpretation of the Islamic succession law, they primarily relied upon a Hanafi text—*al Sirajiya* (Kozlowski, 1985). However, the provisions of this text were subjected to the prevailing customary practices and hence selectively applied. For instance, with respect to devolution of a man's property *al-Sirajiya* provides for equal distribution of property among all children rather than a system of primogeniture (Powers, 1989). However, in applying this law the British administrators made way for the prevailing local customs particularly in cases where it allowed sidelining women and other female heirs from having a share in the property.

Newbigin (2011) argues that even though colonial Muslim law did not always translate into secure legal rights in terms of women's day-to-day life, it nevertheless acknowledged the legal personhood and property-owning capacity of Muslim women (Newbigin, 2011). This was also a significantly distinct Muslim family practice, different from Hindu family practices based on a system of joint family under which individual ownership was not recognized (Newbigin, 2011).

The British administrators were more successful in outlining the Muslim law from the religious scriptures than in Hindu law. This could be attributed to the multiplicity of the Hindu religious texts and huge variance in the customary practices of different regions of the country (Menski, 2003). However, this multiplicity gave scope to the colonial scholars to interpret these scriptures and reshape Hindu law in a way that was more conducive to the British rule (Agarwal, 1994). It was around this time some of the colonial scholars—in particular, Henry Maine—became significant lawgivers of India. Prior to Maine, Sir Henry Thomas Colebrooke took interest in reading and interpreting various Hindu Sanskrit texts that were the standard references for British courts. According to Ludo Rocher, Colebrooke's conception of the Hindu text was based on several misconstructions, because 'he viewed the commentaries of the Hindu Legal text as the work of lawyers, jurist-councils and law-givers, reflecting the actual law of the land' (Cohn, 1996, p. 73). This was analogous to the work of early modern English scholars, who sought English law in varied customs of different parts of Great Britain (Cohn, 1996). Colebrooke came up with an explanation that the ancient sages produced treatises on which the subsequent Hindu lawyers and pandits commented, and these original treatises along with subsequent commentaries on them constituted the body of Hindu legal texts.

In his 1861 work, *Ancient Law: Its Connection with the Early History of Society, and Its Relation to Modern Ideas*, Maine drew a parity between the Hindu Law operating in India at the time and the ancient Roman law. He argued just as in case of ancient Roman law (based on the principle of Patria Potestas), Hindu law also gave power to the male head of the family to complete negation of the claims of individual. Hence, the system was also less favourable to women, because even though it would be possible for the younger male of the family to gain power as the potential head of the family, a Hindu woman would always remain powerless and dependent on her father or husband (Caroll, 1991; Denault, 2009). Emphasizing on the backwardness of the Indian society, Maine argued that such system no longer prevailed in the Western society; India, however, continues to function according to this system. Maine's understanding of Hindu legal system and his work in this area of law brought him popularity, and later in 1862, he became the legal member of Viceroy's Council (Newbigin, 2011).

As a member of the council, Maine also introduced significant legal reforms. The most prominent was to make the Hindu joint family a legal structure. Although in British India joint family existed both among the Hindu and the Muslims as a sociological unit, through Maine's law reform joint family became the primary legal unit of the Hindu society (Newbigin, 2011). The law reform also introduced the concept of individual property right under both Dayabhaga and Mitakshara schools of law. Nevertheless, this was limited to the self-acquired property; the family estate was held as a collective and the nature of devolution varied under both schools (Denault, 2009). With respect to Hindu marriage, the reform upheld the views of upper caste Hindu leaders by positioning Hindu marriage as a sacrament rather than a contract (John and Nair, 1998). Barred from entering her natal coparcenary, a woman had little legal claim to parental support following marriage, when she became the dependent not simply of her husband but of his coparcenary. In this way, the sacramental marital unit worked in tandem with the coparcenary system to support a very hierarchical system of patriarchal legal authority (Cohn, 1996). There was also a judicial system reform in 1864 that led to the establishment of provincial high courts. Simultaneously, all posts for Hindu and Muslim law officers in various moffusil courts were abolished. From this time onwards, the authoritative decisions by English judges transformed Hindu law into a form of English case law (Cohn, 1996). Commenting on similar lines with respect to Hindu law, Menski says, 'The increasing divergence between flexibility-conscious customary practices and precedent-focused official law placed custom in conflict with case law and legislation … [thereby widening] the gap between law and society' (Menski, 2003, p. 178).

Thus, we see that the Hindu and the Muslim laws (with respect to land, property, religion and culture, and other social issues) as practiced for centuries in India were given recognition in law, policy, and administration of the British Raj. Baxi argues that the protection of 'personal' (both religious and customary) law system by the British administrators led to a hybrid formulation of legal system which provided the basis for typical stratagems of 'divide and rule' practices of communalization of governance and politics (Baxi, 2012).

The British colonizers followed a specific stratagem for imposing a system of law in its colonies. It would be wrong to assume that the common law system developed in England was applied equivocally to all the British colonies to facilitate imperial expansion. Arguably, the colonizers created an exception with respect to colonies that had a properly defined civil law system in existence before coming under the possession of British colonizers. For instance, in Ceylon, Mauritius, and Quebec inter alia, the colonizers continued with the existing code of law (Arnot, 1907). In colonies such as India and Australia, where there were considerable indigenous populations and where no formal (uniform) code of law acceptable to the Englishmen prevailed, the common law system was introduced (Arnot, 1907).

Early in its sway the British Empire in India conceived of implanting on the subcontinent modes of law and governance responsible for England's rapid progress and the advance of its people. What we see is that in a contrasting dimension, at some level, the British administrators followed a policy of accommodating Indian society within their administrative scheme and inadvertently undercut their own ideals by adopting most of India's religious and customary law, notwithstanding that they often stood at odds with British objectives (Baxi, 2012). However, these modest adjustments did not obscure their mainstay positions of facilitating the power relation between the colonizers and the colonized (Fanon, 2008; Spivak, 1988). Hence, a more complex analysis is needed to comprehend the impact of introducing the English legal system in India and how did it deal with the indigenous legal institutions.

The difference in the customary practices of the Hindus and the Muslims, which British administrators took into account, also laid down the road for introduction of English common law in India. The First Law Commission report of 1840 stated that neither the Hindu law nor the Muslim law could be the *lex loci* of British India, because these laws were interwoven with religious beliefs and hence would be inapplicable to people professing a different faith (Setalvad, 1960). The Law Commission reasoned that since there were no existing lex loci when British came into the possession of India, the English law should become the lex loci for Indians (Setalvad, 1960).

By this time the British administrators had already established the arbitrary and despotic nature of the Oriental ruler. The task then was to create an empire of law and liberty, 'not empire of men, and certainly not empire of violent men' (Singha, 1998). In response to the crisis of law and order (as portrayed by the British ruler), they engaged in the task of designing a codified rule of law that would provide the colonial state a mechanism to discipline its subjects (Kolsky, 2010). British officials, thus, not only used law to create the colonial state, they also used the language of law to legitimize the rule. Thus, the Law Commission of British India was established in 1834, consisting of eminent English jurists. The commission worked to give India a system of code and important laws dealing with all substantive and procedural aspects of both civil and criminal matters (Setalvad, 1960). Setalvad traces the functioning of the Law Commission in British India and the important laws enacted during the time (see Table 1.1).

Despite a large part of the law having been codified, Setalvad notes that these enactments still allowed scope for applying the principles of English law in India. This is because these codes themselves incorporated principles of English law with variations needed by Indian conditions. 'Indeed the codes explain and clarify the meaning of the rules laid down by them by illustrations which are based on English decisions' (Setalvad, 1960, p. 40).

British scheme of administration of justice would certainly lead to an assumption about an impartial judicial system and equal application of law. Such an assumption, however, elided a very significant fact that establishment of the colonial state and its laws also implied

Table 1.1 Laws Enacted during the British Law Commissions in India

Law Commission	Code/Act/ Regulation	Comments
First Law Commission, 1834 (established by the Charter Act of 1833)	The Indian Penal Code, 1860	It was drafted by the First Law Commission presided over by Macaulay, but was passed later in 1860. It was not based on any prior code in existence and, subject to a few alterations, applies as such till date.
Second Law Commission, 1854 (established by the Charter Act of 1853)	Code of Civil Procedure, 1859	The commission also made proposals for the amalgamation of all courts into one (the Sadar Adalats, the mofussil, and the principal courts in Presidency towns). These proposals were accepted and this led to the establishment of the high courts as the highest court for the mofussils and the Presidency towns.
Third Law Commission, 1861	Enactment of a code for succession and inheritance for Indians other than Hindus and Muslims, 1865; Indian Evidence Act, 1872; Indian Contract Act, 1872; Specific Relief Act, 1877	The Specific Relief Act was based on the English law principles of equity.
Fourth Law Commission, 1879	Negotiable Instruments Act, 1881; Transfer of Property Act, 1882; Indian Trusts Act, 1882; Easement Act, 1882	These laws are still operative in India without any substantive changes.

Source: Authors.

the attempted displacement of a pre-existing order to a significant extent, and that this would be a displacement achieved without the consent of the governed (Kolsky, 2010). Some scholars have delved into the complicated nature of law and violence in the empire. Pagden argues that their actual objective was to expand the British Empire, but at the same time they strove to distinguish their empire from the empires of other European rivals, particularly Spain. Hence, the British rulers used the tool of modernity, reform, and improvement as opposed to conquest by force (Anthony, 1995). Radhika Singha in *A Despotism of Law* offers a similar perspective on the development of the colonial criminal law. She argues that codification of laws should be read alongside the formation of the colonial state. Codification of the Indian law, according to her, 'was neither born solely of an abstract English Political Philosophy nor designed to create a state to rule over only Indians in India. Instead, codification was the official response to the moral, legal and political dilemmas posed by the unruly third face of colonialism' (Kolsky, 2010, p. 9).

Summing Up

The discussion here delves into the process of British incursion into Indian law. It is true that British Empire functioned through law and defined its subjects' life through it. Historians of the past generation have also lavishly praised the British rule in India, for it had equipped India with rapid progress under the rule of law. However, by the time of Independence few among the Indians could have claimed to benefit from the 'European modernization' (Chatterjee, 1993). But the question is, why did India not make any serious effort to dislodge the legal system imposed on it by the British Raj (Galanter, 1989)? The legal system which primarily developed during mid-twentieth century colonial administration was accepted as 'our system' by the Congress leadership and others entrusted with the task of building a new nation state after Independence (Galanter, 1989).

Similar patterns have also been observed in other British colonies of the world. There has been an enormous incorporation of foreign laws in the form of new constitutional orders, reforms, and consolidation and rationalization of existing laws. Galanter argues that legal systems in postcolonial nations are characterized by some common indicators of change brought by modernization. These indicators of change are: (*i*) change in legal rules, which implies that in every modern legal system, legal rules are uniform and unvarying in their application, are moreover, devised in a way to create a valid standard for general applicability; (*ii*) change in institutional arrangements and techniques of administration where older arrangements of dispute settlements are replaced by a network of courts. The system is hierarchical and at the very base is the court of first instance which ensures application of this law. Above are the layers of appeal and review to ensure that there is uniformity in application of national law. These systems can be operated on by qualified professionals such as lawyers and professional jurist; and (*iii*) change in relation between law and political authority. In a modern legal system law is intrinsically connected to the state. The state enjoys the supremacy to deal with all disputes arising within its boundaries. All other non-state institutions work within the supervision of the state (Galanter, 1989).

The Indian legal system is also marked by this cluster of features, driven by the pressing requirements of being 'modern'. Although the postcolonial critics have said much on the unsuitability of the modern British-style law in India, in practice it seems almost impossible to take an absolute departure from the English legal system. Newbigin argues that in British India the relationship with the colonial subject was, in the main, mediated through group identity-access to political office, and law was shaped by a subject's sex and the religious or caste community to which he or she belonged. In the new nation state, this was thought to be replaced by a citizenship-based direct relationship between the state and each and every individual Indian. However, the state–citizenship nexus after so many years of Independence does not live up to this expectation, as many Indians still do not get access to law or to the rights set out in the Constitution (Newbigin, 2011). Hence, we need to understand the postcolonial failures of India through historical engagements with the process of transition marked by both continuities and discontinuities with the colonial past. Therefore, in Chapter II of this book we further delve into the discourse of continuities. We look into details the processes that went into internalization and perpetuation of the claim that India has just one legal system that is based on the British common law system and its gradual entrenchment into the Constitution.

II

Historical and Contemporary Deviations from the State Legal System in India

In the previous chapter, we examined the historical evolution of common law in India. The true significance of the common law system vis-à-vis traditional legal systems prevalent in India prior to its advent was that it constituted a 'fundamental break' from India's ancient legal heritage. Colonization opened the doors for massive legal transplant of Western law into India coupled with a complete metamorphosis of traditional personal laws (Jain, 2007, p. 2). The process of diffusion of the common law tradition into Indian society comprised broadly three markers: first, in the form of English-modelled legal institutions that started out by applying local customary laws but later served as platforms for the second marker of legislative transplants, that is, laws enacted in British India that closely resembled their English counterparts (Singha, 1998, p. 17). These coupled with translation and codification efforts of different Western scholars led to the third major instance of transplantation: the transmutation itself of Hindu and Muslim law (Baxi, 2003).

Owing to its colonial heritage, India has been identified as a common law jurisdiction; although several other legal traditions and cultures are indigenous to its jurisdiction, the state legal system is the most overarching and dominant among them all. Implicit in this proposition is the endeavour on the part of the state to uniformalize all law as a means of projecting itself as most encompassing and comprehensive of all systems and traditions. This positivist normative fixation can be seen in many facets where the range and scope of the state legal system overlaps with other legal systems and traditions.

If the Indian Constitution is considered an aspirational document that embodies the ideals that the state legal system wishes to achieve, then customs, usages, personal laws, traditional legal practices, and institutions are deviations that are waiting to be unified into a single whole such that they are aligned to constitutional principles such as liberty, equality, and fraternity. Such unification, even if ostensibly asserted by the state via a uniform civil code, will never be achieved in the truest sense (Menski, 2008), considering the degree of pluralistic vigour India encompasses (Mendelsohn, 2014). Attempts towards uniformalizing all law have nevertheless been made via quintessential 'model laws' for all communities and regions. This leads to the question as to whether customs, personal laws, traditional legal practices, and so on can be considered components of the state Indian legal system due to their constitutional recognition or are they mere aberrations from it.

Menski describes this push and pull as *Verstaatlichung* (more explicit state involvement) versus *Entstaatlichung* (pulling back of the state). The state's overall engagement with other legal systems and traditions depicts the dichotomy between Verstaatlichung and Entstaatlichung, may it be in the form of codifying any customary law, interpreting and modifying it or striking down any custom or usage as unconstitutional, and so on (2003).

This idea reflects India's highly legally pluralistic nature, where a multiplicity of legal orders on several different planes and levels can be observed. State normative law operates along with laws, rules, customs, and usages among different communities that are classified as such based on some common factors such as religion, language, class or caste, and so on. This is seemingly a 'vertical' categorization wherein the universe of the Indian populace is broadly assorted into different groups such as the ones mentioned above. For instance, Hindu law or Muslim law operate within such groupings, though each of these categories is immensely diverse in its own right. Such diversity within each facet of legal plurality can be seen from region to region and village to village. Hence, variance in the existence and application of legal order can be observed at the basic levels of what we now understand as 'subsidiarity'. Here, a 'horizontal' categorization can be observed in which the multiplicity of legal practices is not just prevalent among different vertical categories of people, but also horizontally at each regional level going right down to the basal village level.

In both the vertical and horizontal respects, one can observe the state's tendency to uniformalize countered by society's tendency to remain steadfast to diversity, the very concept of legality, much like centripetal and centrifugal forces acting and reacting against each other. All the way through the colonial era and later through the postcolonial age, state law has been engaged in this fascinating kind of push-and-pull relationship with other varieties and sources of law.

In this chapter, we have set the contemporary character of Indian law: state and non-state law as the two sides of the same coin in the context of the earlier development of the system during the British and post-Independence periods. This is done by showing how, during the colonial period, several exceptions and deviations from the pan-Indian state legal system existed, which later replicated themselves in the post-Independence period. We look at broad themes or subject areas in which the state legal system does not operate at all or does not operate to the exclusion of other systems. May it be with respect to personal law, tribal law, village-based legal systems (panchayats and traditional legal practices), or several other examples.

Over the course of this chapter, we shall explore the idea of what was arguably the first pan-Indian legal system under the British colonial regime. Herein we show how the British drive to uniformalize all law through the establishment of its legal system in India was rife with several instances of variance and discrimination in application, thereby debilitating the notion of uniform law for all. We also throw light upon the developments around Indian Independence that led to a perpetuation of this colonial trend and, in turn, a perpetuation of its consequences. In the following chapter, we further elaborate the arguments and elucidations put forth here by providing evidence to substantiate the same.

Attempts to Achieve Legal Unification in British and Independent India

As has been noted earlier, since the advent of the East India Company, judicial administration slowly and steadily started falling into its hands among other powers and privileges of state administration and governance. However, after the Company made way for the Raj in 1858, there was an attempt to do a lot more than only justice dispensation. British efforts in creating detailed codes, legislating personal laws after churning them from customary religious practices, establishing their own legal institutions that operated on British procedures and values, all contributed greatly in shaping the pan-Indian legal order.

In this context, it is important to note that this 'pan-Indian legal order' posed to create a uniformity of laws, legal institutions, and generally the system of justice delivery (Baxi, 2012). However, not only were there several contradictions within this state legal paradigm as to its uniformity towards all its subjects which it feigned to bring under one common law system, but also as to its outreach. There were many parts and pockets of British India that were simply kept outside the application of British laws. In this section, we explore these contradictions in the precolonial era that later resonated in the post-colonial era. This is an indicator of the extent to which this foreign system diffused or percolated through the legally pluralistic fabric of India.

Anthropologist Bernard Cohn (1996) notes how after the defeat of the nawab of Bengal at the Battle of Plassey in 1757, the East India Company gained control over the taxation policies and collection of revenue in Bengal. Attempts were made to transform revenue collection to methods that suited the British imagination, and thereby legal practices associated with land, ownership, and taxation became the mainstay of British law. They brought new laws in those legal matters they were directly interested in: for instance, matters of administration of justice (the Civil Procedure Code, 1858; the

Criminal Procedure Code, 1861; the Indian Evidence Act, 1872; and the Indian Penal Code, 1860), security of commercial and land transactions along with revenue related matters (the Indian Contract Act, 1872; the Transfer of Property Act, 1882; and the Societies Registration Act, 1869). In this sense, 'colonial law' comprised a special set of rules (much like the civil law tradition) designed to facilitate transactions of British colonies and traders, and thereby to maintain its imperial domination over India. The implementation of these laws along with the establishment of British legal institutions, while undergoing a unique process of acculturation in India, were efforts in furtherance of the omniscience of the state legal system over all other legal cultures (Halpérin, 2010).

Following Plassey and armed with the victory over the nawab, the Company started appropriating the role of a 'state' in many ways. It could 'wage war, make peace, raise taxes, and administer justice to its own employees and to increasing number of Indians who inhabited the territories in which the company was acting as sovereign' (Cohn, 1996, p. 58); acting like a state led to obvious, intentional interference with the fabric of Indian society.

Between 1815 and 1828, the British government in India recorded 8,134 instances of the practice of widow self-immolation—*sati* (Mani, 1989). The number was significant, and frightening, and led to concentrated legal action to address this practice. This was also a period of slow colonial incursion into education and other social reform by the British, keeping in mind current and future governance considerations. Creating an English-speaking service class educated in the morals and sentiments of Europeans and devising a systematic agenda of social reform targeted to ensure equality between sexes and abolish inhuman practices took shape in these decades right up to the Government of India Act, 1858, when the British Parliament established direct rule over India.

However, British policy in India drew heavily from European cultural, philosophical, and moral considerations of the time. A key administrative consideration, and a key point of frustration for the British administrators, was the diverse population demographic in India. Pluralism of this degree could not be efficiently managed unless strict categories, and uniform systems of law and governance were implemented. However, when viewed historically, despite claims of uniformity and universality, the policies of the British, much like changes in political order in nearly every region across the world, changed under different political figures and their ideological backgrounds. In the years preceding the British Parliament's consolidation of control over India, the European continent was still very much under the sway of Oriental philosophy, which strongly advocated for the preservation of tradition. Policy and governance measures influenced by Orientalism then gave way to Anglicanism, wherein rapid transformation based on Christian moral superiority was encouraged over preservation and retention of traditional frameworks. These currents had cascading effects on the understanding and the implementation of rule of law in India (Vishwanathan, 1988).

'Dismissing the Oriental system as deficient in a strong political tradition (and in this belief Cornwallis was doing no more than echoing a view that was common currency), he turned to English principles of government and jurisprudence for setting the norms of public behaviour and responsibility by which administrators were to function' (Vishwanathan, 1988, p. 88).

Warren Hastings, the then governor general of India, had sympathy with the Orientalist methods, but was dismissed by his successor, Cornwallis, because of several abuses of power that took place under his leadership. According to Cornwallis, the Orient, unlike the West, lacked a consistent political tradition on which efficient rule could be based, and Anglicization was a necessary political move in this context. However, Anglicism received some setbacks from Cornwallis's successors. A new set of British officers would take over Indian administration, and they realized that the preservation of the feudal characteristics of British rule in India could be better sustained by incorporating Orientalism rather than doing away with it altogether. Native culture could not be promoted as a purely defensive measure, neither could it be replaced in its entirety by a centralized structure of British control, rather, it had to be patronized in a more indirect and diffused manner (Vishwanathan, 1988).

The Government of India Act, 1858, brought India under the rule of the British monarch—under feudal aspects of an older order which itself was showing signs of transformation under industrial capitalism. According to certain modes of power in feudal structures, hierarchically lower political systems could be allowed to operate under the eye of the sovereign. The 1858 proclamation, which laid down the rules whereby erstwhile Indian kings and princes would find themselves within a new set of power relations with the British government in India, claimed that Indian princes could hold on to their 'rights, dignity, and honour' (Cohn, 1983, p. 633). Their territorial considerations would be respected by the Crown, and while everyone would enjoy 'the equal and impartial protection of the law', in the framing and the administration of this law, 'due regard would be paid to the ancient rights, usages, and customs' (Cohn, 1983, p. 633). But as it came to be seen over the years, even *after* greater and more uniformly applicable legal mechanisms, everyone did not enjoy 'equal and impartial protection of the law'.

It is a common historical argument that the British followed dual methods of violence and reconciliation while governing India. Violence, to acquire greater control in the face of conflict, and reconciliation, to allow for consensual rule, together contributed to the creation of colonial hegemony in India. However, this dualism reflected in their practice of law as well. Uniform, enforceable law was advocated under the principle of rule of law, while exceptions were allowed at several levels under principles of preservation of and non-interference with traditional practices. The practice of sati, mentioned earlier in this section, demonstrates this logic when we look at British treatment of the practice over the course of a few years. Interestingly, sati was first allowed and later banned. In the first instance, good, consensual sati was differentiated from bad, forced *sati*, and the British government, while selectively making the practice illegal in some cases and some communities, allowed it to flourish in others (Mani, 1989).

Under Oriental methods, the search for a 'real' Indian law led to the reconstitution of Indian legal traditions and principles. Textual forms of knowledge and learning acquired supreme importance and older texts automatically assumed superior positions in the hierarchy of knowledge. In a bid to reach 'true' Indian law, the British went through several layers of translations, interpretations, commentaries, and selective highlighting of what they believed was relevant in the documented histories and traditions of India (Cohn, 1996). The exercise of power and the accumulation of knowledge in the form of language, religious texts, legal texts, and so on were parallel parts of a single project of control and expansion (Dirks, 1996). However, while considerations on fair and equitable governance over newly acquired territory did enter administrative plans, and the proclaimed purposes of equality, civilization, and justice was often the rhetoric, the end aim of the British in India was to maintain a strong hold on their most productive colony.

Despite the rhetoric and the appeal of a uniform legal system predicated on rule of law, exceptions proliferated. It has been argued by historians and anthropologists that British notions of law and justice were instrumental in consolidating control over British colonies (Singha, 1998). Concomitantly, the growth of British territories also entailed more widespread practice of British law, which served to legitimize colonial practices.

> British officials not only used law to create the colonial state (the Permanent Settlement Act of 1793, for example, provided the early colonial state with a legal mechanism to collect land revenues), they also used the language of law to legitimise their rule.... By offering Indians an impartial judicial system and the equal protection of law, Britons assumed that the loyalty of their colonial subjects and the stability of the empire would be secured (Kolsky, 2010, pp. 2–3).

Kolksy argues that while the British in India claimed to introduce, and maintain, a 'rhetorical stance of legal equality, legal practice and conventions placed most Europeans in India above the law' (Kolsky, 2010, p. 4). David Arnold in his work on the colonial prison argues that while Europeans were the obvious exceptions to rule of law, even within institutions and mechanisms of law and order exceptions to standard treatment took place. Europeans and Indians were incarcerated in separate prisons well into the end of the nineteenth century, after India came under direct British rule, and *after* the promulgation of efforts to uniformalize law. Additionally, caste, which the British were wary of ignoring, ensured that Indian prisoners within the colonial prison were each subject to different diets and other social protocols based on their position within the caste system (Arnold, 1994). Kolsky contends that well into the late nineteenth century, and even after the formation of the Indian Penal Code, Europeans in India continued to be treated differentially, against principles of rule of law. Kolsky argues that one of the main reasons the British created the Indian Penal Code in 1860 was to curb what she calls 'white violence', the extreme barbarism of non-official whites, mostly plantation and estate managers and other such Britishers not associated with either the Company or administration.

'The notion of a rule of law as a system of principles designed to govern and protect equal subjects—a notion introduced into India by Britons themselves—was blatantly contradicted by the institutionalization of racial distinctions in the statutory law and by the overt partiality of white police, judges, and juries' (Kolsky, 2010, p. 12).

Also, the Penal Code achieved little. The rate of convictions of white offenders, Kolsky notes, *fell* after the code was implemented. The First Law Commission of colonial India, established in 1834 and led by Lord Macaulay, promised India the 'gift' of codified law to tackle both the misdemeanours of the Company officials and the non-official whites in India, and to make all Indian residents, white and non-white, equal in the eyes of law. Before the coming of the First Law Commission, plural Indian legal traditions, as well as overly complex and discrete sets of Company legal mechanisms, were seen as severely detrimental to good governance.

At the time, the Company administered a plurality of laws, including regional Regulations, Acts of Parliament, Hindu and Islamic law, English common and statutory law, and the principle of justice, equity, and good conscience. In place of this confusing and uncertain system, codification offered a simple and uniform law to which all inhabitants of India (including non-Indians) would be made subject. According to Macaulay, the principle underlying his codification scheme was 'uniformity when you can have it; diversity when you must have it; but in all cases certainty' (Kolsky, 2010, p. 70).

Kolsky points out that what historians tend to ignore is that a concomitant exercise to codify British criminal law was also taking place in Britain during the same time. While British codification was a failure, there were calls to use the *success* of Indian codification as an example to follow the same process in Britain. However, even in India, codification, especially the Code of Criminal Procedure (1861), despite promises to treat all equal under the eyes of law, 'expanded legal distinctions, exceptions, and inequalities' (Kolsky, 2010, p. 73), privileging whites over non-whites.

With respect to personal laws, the British largely followed the policy of non-interference, as they found the prevalent legal system highly chaotic and confusing (Jain, 2007). In the legal institutions that preceded the British, different laws were applied at the village, district, and provincial levels based on customary laws; while in civil matters, Hindus and Muslims were governed by their own personal religious laws that differed from region to region and caste to caste (Williams, 2006), criminal law was much more uniform, as it applied to all subjects under the Mughal rulers. While the ostensible purpose of codification of personal laws was to achieve certainty and uniformity, the real reason lay in furthering the British colonial project (Singha, 1998), and new codes created too did not necessarily have the objective of legal unification *alone* in mind, as they themselves demonstrate.

> Although a codified law was meant to subordinate the [white] non-official and teach him 'obedience' to the law, the Code of Criminal Procedure formally secured to him an elevated status in law to which special benefits accrued. The legal recognition of different rights within the realm of a supposedly universal law was justified by arguments that special circumstances required special legislation. Abstract principles, that is, could not safely be carried to their logical conclusion in colonial India (Kolksy, 2010, p. 73).

Hence, colonialists were, by their very nature, conduct, and style of governance, *discriminating* lawgivers and colonialism implied an unequal treatment towards colonized people by a minority of colonizers (Halpérin, 2010). While, on the one hand, the British legal system established a system of 'rule of law' based on a certain conception of equality, law was never *applied* equally between the colonizers and the colonized. The First Law Commission reflected on the idea of *lex loci* (a sweeping notion of 'law of the land') and proposed to establish English law as the law applicable to persons who were not governed by a particular personal status or to cases that involved persons of different status. Resultantly, the British rolled out the Caste Disabilities Removal Act, 1850, which laid down that no one could forfeit a right on the basis of change of religion or loss of caste; this was owing to the pressure from missionaries in favour of Christian converts. Then came the Indian Christian Marriage Act, 1872, the secularized Special Marriage Act, 1866, the Native Converts' Marriage Dissolution Act, 1866, the Brahmo Marriage Act, 1872, which legalized marriages without the performance of Hindu rituals, Parsi marriage law and law of age of consent (1865 and 1891), succession laws that applied to persons who were neither Hindus nor Muslims (1865), and Sikh marriage law (1909). The British policy of discriminatory lawgiving clearly points in the direction of the existing legal plurality at the time. Not only did the British acknowledge the existence of several legal traditions in India, but also contributed to this existing mesh of pluralism by adding a new set of strings through their legislations and dispute settlement mechanisms in their legal institutions.

On another front, the British classification of 'criminal tribes' (1871 and 1911) ushered a plan to register certain tribes so as to subject them to a special law that places several restrictions on their movement. This separate treatment in order to exclude certain groups from general regulations was another benchmark in building and recognizing a plural legal order in India. Administrative policy of the British also reflected this trend. The Government of India Acts of 1909, 1919, and 1935 allowed for different extents of reservations for different communities, starting with Muslims then later extending to other communities in different provinces. These constituted the *contradictions* of the British policy that was ambivalent between equality and discrimination. As was the case in numerous examples of administration generally, it was so in the case of legal administration, which not only constitutes an important part of the colonial legacy in Indian law, but was also amplified to a large degree after Independence.

For nearly a century prior to Independence in India, special laws were applicable to certain 'backward areas'. These areas were situated in several provinces of British India, and their backwardness was due to the fact that they were mostly populated by tribal and aboriginal populations isolated from the mainstream of Indian society (Shiva Rao, 2010, p. 569). The British administration saw a risk in subjugating these populations to normal laws, a legacy that the postcolonial Indian government has also carries forward till today. Special laws were necessary to protect these populations from getting exploited under the normal laws. Furthermore, a need was felt that the prevalent customs and practices should continue to govern these populations with respect to certain aspects of their lives. This was deemed necessary for their 'sympathetic handling and protection from economic subjugation by their neighbours' (Statutory Commission, Government of India, vol. I, 1930). The Scheduled Districts Act, enacted in 1874, was the first legal measure taken to formulate administrative and judicial institutions and procedures in these areas.

Later, with the advent of the Simon Commission in 1927, the British government modified its policy towards backward regions. The commission felt that perpetuation of isolation from the main currents of progress would not be a satisfactory long-term solution, and that it would be necessary to educate and civilize these people in order for them to become self-reliant. This task the commission saw as extremely complicated and difficult. It was hence recommended that the responsibility for the backward classes would be adequately discharged only if it was entrusted to the Centre (Statutory Commission, Government of India, vol. I, 1930). The flip side of this arrangement was that if these areas were solely centrally administered, they would not be integrated into the provinces and would forever remain detached and separated from them. As a result, a balance was drawn between these two extremes, wherein the Centre would remain responsible, but the central government would use the governors as central agents for administration (Statutory Commission, Government of India, vol. I, 1930). This system was formally adopted via the constitutional reforms of 1935; under the Government of India Act, 1935, such backward areas were termed as 'excluded areas' and 'partially excluded areas'. This formulation ultimately led to the

Fifth and Sixth Schedules in the 1950 Constitution, and special powers of the governor with respect to administration of tribal areas were spelt out under Articles 244, 244A, and 371A.

The differential treatment in the Fifth and Sixth Schedules was first charted by the colonial British Indian government based on broadly two criteria: (*i*) whether the tribe had the ability to manage its own affairs, and (*ii*) whether the tribal region in question had a significant non-tribal population (Statutory Commission, Government of India, vol. I, 1930). When judged by these two criteria, the north-eastern tribes were considered as isolated and also more socially advanced, and hence were given more autonomy to manage their own affairs, while other tribal communities in the rest of the country occupied territories that did not only comprise tribes, but also other populations, thereby negating the factor of isolation. Along with this, tribes not belonging to the North-East were considered socially backward, and hence were placed under the aegis of provincial governors (Kurup, 2008–9), at the risk of ignoring their long historical relationship with non-tribal societies.

The politico-legal issues that tribal communities in India have suffered, such as the right to autonomy, right to seek justice within their own traditional or customary laws, the right to own and exploit the natural resources in their habitat, and so on, have been addressed in the Constitution and through some tribal-people-specific statutes, but there are considerable differences in the way the north-eastern and peninsular tribes are treated in the Indian legal system. Thus, in order to study customary law prevalent in tribal communities in India, one ought to look at these two broad categories of tribal populations separately, keeping in mind the genesis of tribes as a concept in India. Hence, in the nation building process, while India tried to strike a delicate balance between the assimilation versus autonomy debate by leaning towards the latter, it unwittingly accepted the prevalence of multiple legal traditions aside from the state legal system.

The customary village council (also known as the panchayat, meaning a council of elders) holds an iconic place in Indian social and political ideology (Matthai, 1915). Owing to the imagination of Mahatma Gandhi, the concept of a panchayat became the symbol of the ideal indigenous democratic institution that had the potential to be the basis for an authentic Indian democracy (Jaffe, 2014).

Ever since precolonial times, wherein the villages of India were considered 'little republics' within themselves, these village councils or panchayats have undergone a great amount of change. However, the panchayat ideal survived through the colonial era all the way up to Gandhi's involvement in the Constitution-making process and decades thereafter. The credit for conceptualizing the panchayat ideal lies with the British, who themselves idealized the institution in a multifaceted way (Galanter, 1972).

A quick glance into the rich history of village-based and community-level organization in India reveals that these organizations were typically socio-political in nature that carried out public functions, and also served as centres for the preservation of socio-cultural traditions and practices of local habitations (Kashyap, 1998). They also carried out mediation and adjudication of disputes among members of the village community (Klock, 2001). A much relied upon, albeit contested, description of a village panchayat was delivered by Charles Metcalfe in his report submitted to the House of Commons in 1832, where he stated:

> The village communities are little republics, having nearly everything they can want within themselves.... They seem to last where nothing else lasts.... The union of the village communities, each one forming a separate little state, in itself, has I conceive, contributed more than any other cause to the preservation of the people of India ... and is in a high degree conducive to their enjoyment of a great portion of freedom and independence. (Metcalfe, 1835)

Although, these village institutions functioned autonomously, they worked in tandem with higher authorities, such as local chieftains, who, in turn, interfaced with maharajas—each separated in a highly evolved system of power and authority (Metcalfe, 1835). Villages continued as relatively self-governing village republics till the British brought about major changes in restructuring the administrative hierarchy in British India.

In the colonial era, among the first of several attempts made to create a system of local self-government under the British authority and supervision was that of Mountstuart Elphinstone and Thomas Munro. They were both British military officers who fought in the Anglo-Maratha wars (1818–27) and later assumed high administrative positions in the Bombay and Madras Presidencies. In their administrative tenures, the panchayat, and more generally village-based systems of administration and dispute resolution, emerged as a body well capable of managing the affairs of the village community and the Indian analogue of the English jury coupled with European tribunals of arbitration (Jaffe, 2014). These officers put the panchayat's potential to test, and experimented with them in order to make them serve British interests as an instrument of colonial rule as a basic unit of colonial administration which had its own common law tradition (Elphinstone, 1821; Munro, 1807). Yet their experiment failed to churn out the results they were expecting. This plan of panchayat revival had to be dropped by successive governors who were not convinced of the cost–benefit ratio this project had.

A similar story was reiterated in Punjab half a century later, wherein the British allowed for the operation of a unique form of administration, one that was chiefly engineered around the 'village community' that applied customary laws of the region (laws that found their source in religion or elsewhere) to the affairs of a predominantly tribal population that was settled in villages and practicing agriculture (Chakravarty-Kaul, 1996). Just as in the case of the Bombay and Madras Presidencies under the governorship of Elphinstone and Munro, the British encounter with Punjab too had deep-rooted problems and is considered a failure today by many scholars (Dumont, 1966). The failure of village institutions under the control of the British in Punjab can be attributed to the following reasons, which were the same as its preceding models: (*i*) British administrators' oversimplistic and ergo false notion of what a 'village community' truly was; (*ii*) a deep contradiction between the British effort of enforcing customary law through their own courts while also encouraging village institutions to do the same in order to resolve disputes; and most important (*iii*) institutionalizing or formalizing an informal set-up of a village reflected the British's complete lack of understanding of the *structures* that are involved in customary law-making or enforcement (as opposed to substantive state law) (Mendelsohn, 2014). All this made for a profound falsification of the whole enterprise of revival of the panchayat system.

Many experiments with local self-government carried out by the colonial rulers assisted in the survival of the panchayat ideal all the way up to Independence and even later. In the Constitution, Article 40 of the directive principles of state policy was formulated leaving scope for a distant possibility of establishing local self-government bodies at the local level. Post-Independence several official committees delved into the issue of effectiveness and efficacy of rural governance. The Balawantrai Mehta Committee in 1957, the Ashok Mehta Committee in 1977, and the L.M Singhvi Committee in 1986 examined the possibility of vesting official power at the local level. Singhvi's report resulted in the 64th Constitutional Amendment Bill of 1989 proposing an insertion of Article 243 in the Constitution, which mandated a three-tier structure for state administration—a bill that never saw the light of day owing to its blockage in the Rajya Sabha. Finally, in 1992, revamped bills such as the 73rd (Panchayat Raj) and 74th (Nagarpalika) Amendment Bills were passed, and were later ratified by almost all the state assemblies.

Consolidation of the new legal system and systematic reforms of colonial law undertaken by the Indian nation state were oriented both to make the existing Hindu law more equitable and address injustices of colonial law. However, these reform measures drew much from ideas of Western individualism, secularism, and equality between the sexes. Enacted during the 1950s, the Hindu Code Bill, projected to be the modernizing moment of Indian law and envisioned to unify all Hindus under one uniform law, would in fact strip women off their customary rights under the guise of equality between sexes.

In the post-Independence years, the drive to create a uniform legal subject (which also indicated a common national subject) denied women several customary privileges under the tenets of uniformity. Committees convened to examine Hindu law, to create a system wherein all the Hindu subjects of the state could be examined under one legal format. What this achieved, in turn, was the clubbing of several customary rights and laws, indigenous and tribal, under the category of one Hindu law, leading to the dilution of many such laws while maintaining the rhetoric of progress and equal rights.

The Hindu Code Bill not only preserved the customary rights that maintained patriarchal order (such as the undivided Hindu family), but also, at the same time, introduced new responsibilities for women (Agnes, 2008). Influenced by Western ideas of conjugality, women were now equally liable to support their husbands, should the need arise. However, discrepancies remained in inheritance laws, which inevitably favoured men. Moreover, while women were required to provide spousal support to their husbands, the husbands could take legal action on charges of desertion if the wife left the marital home to seek work outside. The same privilege, however, was not extended to women as well. So, on one hand, we have a sense of shared responsibility between men and women, and, on the other, we have a re-inscription of gendered spaces, where the primary obligation of the woman lay first in her home and to her male spouse (Agnes, 2008).

> While the new codified Hindu law of the 1950s attempted to now extend potential economic dependence to men as well, the same law also 'continued to undermine a woman's right to retain her job against her husband's wishes under the ancient notion of the Lord and the Master and granted them [husbands] the privilege of determining the choice of matrimonial home' (Agnes, 2008, p. 11).

Coming to the primal founding document that comprises the highest form of law-making in any polity (Ackerman, 1993), the Constitution of India contains many references to customary law, such as uncodified personal laws of different religious denominations and customary practices among tribal groups. The Constitution acknowledges the application of customary law in broadly two respects: one, under Article 13 (3), which unequivocally includes 'customs and usages' within the ambit of 'law' in force in India, and two, constitutional provisions that allow for the operation of customary law are those that chart out a system of protection of tribal communities and their customs through Articles 244, 244-A, 342, 371-A, the Fifth and Sixth Schedules, and so on.

Concept of 'Law' and Constitutional Provisions under the State Legal System

As a starting point for analysing the nature of the state's engagement with customary law in pursuance of further understanding the true nature of the Indian legal system and its confluence with other systems, one must begin with Article 13. This is because, it is here one can observe the juxtaposition of non-state customary law vis-à-vis Part III of the Constitution, which comprises positive normative state-made rights.

Article 13 reads as follows:

Laws Inconsistent with or in Derogation of the Fundamental Rights:

1. All laws in force in the territory of India immediately before the commencement of this Constitution, in so far as they are inconsistent with the provisions of this Part, shall, to the extent of such inconsistency, be void

2. The State shall not make any law which takes away or abridges the rights conferred by this Part and any law made in contravention of this clause shall, to the extent of the contravention, be void

3. In this article, unless the context otherwise requires law includes any Ordinance, order, byelaw, rule, regulation, notification, custom or usages having in the territory of India the force of law; laws in force includes laws passed or made by Legislature or other competent authority in the territory of India before the commencement of this Constitution and not previously repealed, notwithstanding that any such law or any part thereof may not be then in operation either at all or in particular areas

4. Nothing in this article shall apply to any amendment of this Constitution made under Article 368

On the one hand, Article 13 (1) stands as a touchstone provision that renders any 'law in force' void if it is in derogation to Part III (fundamental rights). On the other hand, Article 13 (3) connotes a specific meaning to the term 'law', and unequivocally prescribes what it shall include and what it shall not within the Indian state legal paradigm. This clause includes inter alia the terms 'custom or usages', thereby indicating that the Constitution makers lay Part III as a qualifying threshold for the operation of custom and usages. Implicit in this provision is a clear recognition of a body of customary law that operates alongside the positivist state law—one that originates from a source other than the state and which is much older than the conception of the Indian nation state. Detailed analysis of the judicial construction of Article 13 has been done in the next chapter.

India's Constitution provides for protection of tribal communities and their customs through Articles 244, 244-A, 371-A to J, and the Fifth and Sixth Schedules. The Fifth and Sixth Schedules provide for a system of 'Scheduled Areas', or tribal regions, which are designed to protect the interests of listed indigenous communities, or 'Scheduled Tribes'. While the Fifth Schedule provides for the administration of scheduled areas and scheduled tribes in the states outside the north-eastern areas of India, the Sixth Schedule, on the other hand, contains provisions for the administration of tribal areas in the north-eastern states of India and grants tribes, considerable administrative autonomy, endowing each regional administrative unit with its own regional council and each district level unit with local district councils. Autonomous councils under the Sixth Schedule are invested with both executive and legislative powers, subject to the approval of the governor, and even judicial authority through traditional legal systems embedded with certain features of federal law.

A study in the Constitution-making history of India can yield valuable insight into the interests of different groups of people that were involved in this nation-building exercise. Even though tribal communities were not at the forefront of Indian politics and constitution-making, they were nevertheless consulted while drafting the provisions that affected them directly. Certain assurances and promises were given by the national leaders of the time, based upon which many tribal communities acquiesced to being a part of the nation-building process (Shiva Rao, 2010, p. 569). As stated earlier, the drafters of our Constitution had certain British legislations and policies at hand in order to chart a postcolonial path in tribal governance for independent India. In spite of there being a provision for considerable amount of autonomy exercisable by the tribes, the fact that the British also exercised control over these groups and territories in their own way was not lost on the Constitution makers (Shiva Rao, 2010, p. 570).

In pursuance of bringing in the views of different stakeholders together, the Constituent Assembly set up different advisory committees, such as those on fundamental rights, minorities, and tribal areas. The North-East Frontier (Assam) Tribal and Excluded Areas Sub-Committee (Sub-Committee [NE]) and the Excluded Areas and Partially Excluded Areas (other than Assam) Sub-committee

(Sub-Committee [EA]) were set up. The reports of these committees throw light on the intention and reasoning that went into making the Fifth and Sixth Schedules. In its report, the sub-committee on Assam noted the highly democratic character of the tribal village councils and the mechanisms for dispute settlement (Sub-Committee, North East Frontier [NE], 1948).

The committee further added:

[I]n the areas where no right of the chief is recognised, the land is regarded as the property of the clan, including the forests.

The committee concluded as follows:

In all the hill areas visited by us, there was an emphatic unanimity of opinion among the hill people that there should be control of immigration and allocation of the land to outsiders, and that such control should be vested in the hands of the hill people themselves. Accepting this then as the fundamental feature of the administration of the hills, we recommend that the Hill Districts should have the power of legislation over occupation or use of land.

On the point of assessing the negative effects of imposing an alien legal system on tribal peoples, the sub-committee on Assam observed:

Some of the tribals such as the system of the tribal council for the decision of dispute afford by far the simplest and the best way of dispensation of justice for all for the rural areas without the costly system of courts and codified laws. Until there is a change in the way of life brought about by the hill people themselves, it would not be desirable to permit any different system to be imposed from outside.

Aside from the separate reports of the sub-committees, there was also a joint report formulated among the Sub-Committees on Minority and Tribal Rights, which only resonated the sentiment mentioned earlier. It observed:

[T]he tribes had their own way of life with institutions like the tribal and village Panchayats (or councils), which were more than capable of administering village matters and personal disputes.

This joint committee further noted that there should be no disruption in usage and customs of the tribals as this would result in greater harm owing to the simplicity of the tribal populations. As in the case of the sub-committee on Assam, the joint committee concluded:

> It [was] essential to provide statutory safeguards for the protection of the land which [was] the mainstay of the aboriginals' economic life and for his customs and institutions which, apart from being his own, contain[ed] elements of value.

The underlying premise of these reports and the Constituent Assembly debates that ensued based on them was that some tribal communities in India had a traditional legal system that was more than sufficient to deal with the complexities of tribal life (Dam, 2006). Whether such a system resembled in any way the state legal system (say in terms of comprehensiveness and procedure) was irrelevant as long as it was purposive and effective. The Fifth Schedule of the Constitution, while not expressly recognizing a right to a traditional legal system, impliedly recognizes customary legal systems or traditions as part of the larger deference principle underlying the purpose of these provisions. And in contrast, the Sixth Schedule expressly recognizes the right to traditional legal system for the people residing in the tribal areas of Assam or its sister states.

Summing Up

In this chapter, a retelling of the interesting story of engagement between the state legal system and other legal traditions in India is done, showing the link between colonial and postcolonial trends. While chasing the ever-receding horizon of uniformalization of all laws and codification of all customary laws, the state legal system evidently continues to stumble and fall several times in its encounters with other systems and traditions.

In the postcolonial context, engagement of the state legal system with other systems and traditions can be analysed in three parts: one, as stated earlier: the scope, nature, and interpretation of Article 13, which not only defines what 'law' is (in the eyes of the state) but also lays down a test that all customs and usages have to be in consonance with Part III. In the next chapter, we shall see in detail how personal laws and customs have been put to this test. In this respect, it is important to note that jurisprudence surrounding Article 13 in no way describes the entire expansive landscape of the state legal system's engagement with customary law in general. In order to put things in perspective, first, it is safe to assume that customary law operates via numerous informal legal institutions within communities, for instance, village-based, caste-based, profession-based, tribe-based adjudicatory and dispute settlement bodies that reflect the true expanse of customary law in India (Mendelsohn, 2014). Only a minority (arguably microscopic) of matters on customary law end up taking legal recourse to institutions of the state. These comprise thousands of cases in different courts in India that involve a component of customary law: may it be cases that define a certain custom, cases that interpret any custom or apply it to a certain set of circumstances, and so on. All these cases stand within the broad purview of the discussion on 'engagement' with customary law. It is hence no surprise that many scholars have analysed different facets of this gargantuan bulk of case law and have reached varied conclusions in their analyses.

The second facet of engagement can be seen in the deference versus development (assimilation versus autonomy) struggle of tribal people that has reached new heights in this day and age owing to increased demand for land, forest and mineral resources, and so on. This debate has broadly been about culture and rights to it. But the presence of traditional legal systems as comprising a part of the culture itself has not received due share of attention. The state continues to dominate the legal arena when it comes to conflicts of interests between the state or its 'mainstream' populace and tribal communities. In any case, there is a constant recognition and acknowledgement of the fact that there exist other parallel systems among tribal communities that continue to operate without having to concern themselves with the state law. Constitutional provisions (Articles 244, 371A to J, Fifth and Sixth Schedules, and so on) that recognize tribal law and self-governance systems are reflective of India's continual attempt to strike a delicate balance between assimilation and autonomy of its tribal people (Xaxa, 2001). In this process, the Indian state has unwittingly accepted the prevalence of multiple legal systems aside from its own.

The third facet lies not in the village-based legal traditions and practices, which the state has constantly engaged with by way of numerous legislations and policies. It is fairly clear that India has a rich history and cultural heritage not only in terms of multiplicity of laws but also the multiplicity of self-organizational structures, which, in turn, have their own laws, procedures, and institutions for settling claims under these said laws. Villages in India have operated independently for several centuries, and evidence of well-organized autonomous legal and administrative village structures date back to several centuries. It was towards the end of the eighteenth century that village self-organizational structures underwent a drastic change. This occurred at the hands of the British that carried out thorough research in the sphere of village councils, institutions, and methods of dispensing justice in order to explore the possibilities of employing them as British administrative units. The British experiment to formalize and institutionalize village panchayats failed owing to an inherent paradox in their scheme. They endeavoured to give colonial state formality to institutions whose success depended on the very fact that they were informal. They institutionalized them in the bureaucratic and governmental sense, and, in doing so, tried to establish some form of uniformity among all these institutions which worked perfectly owing to their autonomy, flexibility, and non-uniform and non-bureaucratic set-up.

Post-Independence, the state has dabbled with different ideas of local self-governance, and has inadvertently perpetuated the Britishers' initial error in assuming that the addition of state-like features such as democratic electoral process, institutional recognition of the village council, and formal adjudication and dispute settlement mechanisms as are carried out in formal state courts would ensure the success of a new revitalized version of an ancient ideal. The passing of the Panchayat Raj Amendment and PESA four years later go to show that India already contained institutions of self-governance, which the state formalized and institutionalized. The problems that such alien imposition has are apparent when it comes to territories in the Fifth Schedule, owing to the fact that tribal organizational systems have still been retained to a large part in these areas. This cannot be said for the other parts of India where Panchayati Raj now operates generally. If nothing, Panchayati Raj has helped in the penetration of state vigilance, organizational style and modes for dispensation of justice, not to mention party politics, right to the grassroots.

In the next chapter, all these three themes will be discussed in greater detail so as to provide *evidence* through this process of engagement on the existence and operation of multiple legal systems and traditions in India.

III

Examples of Alternative Legal Systems in India

The jurisprudence pertaining to customary law is very extensive in our country. Under the influence of Western positivist-centric thinking, it is often erroneously assumed that the state is the only source of law and the only means of legitimate justice delivery (Menski, 2008). This is not true in *any* society, and even more so in a country like India, which exhibits a vast legally pluralistic landscape that is rife with many legal systems and legal traditions (Mendelsohn, 2014). There evidently ensues a constant attempt on the part of the Indian state to *engage* with this plurality (Derrett, 1968). The nature of this engagement may range from tacit acceptance or acknowledgement of other legal systems and traditions to manifestation in callous domination over other such alternate traditions. In the postcolonial era, where the Indian legal system marches forward albeit to the tune of the colonial drumbeats, it becomes imperative to look at the many ways in which the state legal system has interacted with or operated along with these other systems and traditions in India.

This chapter, in continuation with the previous chapter, questions the common understanding that within the territorial divisions of India, people ascribe, for the most part, to a predominant common law tradition, which automatically makes alternate legal traditions either superfluous or at the most secondary. It analyses examples of both state-sanctioned exceptions to formal law and documented community practices and customary norms, which act as an alternate domain of reference for maintaining law and order. The Constitution of India, in keeping with the promise of secularism and legal pluralism in India, includes custom within the understanding of law in India. Apart from official state recognition of and negotiation with alternate legal domains, there has been documented practice of non-state law at the level of the community and the village, in addition to the areas and communities outlined by the Constitution. This chapter takes a closer look at the treatment of customary and personal law under the Constitution, and judicial engagement with non-state legal practices, along with a close examination of constitutional privileges given specifically to tribal groups in India. In addition to the state's negotiation with and occasional appropriation of alternate legal traditions, this section also looks into anthropological and sociological notes on informal and community-based mechanisms of law and order in India.

The State Legal System's Different Conceptions of 'Law' through the Scrutiny of Article 13

While it has been previously argued that Article 13 can be implicitly read to accommodate 'custom and usage' alongside state law, in several cases before the Supreme Court and high courts, Article 13 has been invoked time and again for any custom or usage to be declared unconstitutional. The courts, while shaping the judicial construction of Article 13 (3), have meted out a differential treatment towards different spheres or branches of customary law. The extensive realm of 'customs and usages' comprise several facets, such as religious personal law, tribal customary law, caste-based, trade-based, and village-based customs, and so on (Galanter, 1981, pp. 1–47). As per the specific *legal* meaning and scope of Article 13 (3), uncodified religious 'personal laws' are not read within the ambit of 'customs and usages' in the *legal* sense (Jain, 2010; M.P. Singh, 2017). Personal laws are laws (such as the Hindu Law, Muslim Law, Christian Law, and Parsi Law of marriage and divorce) that govern the private affairs of members of the concerned religious community. They are ancient systems of law that are deeply connected to customs, though customs are not their only source (Seervai, 2003, p. 677).

Many judicial decisions, having employed the rules of constitutional interpretation, have taken the view that personal laws are not covered within the ambit of Article 13. In the *Narasu Appa Mali* case (AIR 1952 Bom 84), Chief Justice Chagla and Justice Gajendragadkar of the Bombay High Court laid out several reasons as to why personal laws cannot be included within the ambit of Article 13. The ratio of this case stands as a landmark precedent that is continually cited in judgments even today. Cases that followed, such as *Krishna Singh* v. *Mathura Ahir* (AIR 1980 SC 707), the *Ahmedabad Women Action Group* case (AIR 1997, 3 SCC 573) and the *P.E. Mathew* case (AIR 1999 Ker 345) kept to the distinction between personal laws and other customs toeing the line drawn in the *Narasu* case. This means that the threshold usually applicable to customs (that they are not allowed to violate fundamental rights) does not *per se* apply to personal laws. It is for this reason that personal laws are delicately *allowed* to operate in spite of features such as polygamy, unilateral talaq, and differential succession rights among men and women, which are arguably in derogation of fundamental rights.

This leeway certainly does not exist when any religious personal law is *codified*, as it will not preclude the application of Article 13 as an Act of Parliament or state legislature. This means that any Act once codified will stand the test of Article 13. It is, therefore, no surprise that when challenges to codified personal law were made, they succeeded in most cases. In cases such as *Amini E.J.*, (AIR 1995 Ker 252), *Mary Sonia Zachariah* (1995 [1] Ker LT 644 [FB]), *Githa Hariharan* (AIR 1999 SC 1149), and *John Vallamattom* (AIR 2003 SC 2902), provisions of codified religious personal law were struck down owing to their violation of fundamental rights. However, there are exceptions to this: in the *Ahmedabad Women Action Group* case, the Supreme Court chose not to interfere with even codified provisions of the Hindu Code, stating that it involved questions of public policy and governance; as a result, the legislature and the executive is best suited for making any change in the nature of the law via an amendment. Striking down any provision seemed too drastic a step to be taken; and there are many other cases that show an anomaly in the judicial attitude towards cases in which codified personal laws were not mechanically read within the ambit of Article 13, but were handled more delicately, as was the case with uncodified personal laws. These cases include *Maharshi Avadhesh* v. *Union of India* (1994 Supp [1] SCC 713), *Reynold Rajamani* v. *Union of India* (1982 2 SCC 474), *Pannalal Pitti* v. *State of Andhra Pradesh* (1996 2 SCC 498), and so on.

It is expedient here to state that even when it comes to *uncodified* personal law, in some exceptional circumstances the apex court has struck down certain laws by virtue of Article 13. This happened in *Masilamani Mudaliar* v. *Idol of Sri Swaminathaswami* (1996 8 SCC 525). Interestingly, though, around the same time as the *Ahmedabad Women Action Group* case was marking a new trend for codified personal law, this case endeavoured to set a new trend for uncodified personal law. In this case, a Hindu custom precluding women's propriety rights was held unconstitutional. This case stands out in many respects, as it is one of the few instances wherein the court explicitly reasoned that personal laws should generally stand the test of Article 13, thereby ignoring the *Narasu* precedent. However, when dealing with matters of personal law, by and large, the courts have followed a dichotomous approach, by exercising restraint in matters that involve a challenge to uncodified personal law, thereby following the dictum laid down in *Narasu*; and except for some cases, the courts have done the same in matters involving a challenge to even *codified* personal laws. In *Shayara Bano* v. *Union of India*, decided on 22 August 2017, the Supreme Court has reiterated its stand in the Narasu case holding Hindu and Muslim personal laws beyond the can of law in Article 13.

Having delved into the trend of leaving personal laws outside the scrutiny of Article 13, it is now important to gauge the judicial attitude towards cases where customs and usages (that do not amount to 'personal laws') are challenged. Herein, in the landmark case of *Gazula Dasaratha Rama Rao* v. *State of Andhra Pradesh* (AIR 1961 SC 564), the Supreme Court struck down a custom of pre-emptive succession right to a property that violated Part III of the Constitution. In many cases up till 1996 (leading up to the case of *Madhu Kishwar* in 1996), the Court followed the *Gazula* ratio. It is arguably the equivalent for customs and usages of the *Narasu* case. In cases such as *Kahaosan Tangkhul* v. *Simirei Shailei Khullakpa*

(AIR 1960 Assam 48), *Sant Ram* v. *Labh Singh* (AIR 1965 SC 312), *Sheikriyammada Nalla Koya* v. *Administrator* (AIR 1967 Ker 259), and *Atam Prakash* v. *State of Haryana* (AIR 1986 SC 859), customs observed by different communities in question were struck down. Thus, there is a clear distinction between the way personal laws and customs are treated by the judiciary.

In the famous *Madhu Kishwar* case (1996 [5] SCC 125), the Supreme Court chose not to declare the custom among the tribes of the Chhota Nagpur area that precluded women from inheriting property to be unconstitutional under Articles 14, 15, and 21. It adopted a sensitive approach by reading down certain statutory provisions, stating that customs of tribes that have been operative since hundreds of years cannot be held invalid all of a sudden. It also stated that religious personal laws will not be made applicable to tribes even if there is an intersection of tribal and Hindu identities among them. This hesitation to assert the superiority of the normative state law (in this case, fundamental rights) over customary law marks a clear distinction in the judicial application of Article 13. Since 1996, courts have become increasingly wary of striking down customs and usages without any reasonable explanation.

This kind of judicial restraint was also seen in the famous case *Ewanlangki-E-Rymbai* v. *Jaintia Hills District Council* (2006 [4] SCC 748) where the right of a tribe to determine its own rules of membership was respected, even if it conflicted with an individual's fundamental right. Citing *Madhu Kishwar*, the court steered clear of striking down this custom even when it technically had the power to do so. In the same year, the Gauhati High Court in an interesting case did not strike down codified customary election law after it was alleged that it is discriminatory as it favoured a hereditary right to office (*U Fairly Syiem* v. *Khasi Hills Autonomous District Council* [WP no. 5866 of 2006 [PS], Gauhati High Court).

A long chain of cases that threw light upon customs having the force of law in India started from the *Gazula* case in 1961. And since then, instead of exercising the power vested in Article 13 to pronounce any custom as unconstitutional if it violates Part III, the Court has taken a position that is anything but activist. It has declined to get involved in such matters altogether, and has allowed customs to operate despite their derogation to Part III. Furthermore, with respect to personal laws, from the very beginning, in the *Narasu* case in 1952, the Court held that they were intentionally kept outside the purview of Article 13, and thus could stand in derogation to Part III. This position has constantly been challenged by numerous petitioners who have contested that the provisions of certain personal laws constitute gross constitutional violations. On some of these occasions, the Court has very reluctantly adhered to the *Narasu* ratio, on others it has refused to observe it altogether; however, largely, this position still holds true more unequivocally than in the case of customs having the force of law.

The trend that emerges from the cases summarized earlier, and so many others that have raised similar questions of law, can be related to Baxi's idea of written and unwritten constitutions, and how constitutional interpretation favours one of the two in any given instance (Baxi, 2012, p. 181). He states that behind each written constitution lies an unwritten one; while the former is a result of a colonial legacy of political and social action, the latter comprises usages, traditions, protocols, and practices that resist codification. This he claims is the true constitution. Judges while interpreting the constitution, or in this case carrying out the function of judicial review, privilege either the written or reinforce the constitution (Gardner, 2011); this is manifested through judicial self-restraint by declining to address basic violations of rights on the differently named doctrines, such as of the separation of powers, political questions of the state, or margin of appreciation towards other organs of governance.

This brings one to the question of whether customs and personal laws are considered components of the state legal system or are they mere aberrations. If the Indian Constitution is considered an aspirational document that embodies the ideals that the Indian legal system wants and hopes to achieve, then customs and personal laws are deviations that are waiting to be unified into a single whole—one, which is more aligned to constitutional principles such as liberty, equality, and fraternity. Such unification, even if ostensibly asserted by the state via a uniform civil code, will never be achieved in the truest sense (Menski, 2008), considering the degree of pluralistic vigour India encompasses (Mendelsohn, 2014). Attempts towards unification can be construed through the enactment of religion-neutral law (such as the Special Marriage Act, 1956) that inter alia adheres to constitutionally cherished principles of equality and freedom. The state quintessentially introduces such laws as 'model laws' for all communities. When personal laws of different communities resemble this model law, they seem to have assimilated themselves into the state Indian legal system. In the case of personal laws that drastically differ from the model law, it stands out as an aberration or a separate legal tradition. However, one must keep in mind that the discussion on unification lies within the universe of state legislated law and does not account for all the affairs of an individual's life that are regulated by rules, procedures, and institutions that bear no resemblance to, deference to, or compliance with state law.

Tribal Legal Systems and Traditions as Exceptions to the State Legal System

Common criteria for identifying communities as tribes in India range from 'geographical isolation, simple technology and condition of living, general backwardness, to the practice of animism, tribal language, physical features' (Xaxa, 1999, p. 3,589), and so on. However, these are a series of categories that have developed based significantly on inputs from early anthropological accounts of tribal societies across the world and administrative and law and governance contingencies. Communities which have come to be historically identified as tribes nearly always have a different system of political and kinship ordering from larger political systems. However, this does not imply that reciprocal relations and some levels of integration did not exist between tribal and non-tribal India. In India, therefore, it can be argued that by grouping more than 400 tribes under uniform state categories can lead to several dissonances on ground.

Tribes in anthropology came to be known as communities characterized predominantly by pre-industrial modes of economy and organization, with lower levels of technological development in comparison to their rural settled cultivator counterparts, as well as the urban populations. However, the concept of a tribe as it ossified over the course of documented Indian history is often considered to be a British-colonial import, based on information gleaned from studying mostly 'simple, pre-literate, small-scale, and isolated societies in Australia, Melanesia, the Pacific Islands, North and South America, and Sub-Saharan Africa'

(Béteille, 1986, p. 297). The contention of tribal scholars in India, such as Andre Béteille and Virginius Xaxa, is that a social group corresponding to European definitions of a tribe could not be applied to all communities which are identified as tribes in India, and 'ethnographic material from India did not figure prominently in the general discussion regarding the definition of tribes' (Béteille, 1986, p. 299).

When encountered with culturally dissimilar Indian communities, the British at first used the words 'caste' and 'tribe' interchangeably (Xaxa, 2008). Later, several different, often opposed, categories were used to demarcate tribal society in India from non-tribal societies. Several classified tribes were not geographically isolated and demonstrated a long relationship with mainstream Indian society, but showed a lower level of technological development than their mainstream counterparts. Moreover, several tribes that were isolated and inaccessible showed greater degrees of technicity and often dominated non-tribal societies in their region (such as in the case of the Ahom in Assam). While the Constitution under its broad divisions of tribes of the North-East and tribes of Peninsular India tries to accommodate for these differences, a general understanding and common rhetoric of tribes being backward and obsolete social systems prevails.

It is important here to note that the representative of the tribals in the Constituent Assembly debates, Jaipal Singh Munda, belonged to one of the numerically dominant Peninsular tribes of India. His specific location within the tribal heterogeneity in India was, in fact, often used to destabilize his arguments and overrule his suggestions. Whether the other members' attitudes towards tribes as the backward counterparts of mainstream Indians were a reaction to Singh's particular identity is difficult to state; however, during the course of the debates, despite the careful considerations on creating two Schedules for different types of tribes in India, dialogue between the members of the assembly casually referred to *all* tribes as isolated and backward. When Singh advocated for autonomy for tribal republic in India, dissenters in the Assembly shot him down, arguing autonomy would deepen isolation despite the presence of underlying assumptions that Peninsular tribes in India were, in fact, *not* isolated.

An excerpt from K.M. Munshi, Singh's primary foil in the debates, clearly shows (*i*) the assumed inferiority of tribes in India, and (*ii*) their isolation and separation from mainstream Indian life.

The policy behind this, as has already been pointed out, is the same which my friend, Mr. Jaipal Singh, has at heart, *viz.* that these scheduled tribes in course of time might be raised to the level of other Indians in the Provinces and might be absorbed in the national life of this country. (Constituent Assembly of India Debates, Volume 9, K.M. Munshi)

However, as tribal studies scholars note—and the Constitution in its categorical distinctions demonstrates in the Fifth and the Sixth Schedule also accepts—that a tribe in India, contrary to early anthropological and other scientific criteria, is not always at once isolated, with lower levels of technicity, autonomy, and so on. Contrary to the logic of isolation and peripheral existence, which is often misplaced on to heartland tribes of India, India demonstrates a long history of coexistence of tribal and non-tribal societies, of 'tribes' and 'civilization'. It has also been reported that tribal dynasties would also compete to be included within the Hindu order and a new caste or sub-caste would be created as a result. However, importantly, Béteille also notes that in ancient and medieval India, 'despite changes in fortune of individual tribes and despite incursions into tribal territories by Hindu kings and Hindu ascetics, the tribal identity never became fully effaced in any of the major regions of the country' (Béteille, 1986, p. 309). Despite assimilation, tribal culture retained its integrity.

A historical view of tribes in India, such as the one advocated by Xaxa and Béteille, upends the predominant evolutionary logic that governs most conceptions regarding tribes. Tribal systems—or those communities in India which came to be known as tribal for myriad reasons—were considered evolutionary lower forms of social organization whose fitting teleological end was absorption within the Indian state, specifically the Hindu majority. While tribal communities over long periods of time vociferously differentiated themselves from mainstream India, and continue to do so, with Independence and the making of a new nation, their numerous internal differences too were made largely uniform and consistent under state definitions. Keeping in mind the concept of tribe in India, several scholars, therefore, prefer to use the term Adivasi instead. However, the use of the term 'tribe' continues in official documents.

The Adivasi history of cultural difference is an obvious indicator of their preference for customary practices over state-ordained ones, be it in the realms of economics, law, kinship, and personal practices or even political movements. However, assuming an evolutionary bias in state policies, rather than taking into consideration treatment of different Adivasi communities based on historical needs and differences, locates them lower in the stages of social development and superimposes state logic as a naturally higher and more evolved process, to which Adivasis are ordained to eventually adhere. Lack of compliance with state logic then comes to be viewed as deviation from rule of law, and, in some cases, even against national interest. Evolutionist thought and single-minded agendas of progress stubbornly continued (and continue) to locate Adivasis as mainstream India's evolutionary inferior rather than its historical foil.

In the years after Independence, driven by large-scale industrialization agendas with the projected aim of national good, mechanisms of the state were leveraged to occupy resource-rich areas. Areas with high concentration of Adivasi population are usually resource rich as well. A report by Centre for Science and Environment, New Delhi, illustrates this overlap. According to the 2008 report, 'Keonjhar, Orissa, produces the maximum amount of iron ore in the country ... the district also has 39 percent of its geographical area under forests; 45 percent of its population is tribal' (Centre for Science and Environment, 2008, p. 7). Much like Keonjhar, the report outlines fifteen further districts with similar overlaps, across India, showing the apparent convergence of Adivasis, their land, and the state's expropriation of resources. Scheduled areas, natural resources and forest cover, and high percentages of Adivasi populations have a historical confluence in India.

Under the doctrine of eminent domain, territory could be acquired by the state for the public good. Adivasi territories, already targeted for their resource potential during the colonial period, were targeted anew under the Independent Indian state. In consonance with aggressive development targets, resources were mined and collected in unsustainable ways, deeply affecting those traditional, sustainable synergies indigenous populations already shared with their environments. These areas became the targets for achieving India's ambitious development agendas, leading to massive displacement and dispossession among the Adivasis.

Appealing for reform and greater justice could be done only on the limited and limiting terms of the state, and when the state itself was being contested, it led to a proliferation of movements contesting the validity of state procedures by using informal or non-state logics. The state itself was the architect of citizenship and the rights it entailed and, therefore, movements needed to borrow from custom and local tradition, as well as international conventions, *outside* of the state. Plural legal conventions had to be marshalled for movements urging justice for dispossessed Adivasis, and customary laws and non-modern means of advocacy and protest had to be leveraged (Sundar, 2011).

Adivasi movements for greater justice created 'a bricolage of legal claims based on notions of "custom" enshrined in local tenure laws on the one hand, as well as universalist constitutional principles, court judgements and international conventions on the other hand' (Sundar, 2011, p. 422). Where processes and categories of the state seemed insufficient, Adivasi movements resorted to practices and principles of law and order present outside the formal state. Adivasi histories of synergy and continuity with their civilizational counterparts are often ignored in the making of modern socio-legal systems. In cases where due recognition is given to Adivasi communities and their cultural integrity, those communities with demonstrated and systemic political and legal traditions are inadvertently privileged. When the state, at best, partially recognizes Adivasi communities and their socio-political systems, state legal systems, under this conception of indigenous traditions, continue to be but one alternative rather than the go-to systems for the maintenance of law and order in these communities.

While India has a remarkable diversity of tribal communities, they share similar traits across many regional variations, such as being relatively more homogenous and more self-contained than the non-tribal social groups (Grigson, 1944). As a result, India's legal and political history has been marred by tensions (both perceptible and obscure) that pervade between tribal and non-tribal groups, on the one hand, and the tribes and the state, on the other (Kurup, 2008–9, p. 95).

The state legal system in India in this context has endeavoured to balance the assimilation of tribal peoples into the mainstream along with the preservation of their independent identity; this means that the contours of special provisions in the Constitution and certain special laws allow tribal communities to preserve their way of life without compromising development. This echoes the same contradiction that is evident in the case of personal laws and customs. While tribal communities are given a fair deal of autonomy when their grouping and organizational structure is crystallized (in other words, when they are viewed to be capable of self-government), their mainstreaming is viewed as desirable eventuality of this political process (Xaxa, 2001, p. 202). In the case of personal laws and customs, leeway, exceptions, and recognition is given, yet the desired outcome or endgame of this multiplicity of laws and legal systems is a uniform civil code that promises to either bring uniformity or encompass personal laws and customs and usages within the fold of state law.

Due to this contradiction, many scholars have argued that autonomy in governance was given to certain groups only to ensure the most convenient and efficient form of administration, and as such, such autonomy is no more than an innovative system of decentralized administration rather than evidence of true self-government (Hooja, 2004, p. 19). This is so, because, the state continues to have a looming presence through certain constitutional functionaries like the governor and the State Council of Ministers (Basu, 2002, p. 1709). Furthermore, the state always claims the last word in terms of adjudication of disputes and resolving administrative conflicts. However, irrespective of the extent of the state's involvement in tribal affairs, it must be noted that autonomy over assimilation for some tribal populations was chosen not only as a charitable act on the part of the state, but also as a necessary measure, considering the high capacity of self-government and management (including management of legal affairs) exhibited by some tribal communities of India (K.S. Singh, 1995). The extent of legal and juridical sophistication exercised by some of the tribes rendered the rules, procedures, and institutions of the state rather irrelevant for them. However, the category Scheduled Tribe, despite such considerations that may have taken place while autonomy was being accorded, continues to be associated with the stigma of backwardness, primitivity, and isolation, both in the formal and informal spheres of law and governance.

The granting of autonomy to tribal communities (albeit to different extents in different circumstances) in our Constitution constitutes 'recognition' of other legal systems, which is based on a sociological founding principle that 'legal systems' cannot be viewed in isolation within the tribal context, but must be analysed as part of a distinguished culture (Zimmermann, 1996, p. 601). If a legal system is an element or attribute within the meaning of the term 'culture', then it can be compared with the other legal systems surrounding it (in this case, the state legal system), even if it cannot be viewed in absolute isolation from culture's other elements and attributes (Dam, 2006). This will show how traditional practices and customs are not only expressions of a culture, but also a means of adjudication of claims and dispute resolution.

Recognition of distinguished legal systems can be inferred from the Constitution as the act of granting administrative autonomy, which is an expression of deference towards tribal cultural systems; and as stated earlier, a legal system is but a part of this tribal culture. Hence, when evidence is sought for substantiating the proposition, one must not only look at the provisions of the Constitution and statutory instruments that endow or recognize tribal cultural autonomy, but also the instances wherein the state's interest (as being a form of mainstream or majoritarian culture) conflicts with the tribal interests. This conflict may manifest in the way of historical struggles, incidences, events, and case law that evince the distinction between two systems and not merely the interpretation of some constitutional or statutory provisions (Narwani, 2004, p. 31).

In the constitution-making process, some of the debates and discussions held among members of the Constituent Assembly show that India attempted to consciously reject the assimilation model in favour of the autonomy one (at least with respect to tribes that were identified to have a 'distinct' culture) (Constitutional Assembly Debates, 1949). Upon adoption, the Fifth Schedule of the Constitution, while not expressly recognizing a right to a traditional legal system, implicitly recognizes customary legal systems as part of the larger deference principle underlying the purpose of these provisions. And, in contrast, the Sixth Schedule expressly recognizes the right to traditional legal system for the people residing in the tribal areas of Assam or its sister states. Despite clearly stated ideals of assimilation, India at the time of nation building did consider its plural history, albeit partially. However, this was not always uniformly followed, and conceptual confusions about the status and situation of tribes vis-à-vis Indian society often informed the decisions of the Constituent Assembly.

Implications of Panchayati Raj in India

As examined in the previous chapter, panchayats have long been considered the ideal social order and administrative sub-unit both under colonial rule and after. Panchayats seemed to be micro-level representations of democratic processes and villages the basic constituent units of the Indian state. The Amendment Acts that introduced Panchayati Raj meant to instil democratic practices at the very grassroots of the Indian polity, creating mechanisms for elections and reservation for members of scheduled tribes, scheduled castes, and women. However, one striking feature of the Act is the quantum of control exercised by the state government right from the electoral process to the functioning and operation of the panchayats. This is because under the Indian Constitution Panchayat Raj is a state subject, and state governments have shown the utmost reluctance in effectively devolving adequate powers and resources (Rajput and Meghe, 1984).

While the notion of allowing democracy to seep into the lowest rungs of the Indian political system is seemingly appealing, democracy manifests as a game of political parties and numbers. There is hence an inevitable nexus between the interests of the ruling party in the state and the administration at the local level, that is, there always is an inexorable push from above to delay, derail, and defer devolution of interests that will not align with those of the state (U. Singh, 2009). It is hence no surprise that only in states where the political authority has demonstrated an over-riding political will (either owing to a high standard of political maturity or owing to assuredly similar political inclinations at the state level and local level) has the 1992 Act been implemented in its true spirit.

Since its operation in the ancient times, village councils have come a long way in becoming instrumentalities of the state itself. Their semi-autonomous nature and informality in adjudicating claims and settling disputes has now, over several centuries, been replaced by a formal institutional framework that operates formally at the behest of the state.

In 1992, the 73rd Amendment was intended to apply only in non-tribal rural areas. With the introduction of the Panchayat (Extension to Scheduled Areas) Act (PESA) in 1996, however, Part IX of the Constitution was extended to the Fifth Schedule territories (albeit not to Sixth Schedule territories). As a result, state governments had the power, much like in the case of other areas, to foster tribal self-government through Panchayati Raj institutions. The Fifth Schedule was not amended following the enactment of PESA and this has resulted in a unique scenario of conflicting constitutional mandates, wherein one prescribes autonomy to manage one's own affairs and the other imposes a state controlled scheme of administration with the intent to introduce concepts of democracy, accountability, and state-styled governance (Kurup, 2008–9, p. 99).

According to the PESA, any territory within the Fifth Schedule 'comprising a community and managing its affairs in accordance with traditions and customs' could exercise limited self-government (Section 4[b]). Owing to the enactment of PESA, communities in the Fifth Schedule areas were directed to follow democratic elections, conform to the hierarchical panchayat system stipulated in Part IX, and exercise the powers thought necessary to enable them to function as institutions of self-government. In order to retain some consonance with the spirit of the Fifth Schedule, state governments were to ensure that (*i*) the laws applicable to panchayats conformed with the customary law, social and religious practices, as well as traditional access and management of community resources and (*ii*) the *gram sabhas* (village assemblies not understood in the traditional sense but comprising those members whose names are included in the electoral rolls for electing the panchayat at the village level) were competent to preserve the customs and traditions of the people, their cultural identity, community resources, and the customary mode of dispute resolution.

Many a statesman hailed the PESA as a logical extension of both the Fifth Schedule, on the one hand, and Part IX of the Constitution, on the other (Aiyar, 2012, p. 227). However, the enactment of the PESA resulted in a repetition of the errors similar to the ones committed by the British. Village councils that once resembled republics in themselves were completely made devoid of their independence and indigenous system of administration and adjudication owing to British remodelling (George and Sreekumar, 1994). Hence, the effect of Panchayati Raj in 1992 produced mixed results: in some states, it worked well to strengthen and democratize local institutions, in others it failed (in a way that the programmatic state-supervised development competed with the already established village administrative system), and in many states, it never was implemented to be anything more than a penetration of state party politics at the village level (Kurup, 2008–9). However, when it comes to the Fifth Schedule territories, they still retained their systems of indigenous governance. They bore great resemblance to 'village republics' that Metcalfe and his compatriots observed in the villages of India at that time (Cohn, 1965, p. 96).

Hence, the implications of the PESA on tribal populations was very dire and led to the debilitation of traditional legal systems at the hands of the state. The PESA is seen by many activists and scholars as a prime example of the state's attempt to monopolize power, rather than share it with its populace (Samal, 2003). In fact, the very idea of imposition of state administration in tribal areas was frowned upon by the first commission on scheduled areas and scheduled tribes. After over two decades of PESA's operation, many tribal regions previously administered by traditional councils and organizational structures have now had to cope with an entirely new power dynamic within them. They have also settled into a state-styled mode of governance that is predicated on the belief that state-initiated development carried out on the basis of values such as democracy through the majoritarian electoral process, transparency and accountability to higher governmental functionaries, and so on was the only solution for administering primitive tribal societies (Briggs and Sharp, 2004). Furthermore, states that did make attempts to devolve decision-making powers upon tribal communities have also largely been unsuccessful owing to the fact that at the end of the day, the primary responsibility for implementing PESA via distribution of funds and allocation of resources remains the prerogative of the state government. This echoes the same issues faced by the Presidencies of Bombay and Madras, as well as the erroneous experiment with village councils in Punjab, where a misplaced view of what self-government truly means gave rise to a situation in which the state imposed its system of governance on a population as a largesse hoping that they will be thankful and learn to adapt to the state's methods in due time.

It has also been argued that The Scheduled Tribes and Other Traditional Forest Dwellers (Recognition of Forest Rights Act), 2006 (FRA), which came into force in 2008, too has fallen prey to the inadequacies of the PESA. This Act, unlike any of its predecessors, aspires to undo the 'historic injustice' meted out to communities dependant on the forest by recognizing their customary forest land rights, that is, their legal right to hold forest lands upon which they have been residing and cultivating, and by extension recognizing their rights to use, manage, and conserve forest resources as accruing thereto (Dash and Kothari, 2013). The Act unequivocally acknowledges (in its preamble) that forest dwellers are 'integral' to the survival and sustainability of forests owing to their role in biodiversity conservation. Interestingly, this legislation stands to signify the culmination of decades of wrongful land alienation and eviction of forest-dwelling communities from their ancestral homes (Khare, 2012). Furthermore, it is not only a combination of the environmental and sustainability agenda but also the struggles that tribal communities have suffered surrounding the insecurity of tenure and lack of established rights over forests, which has, in turn, led to their marginalization and displacement.

A major contradiction in the implementation of the PESA, as pointed out by many scholars, is that it cannot work in isolation without a comprehensive roadmap towards greater tribal control over natural resources, including water, forest produce, and so on (Kurup, 2008–9). The organizational structures of many PESA-inflicted areas is that of a traditional tribal system of self-organization and adjudication and dispute settlement, and such systems are inherently linked with control over land and forests. The stronger the link between these communities and their ancestral forests rights, stronger the level of empowerment in socio-cultural terms and oftentimes in economic terms (Sunder, 2006). There is, hence, a clearly visible link between the legal systems prevalent in village communities, state's imposition of Panchayati Raj and PESA, and the enactment of FRA as a means to assuage past wrongs committed by the state towards divesting tribal communities of their rights. Unfortunately, when it comes to the field implementation, in the 10 years that the FRA has remained in force, it has proven to be yet another Act that imposes state superiority over indigenous and traditional systems, as its realization lies in the hands of the state forest bureaucracy that is not yet ready to consider any other system of forest management as legitimate (CFR-LA, 2016).

As illustrated, the assertion of the state legal system as the primary mechanism for resolving disputes has had a long history in India, which traditional, non-state institutions intermittently question. As the incursions of PESA and FRA show, the state often models its own practices based on input from the non-state mechanisms. Community practices, custom, and other such informal mechanisms of social control are acknowledged, incorporated, and often ignored by the state. However, they persist in governing the lives of the people, often despite the incursions of the state.

State Legal System's Negotiation with Traditional Legal Practices in Other Scenarios

Much the same trend of transplanting general models onto disparate local contexts can be noticed in the sector of legal reform around the same time as the enactment of the 73rd and 74th Amendment Acts. Since the colonial era, certain indigenous legal institutions such as the traditional *lok adalat*s and *nyaya panchayat*s were exempted from strict procedural rules, and employed adjudicators who were among members of the village council or elected popularly and were located geographically close to potential claimants, at the village level. This changed with the advent of the Legal Services Authority Act, 1987, and later the Gram Nyayalayas Act, 2008. Many states had previously passed their own laws on carrying out justice via traditional nyaya panchayats until the central laws formalized the indigenous informal systems. Similarly, states employed a three-tier administrative system vesting powers at the village level right from Independence up till the point when the Panchayat Raj Act and PESA were enacted.

From traditional village councils to formal panchayats, from nyaya panchayats to gram nyayalayas, and from traditional village-based lok adalats to formal permanent lok adalats indicates a trend of increasing state role in the judicial and political systems to not just a large horizontal sphere of subject areas, but also a vertical top to bottom impact that has today reached the last frontier of 'subsidiarity'. While considering the functioning of nyaya panchayats in some states, Baxi and Galanter chart out a very dreary picture of dismal performance (Baxi and Galanter, 1979). They explain how not only did the adjudicators not know the exact nature of their role, much less, they were also not trained in record keeping, using evidence, and applying law, and resultantly could not assert jurisdiction over and above the state judicial institutions that already exercised plenary jurisdiction in that area or region. Their views were further reinforced by the time Meschievitz and Galanter carried out empirical research in 1982, wherein they stated that nyaya panchayats were as good as non-existent given their infrequent promulgation (Meschievitz and Galanter, 1982).

In the case of the decline of nyaya panchayats, scholars such as Galanter, Meschievitz, and Krishnan pointed out several reasons that led to the decline of their use (Galanter and Krishnan, 2004). One, indiscriminate use by Indian policymakers of the 'panchayat ideology', which was employed owing to political reasons at the Centre along with a general inclination to avoid serious engagement with the nature of disputes and law in rural India. Second, nyaya panchayats failed because they symbolized an unappetizing combination of the formality of official law with the political malleability of village tribunals. This experience continued with the passing of the Gram Nyayalayas Act, 2008, which further entrenched the state's modus operandi into the rural pockets that thrived on informality and autonomy (Bail, 2015). According to these scholars, the nyaya panchayat experience holds valuable lessons for the design of rural political and judicial reform in India. The Panchayat Raj, and even more so the PESA, are attempts to recreate an idealized traditional institution, the village panchayat, and, at the same time, imbue it with an adherence to the substantive and procedural law of the country. Is this an attempt to bring different legal orders within the fold of the state common law system? Either way that response unfurls, it is an allusion to the idea of plural culture of politico-legal institutions, procedures, and rules.

The impulse of recreating an idealized Indian past within the modern legal system has led to several institutional failures in addition to those of the permanent lok adalats and the nyaya panchayats. Public Interest Litigation (PIL) in India has also been considered another such failed 'Indian' adventure within the formal legal system. PILs expanded the scope of participation in the legal process to non-professionals. Effectively, anyone who 'may be witness to constitutional neglect and lawlessness' (Bhuwania, 2017, p. 2) could file a writ petition in the higher judiciary in India. Simpler procedures and relaxed rules gave to the PIL a collaborative character. The potential of public participation and access combined with non-adversarial procedure seemed to bring PILs closer to indigenous systems of dispute settlement, which, as several scholars note, are more collective and compromise-oriented than the state legal system. Here was the state legal system attempting to make amends for its formal, inaccessible nature by presenting PILs as 'providing substantive, popular justice, unmediated by legalese and with an emphasis on questions of fact rather than law' (Bhuwania, 2017, pp. 10–11).

Scholars such as Galanter (1968) have argued that over time the modern common law system in India has come to appropriate distinctly indigenous characteristics, and PIL came to be seen as one of those instances of indigenous transformation of imported, modern processes. Much like the discourse around nyaya panchayats, where again it was believed that formal state institutions structured on indigenous principles would allow for better operation of the originally British legal system in India, PILs too seemed to incorporate indigenous principles onto the logic of the common law system (Bhuwania, 2017).

PIL procedures in India, Bhuwania argues, began exhibiting symptoms of a model in which 'commitment to principles of law in Indian judicial discourse mattered less and less, [and] what mattered was commitment to an ideology' (Bhuwania, 2017, p. 117). Over time, PILs in India came to exhibit decidedly 'irrational' properties as well. In a case brought before the Supreme Court in March 2007, hawkers' organizations questioned a Municipal Corporation of Delhi (MCD) scheme that sought to *first* identify sites in the city where hawking could be allowed, and *then* invite applications from vendors to avail of hawking rights in these identified zones. A member of the hawkers' organization suggested an alternative in which the MCD could *first* survey and map already existing hawking zones, and formalize them based on the survey findings. The Court dismissed this logic, arguing that allowing this would enable a proliferation of hawking, and informal vendors would take over the city, even the Supreme Court premises. In another similar case at the Delhi High Court regarding slum dwellers close to the Court premises, judges again expressed fears of squatters encroaching on high court territory. It seemed that the popular promise of PILs here was being undermined by the judges' own fears of their inconvenience and their private visions of a 'hypermodern' Delhi.

This system, Bhuwani argues, is a direct departure from Max Weber's terms of reference for modern, formal, rational legal systems—the logically highest point for any legal system to arrive at over time (Weber, 1968). Emphasis on fact and substance over law and general legal guidelines denoted a return to prior, premodern version of *kadijustiz* (Weber's term for 'administration of justice which is oriented not at fixed rules of a formally rational law but at an ethical, religious, political, or otherwise expediential postulates of a substantively rational law') (Bhuwania, 2017, p. 134). PILs in their transformed state tried to achieve 'social' outcomes—they, therefore, referred to ideological realms outside the juristic, making them substantive according to Weber's logic. Arbitrary use by judges for individual agendas also made them irrational—locating them at the bottom corner of Weber's fourfold distribution of legal orders (Bhuwania, 2017).

Bhuwania's pinpointing of the higher judiciary's intentional disregard for formal procedures and attempt to further its own arbitrary ends indicates a certain kind of corruption. However, his uncritical acceptance of Weber's evolutionary highest formal rational legal system as the logical prototype of all modern legal orders ignores that Weber was inadvertently privileging *all* Western systems. Weber's vision of a modern legal system was also undeniably a Western legal system. However, Bhuwania also indicates how rather than enhancing indigenous institutions, the Indian state has focused more on 'Indianizing' these other institutions of Western import by introducing a component of an ideal Indian past (such as in the case of nyaya panchayats and the application of 'panchayat ideology'). If the formal legal system in India conforms to the Weberian prototype, which is defined in opposition to indigenous systems with less regard for formal procedures and greater emphasis on fact and substance, Indianizing them, in a way, is then predestined for failure. Bhuwania indicates, albeit only in passing, that in India, the non-state legal system was not empowered, rather, 'the state institutions themselves were transformed and made to behave according to inchoate ideas of what informal "traditional" institutions were like' (Bhuwania, 2017, p. 33).

Bhuwania, while critical of this degeneration of courts into 'kadi justice', goes on to refer to Partha Chatterjee's explanation of why this phenomenon exists in countries with colonial pasts. Chatterjee (2011) is arguing that under the creeping logic of general and standard principles, cultures became commensurable and reducible to a common standard. The first wave of colonialism in the Americas did not necessitate the incorporation of local order with European ones, as indigenous American communities 'were not regarded as having a credible political society at all that needed to be integrated into the new imperial formation' (Chatterjee, 2011, p. 4). But European expansion in the Eastern hemisphere could not disregard existing Oriental political institutions. To deal with cultural and political differences Bentham, argues Chatterjee, proposed that since human nature was fundamentally the same universally, English principles *could* be applied to India. However, since there existed concrete difference in English and Indian conditions, changes needed to be made. But Bentham also believed that these differences were just differences of variance, and these differences were 'amenable to more or less precise and detailed qualitative or quantitative comparison—that is to say, they were all subject to some common measure' (Chatterjee, 2011, p. 7). Essentially everyone was the same, they just deviated in degrees from the common standard—cultural difference could be 'plotted as deviations from a standard and hence normalised' (Chatterjee, 2001, p. 7).

Chatterjee here is referring to Ian Hacking's (1990) two ideas of what 'normal' could mean. While normal meant what was right, and what was good, it also indicated an empirical average state. The statistical conception of 'normal' allows for a proliferation of exceptions to the norm, without questioning the norm itself. So, while the British themselves performed several exceptions to rule of law, their general legal principles were not greatly compromised. Even in independent

India, which allows access to land, electricity, and water to 'illegal' colonies, in this case 'the particular illegality associated with a specific population group may be treated as an exception which does not disturb the fundamental rule of law' (Chatterjee, 2011, p. 14). The general Western model, under this understanding, is not threatened by incorporating non-Western models under its fold, and the regular normal is not disrupted by the presence of irregular exceptions. The condition of the Indian legal system and its many classificatory confusions can be understood under this statistical framework of understanding what is 'normal'. Under this framework, the Indian legal system can potentially still identify as a common law country while accommodating a host of qualitatively heterogeneous exceptions. However, identifying practices as deviations from a set standard does not necessarily negate difference altogether; variations of the same do not dismiss the presence of real heterogeneity (Canguilhem, 1991). In addition to this, state exceptions can be conclusively counted as evidence of India's significantly different indigenous conceptions of law and its practice. Coupled with the vast network of informal legality in India, continued identification of the Indian legal system with the common law family continues to raise questions.

A Brief Examination of the Structure and Procedures of Informal and Community-Based Mechanisms of Social Control

In marking the theoretical separation between state and non-state legal systems, Baxi (1986) recognizes his debt to Bernard Cohn, one of the early writers on the Indian postcolonial period. Cohn (1965) observes differences in India between what he calls 'local law-ways' (norms that govern social behaviour in restricted political systems where nation state authority may be acknowledged, but does not play a strong role) and 'lawyer's law' (which, borrowing from Galanter [1964], can be referred to as rules and behaviours in statute books and law reports).

Local law-ways exist at the levels of the kinship groups, the caste groups, and the single- and multi-caste village groups. The presiding authority of the caste group is the caste panchayat or community council, and that of the multi-caste village is the heterogeneous village panchayat—the basic unit which the British and Indian governments appropriated while formalizing panchayats in India. The structure of the council differs depending on the structure of villages. While in single-caste villages with small populations the caste norms and the village norms are coterminous, and the presiding council may be composed of the same caste as the petitioners, the same cannot be said for multi-caste villages where heterogeneity necessitates the presence and authority of a single dominant caste, which occupies a position of power. However, as Cohn notes, not all Indian villages have a caste-based panchayat. Villages without a dominant caste often have a single authoritative individual as a village head—usually a man with economic and political dominance who also relates to the ideals of just and good man, one who will be able to offer both protection and justice (Cohn, 1965).

In multi-caste villages, intra-community disputes are usually settled by a heterogeneous panchayat using the customary laws of the community in question, but in inter-caste and inter-community quarrels, compromise is encouraged. This compromise may sometimes come at the cost of the customary practices of one or both communities. Numerically insignificant caste groups, as well as lower castes in the varna, often do not have their own panchayats. Lower caste groups residing in multi-caste villages rarely find place or representation within panchayats, and as the documented history of panchayats show, women too are under-represented. In the absence of a caste panchayat, community elders often gather and arbitrate small matters, and larger disputes are referred to regional caste groups (the next level after the village caste group), dominant castes, or even supernatural entities.

The People of India volume on the state of Himachal Pradesh reports how several villages follow a village deity (*deota*). The deota speaks through its oracle (*gur*). Often, the gur, the traditional councils, and the statutory bodies work together to maintain social order. In several villages, the oracle has the ultimate decisive power. And in some cases (for example, the Pajiara community), the oracle, or the temple manager, in accordance with his high social status, is often the *pradhan* of the statutory panchayat as well.

Among the Pajiaras, 'There are Jati councils and regional sabha of the community, but the word of the oracle is considered final. Gram panchayats also exercise control, and in many cases the Pajiaras have control over the village panchayat. Many pajiaras are nominated or elected as presidents of their Gram Panchayat' (People of India, Volume XXIV, Himachal Pradesh, 1996, p. 439).

However, well into the 1950s, there were villages in India where nearly constant conflict made subscription to a single legal system, either state or non-state, difficult. Namahalli, a multi-caste village without a dominant caste, experienced what Cohn calls 'pervasive factionalism' in the 1950s (Siegal and Beals, 1960). There was no one clear contender under whose jurisdiction the village could function. The village council, different caste groups vying for dominance, and the backdrop of a system of courts and statute law all competed for primary authority in settling matters of social order. It was in this context that an offender refused to follow the pronouncements of the village council, claiming they had no 'legal' authority, and claimed if forced to follow their edicts, he would be compelled to take his case to urban law courts. The village council, recognizing that the courts of law seldom delivered equitable justice within a reasonable time frame, did not press the matter and the offender walked free. 'The traditional legal system was rendered ineffective by the new legal system, but it was not replaced by it', claim Siegal and Beals (1960, p. 408). Here, the village, seemingly ungoverned by traditional methods, had not yet transformed sufficiently to transition to the new legal system. Beals would revisit the village in 1959, where 'new forms of cooperation which were based on a new economy of urban wage work had emerged' (Siegal and Beals, 1960, p. 408), and social transformation had effectively halted the 'pervasive factionalism' present when conflicting systems were simultaneously in place.

Cohn claims seeking settlements outside caste rules was not necessarily a 'new' development or a development unique to the establishment of a new nation state. Sovereign powers have always been a possible avenue of appeal regarding decisions of local community authorities. It is not necessary that alternatives to older forms of law were found only when the state came in and established its presence and the promise of a uniform legal system. Even customary law was not always binding on the people of the community. Citing a case from the 1950s of the village of Senapur, where several lower caste members claimed to engage in sexual and marital relations in open defiance of customary caste norms, Cohn notes that in this instance, the numerically significant and politically powerful lower caste could flout customary law with little fear of redress of the caste and community councils.

Cohn also notes that exceptions to caste rules were being made as early as 1796. A 1796 decision of the Bengal Sadar Diwani Adalat shows that exceptions based on personal influence can and have been made even in times where custom in Indian communities was thought to be considerably more 'rigid' and premodern. Adherence to tradition was not an unreflexive state of the Indian communities, and neither was tradition or custom inflexible. Common logic of power, economic authority, and what could be considered universal notions of ethics (as in the case of the headman who was a just and good man, morally and ethically superior, in addition to possessing power and economic wherewithal) often had the power to supersede community and caste strictures. When a situation of non-compliance could not be redressed using caste norms, the village council encouraged a settlement—a compromise of sorts—one where an amicable resolution could be achieved, one which often resembled the achievement of some sort of equity. Indian custom and tradition, however, were understood by the British to be relics out of place in a modern vision.

To understand the true nature of legal cultures in India, the British interpreted, transformed, and fixed otherwise flexible customary practices. Customs were not always immemorial or inflexible. Non-state legal systems based on customary law and social norms, Cohn indicates, often run contrary to their own rule books and incorporate the principles of compromise and settlement, based on a logic of power and authority, which may have little to do with tenets of traditional and customary caste pollution and be closer to the implicit dimensions of authority and power vested in modern nation states.

The tribe to which Jiswant Roy belonged did not think it proper to expel him from their caste. Besides Jiswant Roy had so much pomp and parade about him that none of the people belonging to his caste dared take notice of his faults, or even to mention them in his presence. Moreover, the witnesses of the Nagar caste who were brought forward by the appellant said that any who had a mistress would be expelled from their caste…. Yet Jiswant Roy and Bhugwunt Roy have not been expelled from their caste. On the contrary, they on all occasions eat with them and attend their ceremonies whether of rejoicing or mourning and particularly desire them to come to their houses on similar occasions. They dare not, however, take notice of their faults, nor even contradict them and much less expel them from their caste (Cohn, 1965, p. 101).

Moreover, the state legal system in India does not always resemble the vision of efficient and equitable modernity. Cohn also goes on to say that courts in India are approached to compete for social status. Courts are not approached, Cohn argues, to achieve practical resolution of matters, rather, they are used as symbolic performative areas to 'harass one's opponents, as a punishment, as a form of land speculation and profit making, to satisfy insulted pride, and to maintain local political dominance over one's followers. The litigants do not expect a settlement that will end the dispute to eventuate from recourse to the state courts' (Cohn, 1965, p. 105). Rather, it is often the case that after several rounds in the state legal machinery, it is a local council which eventually encourages a settlement by the parties involved.

What Cohn's examples seem to demonstrate is that it is perhaps not always beneficial to view the state as an overarching system that incrementally adds on those local customs and world views previously outside its scope. There is a much more complex interplay of forces at work here. For local villages and communities whose systems of dispute settlement and adjudication do *not* require authority from the state, the state legal system and judicial institutions become tools for attaining symbolic and performative outcomes rather than outcomes of practical justice.

In another, more recent example of community law, Upendra Baxi and L.M. Singhvi examine the operation of a lok adalat in Rangpur before the formalization of lok adalats in India. In their 1976 paper, they note the curious way in which the lok adalat, part of the informal legal domain, administers and upholds order by emphasising on collective agreement in the settlement of disputes. Rangpur's adalat derived legitimacy from community consensus in addition to an indirect recognition from the state's law enforcement bodies—most members of the community under its jurisdiction referred their matters to the adalat and relied heavily on it for mitigating conflict, sometimes with approval from the local police as well.

While the main function of the adalat was to settle disputes, people also approached it to arrive at 'a just and fair compromise' (Baxi, 1976, p. 84) wherein blame and retribution were not always individual, or absolute, or irrevocable. The adalat at Rangpur enjoyed tremendous success for a short period of time, and even within the bounds of the 'institution', disputes were settled differentially. In a case where the second in command of the head of the adalat followed procedures distinct from the head without raising questions on the institutional integrity of the adalat or the legitimacy of the compromise. Hearings were public, motivating a kind of public consensus regarding the outcome as well. Baxi notes that public presence itself acted as a kind of sanction even in cases where explicit public *intervention* did not take place, since the presence of large numbers legitimated outcomes and gave it community approval.

Sanctions in the adalat were seldom elevated beyond compromise, the distribution of sweets to all present, return or recompense of loans, and restitution of land. The public aspect of the hearing and the settlement of disputes itself acted as a sanction. Documenting the hearing processes, Baxi notes that if 'by sanction then one really means coercive consequences attached by way of specific execution to breaches of authoritative decisions, there are very few situations where such direct and specific sanction process can be said to be present' (Baxi, 1976, p. 84). The formal dispute settlement processes in the adalat were reversed, claims Baxi. A sanction was not imposed after the matter had been settled, rather, bringing disputes for public airing was itself a sanction, rendering a formal sanction in the end of the hearing moot.

There are several ways in which the lok adalat, part of the informal dispute settlement space in India, recalls characteristics close to the indigenous legal systems of Cohn's description. Differential processes and community involvement are both characteristics that align with indigenous legal systems in India. The adalat at Rangpur embodied within its institutional boundaries those very aspects which made people amenable to approaching it for conflict mitigation and

dispute settlement. Unlike the 'overorganised, formalised procedures, distance, dilatoriness, and expense of [formal] legal recourse'
(Baxi, 1976, p. 92), the lok adalat was comparatively fluid and less
individuated.

Communities which depend on customary laws and related
aspects for social control function in India based on several attributes,
of which the promise of swift and more equitable justice is one. In
several anthropological and historical descriptions, they are often
primary, and it is often the state legal system which is considered a
(rarely visited) alternative.

Earlier we have noted how religious personal laws are not *legally*
classified as 'law' under the definitions outlined in Article 13.
However, the state legal system, often to reduce administrative costs
and increase administrative efficiency, encourages certain alternate
methods of resolving disputes, which rely on religious personal law,
among others. The permanent lok adalats, mentioned earlier, are a
part of one such alternate method. Sharia courts (or Darul Qaza),
which govern using religious law, often come under such recognition
as well, although they have not yet been formalized by the state. Such
alternate systems of settling disputes draw from a rich, non–common
law heritage.

This distinction was starkly expressed in a 2005 PIL submitted
to the Supreme Court, in which the petitioner claimed that Sharia
courts were operating as *parallel* legal systems rather than operating
in a supporting or additional capacity to the state legal system. The
petition implicitly acknowledged the legitimacy of *only* the state legal
system and was filed in reaction to what the petitioner perceived was
a threat to this legitimacy (*Vishwa Lochan Madan* v. *Union of India
& Ors*, 2014 [7] SCC 707). The petition, submitted to check what
was felt to be an encroachment by the Sharia courts into the territory
of the formal judicial system, asked for the disbanding of the Darul
Qazas and requested an end to Islamic judicial training itself, reading
it to be incompatible with the state legal system.

In a move which upheld the legal viability of the Sharia courts, the
Supreme Court's verdict, while recognizing that it had jurisdiction
over cases of criminal nature, also went on to recognize that within
the purview of family and personal law, Muslim law could prevail.
Darul Qazas, the Court maintained, do not administer criminal

justice and essentially function as an 'arbitrator, mediator, negotiator or conciliator in matters pertaining to family dispute or any other dispute of civil nature between the Muslims' (*Vishwa Lochan Madan v. Union of India & Ors*, 2014 [7] SCC 707, pp. 6–7). Moreover, the Court mentioned, the decisions of the Darul Qaza in the form of *fatwas* (the PIL was also asking for a closer examination of fatwas, or judgments based on Islamic law by authoritative bodies) were largely advisory and not enforceable, and Muslims could not be compelled or obligated to follow them. The 'real' adjudicatory authority, the Court seemed to imply, existed with the state legal system, and by that virtue, the Sharia courts were not operating parallel to the law or challenging it in any form.

While the central government was careful to note that fatwas and Sharia courts were not illegal, because they never had legal power to begin with, the 'government acknowledged and encouraged the establishment of informal *sharia* courts in the name of protecting religious freedoms, and also—perhaps—financial and administrative efficiency' (Kunkler and Sezgin, 2016, p. 998). This, coupled with a statement from a Darul Qaza member, actively discouraging Muslims from entering the state legal systems at all, question the translation of such technical distinctions such as those made by the Supreme Court in the PIL into local realities. Given below are excerpts from interviews with a Darul Qaza members:

> The Indian courts are not qualified to interpret the *sharia*—especially when the judges are non-Muslims.... When there is a *sharia* court, if one goes to civil courts ... [this] will be *haram* or a sin.... Muslims have to come to *sharia* courts .... (Kunkler and Sezgin, 2016, p. 997)

The domain of alternate dispute resolution is, in effect, a recognition of not only how the non-state legal system can lessen the burden on the state legal system, but also how the non-state domain can perform functions and outcomes not significantly different from the state domain. Weber (1919), in his essay on what the political domain constitutes, attempts to set the definition of the modern state. While a state may have a social and economic identity as well, what makes it *political* is that it '(successfully) claims the *monopoly of the legitimate use of physical force* within a given territory.... The state is considered the sole source of the "right to use violence"' (Weber, 1919, p. 1). For Weber, the state's very existence is premised on being the sole dominant authority, whose power can be supported by 'means of legitimate (i.e. considered to be legitimate) violence' (Weber, 1919, p.1). Where do we then locate non-state dispute resolution bodies and institutions such as Darul Qazas?

Legitimacy, from the perspective of the state, continues to lie with the state itself as long as local bodies such as the Darul Qazas do not use the power of force to support their decisions. Any domination, argues Weber, must rely on 'inner justifications' to legitimize its presence. While traditional authority or what he calls 'the authority of the "eternal yesterday"' is one such justification for any domination, legality, or the 'belief in the validity of legal statute and functional "competence" based on rationally created *rules*' is another (Weber, 1991, p. 2). The Indian legal system has attempted to account for tradition and the authority of the 'eternal yesterday', while at the same time reserving the right to force.

While fatwas may not threaten the structural integrity of the formal legal system, since they are considered not to have legal force, hegemonic structures are arrived at through social forces as pressures of compliance as well. Moreover, while the formal legal system may have, in Weber's words, legitimacy born of legality, Islamic law in India contains legitimacy born of tradition. The modern Indian state's identity comes under further scrutiny in cases such as that of the Salwa Judum (a state-sponsored local vigilante group organized in 2005 to counter Naxalite violence in Chhattisgarh in India), where force is no longer the domain of the state alone. In the Naxal swathes of central India, the state's presence is arguably minimal (Sundar, 2006). In such conditions, while Maoist insurgents fought to establish parallel state structures, Salwa Judum, a civilian army, was given arms and the state's endorsement to practice violence—in other words, the state transferred the responsibility to enforce rule onto a civilian army. When the operation was started under government orders, its 'people' aspect was emphasized. An informal organization, its members 'were armed by the state in the hopes that they would use the weapons to engage the Naxals in combat' (Miklian, 2009, p. 442).

Sundar writes this article in 2006, and in 2011 the Supreme Court went on to state that 'no wielder of power should be allowed to claim the right to perpetrate state's violence against any one, much less its own citizens' (*Nandini Sundar & Ors* v. *Government of Chattisgarh*, AIR 2011 SC 2839, p. 4). Although Sundar argues in 2006 that 'the government's support for vigilantism, is not an abdication of the claim to being a legitimate state, but an expansion of options or greater market choice in the use of violence' (Sundar, 2006, p. 35), the Supreme Court, through its ruling, recognizes the sharing of power with non-state bodies as a challenge to the state's own legitimacy. Several such examples, even in contemporary India, demonstrate the fuzzy lines between state and non-state legality in a milieu where both tradition and legality compete to give legitimacy to different domains.

IV

Conclusion

Émile Durkheim, in his analysis of the division of labour in society, assumes an intricate and inevitable relationship between law and society (1933). The role of law, in Durkheim's conception of industrial and pre-industrial societies, was to order and to organize. While economic relations arising from the division of labour, for Durkheim, gave rise to different forms of solidarity (the binding power of society), law for him was the main organizing framework for the societies in question. Simple, pre-industrial division of labour gave rise to mechanical solidarity. Since tasks were isolated in pre-industrial society, and each artisan or labourer was involved in almost every step of the production process, labour interaction was minimal. Social bonds could not be created in this environment of isolated, individually owned production chains, and solidarity had to be enforced *mechanically* through the top-down enforcement of group norms and values (Durkheim, 1933).

However, in industrial societies dependent on complex divisions of labour, organic solidarity was what bound society. With the advent of industrialization and complex divisions of labour, the production chain was split into several components, with each labourer in charge of only one aspect of the entire production chain. The final product was dependent on the individual labour of every member in the chain, promoting interaction and interdependence. When individuals began performing greatly differentiated tasks, this newly created dependence based on complex, interlinked labour led to a kind of interior, organic solidarity (Durkheim, 1933).

But the concept of solidarity came replete with questions regarding its applicability in real-world scenarios. In what was claimed to be a study furthering the empirical science of society, the concept of solidarity could not be easily quantified or typified. Durkheim's solution to this problem was to suggest that the framework of law present in each society could act as an indicator of the type of solidarity present in the society. According to this understanding, classifying the legal system present in a society could potentially tell us what form of solidarity existed in the society in question, which could then tell us whether the society was pre-industrial or industrial, traditional or modern. Studying the legal system, therefore, indicated Durkheim, could reveal the stage of development the society was at, and thereby lead to important inferences about the nature of the society.

Societies with systems of law characterized by heavy penal sanctions indicated the presence of a high level of mechanical solidarity. Crimes in these societies needed to be sanctioned with severe, often asymmetric, penalties, since misdemeanours under this form of social organization offended the collective more than the individual, and it was the collective sensibilities that needed to be reassured. Pre-industrial societies, therefore, Durkheim argued, could be recognized not only by simple divisions of labour, but also by their characteristically harsh punitive orders.

Societies with organic solidarity, on the other hand, were characterized by restitutive or restorative systems of law, where emphasis was not on redressing the shock of an upset in the collective consciousness, but on restoring the situation to its prior state. For example, under penal and repressive legal systems, the punishment could be severe for even small crimes, such as death or dismemberment for theft, and could extend to members of the offender's family as well. However, under restitutive systems of law, sanctions such as compensation for theft took the place of physical punishments. While death in the form of capital punishment did exist, it was practised only in exceptional cases.

Law and Society in the Views of Henry Maine, Eugen Ehrlich, and Friedrich Karl von Savigny

Durkheim's indicative models, where primitive society referred to a particular legal type and modern society referred to another legal type, is close to Maine's (1861) analysis of the law in different societies. According to Maine's descriptions, if 'the individual is conspicuously guilty, it is his children, his kinsfolk, his tribesmen, or his fellow-citizens, who suffer with him, and sometimes for him' (1861, p. 52). Sociologists and anthropologists before (as well as after) Durkheim keenly invested in the rise and cross-disciplinary acceptance of evolutionary theory. Maine's theory of the development of law in the simultaneous development of human society follows the evolutionary canon as well. The problem most of these theorists contended with was tracing the origins of society, and thereby the origins of law, much like the celebrated origins of the species, to first historicize the current state of their societies and subsequently offer insights for its future progress. These models had the promise of giving a systemic and structured understanding of how law and society functioned over time.

Pre-industrial societies presented a tempting ground for observing what was considered to be a prior stage in human development conveniently present in contemporary time (Fabian, 1983). These were the societies, the objects of anthropological study, which could offer a glimpse of the origins of law. Much of what is now considered the Global South came under anthropologists' attention as possible (albeit misread) example of a pre-modern simplicity. In complex industrial age, Maine argued, contemporary society in its totality could be understood correctly only by studying 'the particles which are its simplest ingredients' (1861, p. 49), and since these particles were no longer present to be observed and understood within modern society, and since it was generally understood that different societies progressed at different rates, these observable units could be found in 'civilisations less advanced than their own' (p. 49).

Maine also made the claim that the fundamental unit in ancient society was the family, unlike modern society where it is the individual, and within ancient society, it was the law of the father that could be seen as the earliest vestiges of law. The emphasis on family and community, not to mention patriarchal ordering of society, are common notions regarding indigenous Indian legal systems as well. Legal formations in pre-industrial society, according to Maine, with their close emphasis on family and community, were governed by status, where those categories of people who had a lower position in the hierarchy of power were 'subject to extrinsic control on the single ground that they do not possess the faculty of forming a judgement on their own interests'. Progressive legal orders were premised on contract, and it was this capability of forming judgements in their own interest—or in other words, 'the free agreement of Individuals'—which was also the prerequisite for the first forms of contract (Maine, 1861, p. 69).

A few decades after *Division of Labour*, Durkheim's contemporary Eugen Ehrlich also made important contributions in expanding the understanding of law. By introducing the phrase 'living law', which encapsulated state as well as non-state aspects of law, Ehrlich pointed out how normative standards of behaviour, regardless of whether they were officially recognized or legitimized, had roots in social life. For Ehrlich, 'the living law is the law which dominates life itself even though it has not been posited in legal propositions' (Ehrlich, 2001, p. 493); it was the socially shaped matter of state law, customary practices, and other normative patterns which ordered human society. Similar to Durkheim's conclusions about how legal frameworks could indicate the nature of the society they inhabited, Ehrlich too pointed out how different types of law indicated different relationships with the environment they inhabited, the main difference between Durkheim and Ehrlich being that the former was speaking in terms of social whole where one society indicated the presence of one legal order, while the latter argued that different types of law (all a part of living law) could exist within the social whole.

While Durkheim's divisions have been criticized due to their overt emphasis on structure and classification and their subsequent lack of applicability in several real-world contexts, they illustrate an important view—society and law share a mutually dependent relationship. Ehrlich's arguments too have been empirically tested and found to be lacking—for instance, 'empirical research showed that different forms of law, such as that to do with labour relations, did not necessarily correspond to particular forms of social organisation in ways that would be expected' (Nelken, 2008, p. 448). Moreover, the description of the lok adalat as outlined in Chapter 3, despite belonging to the type of society Durkheim called pre-industrial, definitely possessed some of the attributes of a modern legal system of Durkheim's definition.

Maine's evolutionist thought—an outcome of his ethnographic heritage—also contributes to generalizations and misrepresentations about the realistic nature of the Indian legal system. Although predictions based on the relationship between law and society do not always hold, Durkehim, Ehrlich, Maine, legal historians, comparative law theorists, and other sociologists of law all point to the need to see law as formed by and related to the social space it inhabits. Durkheim's placement of law as a social tool, or law as an indicator of social reality, does not necessarily prove the latter's supremacy over the former, or vice versa, rather, it leads us to the unquestionable and intricate relationship between the two.

In addition to sociological and anthropological scholarship, scholars of the historical school of law have vigorously argued that legal systems are cultural institutions which stand out not just as distinguished processes in their own right, but also as distinguishing characteristics of a community (Kantowicz, 1937). The founder of historical jurisprudence, Friedrich Karl von Savigny, propounded that law was not *made* but *found*, thereby establishing an interesting relationship between a culture and its legal system (Bodenheimer, 2011, p. 72). The law of any society is intricately linked with the experience of the people and groups within society, such that it develops over a period of time. Savigny explained this through his analysis of Volksgeist in the tradition of the German legal system and its substantive differences from Roman law. The historical school's assertions are particularly relevant when put in the context of Indian tribal communities, wherein law is not an abstract set of rules that can be classified (as is the case with state law that is classified as family law, commercial law, criminal law, and so on), but rather is an integral part of the community, having deep roots in the social and economic habits and attitudes of its past and present members.

If law and society have an inextricable relationship, our research then leads us to the social bases of state and non-state law. Upendra

Baxi (1986) marks a difference between two forms of legal intervention in the Indian legal universe—the state legal system, comprising the body of formal, codified law, practised in and by statutory local bodies and courts of law and other state-recognized arbitration spaces, and the non-state legal system, comprising the systems and processes of traditional justice, tribal councils, and informal bodies of dispute management. Baxi's two categories also presume a failure of the state system (despite its claimed religious and cultural accommodations and sanctions and exceptions) to penetrate to the level of *all* Indian communities. This could be the result of the partiality of the common law heritage.

We come to understand that the state legal system is not omnipresent, nor is it all powerful, and is not the mirror of the society it is applied to. This raises questions on the relationship between 'law' and the society it inhabits. If state legal systems fail to resonate with the societies they are intended for, do non-state legal systems then 'fill' the gaps revealed by the limits of the state? Baxi here also makes a preliminary assumption—the Indian legal universe contains within itself several different ways of maintaining social order. The formal legal system, deriving from the relics of the British common law system, and codified aspects of Hindu and Muslim Law, cannot be seen as the one determining system under which Indian nationals can be governed. Customary or traditional law, as encompassed in the non-state legal systems, does not necessarily come second to the legitimacy or the authority vested in the state legal system, neither does it always refer to a premodern state. It is contemporaneously followed across the country, and is often the preferred mode of settling disputes.

Traditional systems are often seen as necessarily giving away to make way for modern models of order maintenance. However, here, we have both traditional and modern systems sharing the same space of operation. What could then explain the continued demand for tradition in the face of a powerful and transformative modernity?

The cultural approaches of Bernard S. Cohn and André Béteille view the state legal system and the non-state legal systems as structurally incompatible in terms of values and ideals. The assumption implicit in this is that non-state legal systems are closer to the communities within which they are practised, and the state legal system alien. In particular, many also assume that formal state legal systems individualize while traditional systems give primacy to the coherence of the social group and the local collective. Non-state legal systems, according to this approach, prevail due to a 'correspondence' with the 'structure of the community it represents' and are, therefore, more in tune with the societies they are located in (Baxi, 1986, p. 24).

While the formal legal system is oriented towards equalizing and homogenizing, the community in India is one organized on formal hierarchies and segmentations which resist such homogeneity. A structural misfit between the state legal system and the community it aspires to deliver justice to can then explain the tendency to rely on non-state legal systems.

In an article exploring what he considers the gradual 'displacement' of the Hindu legal tradition with British common law, Marc Galanter draws attention to a group of legal universes called 'dualistic or colonial-style legal systems', wherein the official law 'embodies norms and procedures congenial to the governing classes and remote from the attitudes and concerns of its clientele' (1968, p. 84). These, again, closely follow Baxi's (1986) classifications of two domains of legality in India—official state, and informal non-state— in continuation with Galanter's claim that a kind of 'legal colonisation from within' (1968, p. 84) persists in India since the departure of the British, which allows this separation to continue.

When examining the stated distance in India between law in statute and law in practice, we are brought immediately to all those legal universes where both state and non-state, modern and traditional, and formal and informal domains of law coexist. It is in such a dualistic system of law, research seems to suggest, where national legitimacy is claimed by that body of law which does not entirely resonate with the people for whom it is intended, that alternate domains of legality acquire both local legitimacy and functionality (Cohn, 1965; Galanter, 1968).

While Galanter and Cohn write about the tensions of indigenous tradition and imposed law in India, Benton (2004) looks at colonialism as a global enterprise that has allowed for different forms of legal pluralism to flourish across geographically disparate countries and continents. Locating her first example of pluralist legal regimes which fought for power, recognition, and legitimacy in the fifteenth-century Iberian Peninsula (southwest Europe), Benton illustrates the dilemma of a North African legal scholar. Increasing Christian penetration into erstwhile Moorish pockets was leading to an outmigration of Muslims. While the scholar in question wanted to stay on under Christian dominion and advocate for the remaining Muslims, their legal order, and their way of life, Islamic muftis were urging all good Muslims to flee the land, arguing that the 'central rituals of Muslim religious life would be threatened—the collection of alms, the celebration of Ramadan, the daily prayers', and so on (Benton, 2004, p. 1). People like the African scholar of Benton's description chose to stay back to help their people, and 'their actions as agents seeking to reinforce one legal authority by representing cases before another, were remarkably common in territories of imperial or colonial conquest' (Benton, 2004, p. 2).

Benton goes on to say that 'wherever a group imposed law on newly acquired territories and subordinate peoples, strategic decisions were made about the extent and nature of legal control' (2004, p. 2). Indigenous systems were retained as well as limited, in addition to the imposition of foreign law, to maintain social order leading to complex systems of law where indigenous law, much like in contemporary India, fought for 'accommodation, advocacy within the system, subtle delegitimization, and outright rebellion' (p. 3).

Such systems, states Galanter, are symbolic of situations where an alien system of rule introduced by the colonizer was superimposed on to the fabric of diverse local traditions. The Hindu system, argues Galanter, which was inherently flexible and relatively less static than the European systems, was one of the many local traditions the British in India sought to replace. The British in India, says Galanter, borrowing from Weber, performed an 'expropriation of law'—where the government alone claims the 'power to find, declare and apply law' (Galanter, 1968, p. 68)—and this continued well into independent India. He locates the beginnings of British expropriation of law in the post-1772 era, when a system of courts in Bengal encouraged a process where 'authoritative sources of law to be used in governmental courts were isolated and legislation initiated', initiating the capture or the expropriation of law into the hands of the colonial government (Galanter, 1968, p. 68). The next logical step in the trajectory of expropriation was characterized by codification and rationalization of the system, wherein sources of law became further fixed. The third phase of expropriation continues in post-Independence India where the same measures persist, culminating in greater rationalization and a unified judiciary. Galanter also mentions that codification of nearly all domains of commercial, criminal, and procedural law was more or less complete by 1882. Interestingly, none of the codes referred to pre-British Indian law. Galanter's claim is that 'there was no borrowing from Hindu, Muslim, or customary law, although there is occasional accommodation of local rules and there are adjustments and elaborations of the common law to deal with the kinds of persons and situations and conditions found in India' (1968, p. 69). One of the reasons mentioned for this oversight is the inability of the British to find authentic sources of Hindu law. Even the shastras were considered only a part of the law, and Hindus for a large part were also governed by informal and customary law (Galanter, 1968).

Hindu law, Galanter asserts, was traditionally flexible, inclusive of but never reducible to just the content of the shastras or custom, and difficult to define. Unwritten custom was inherently incompatible with the court systems introduced by the British, resulting in an elevation of written law and a diminishing of other components of law in India. The British, Galanter goes on to state, applied their own rules of custom to Indian society, where 'to prevail over written law, a custom must be "proved to be immemorial or ancient, uniform, unvariable, continuous, certain"', and so on (Poitevin, 2010, p. 38). To be admissible in court, custom needed to conform to all the listed ideas, but with the monopoly to declare what was lawful and unlawful firmly in the hands of the government, it was relegated by official discourse to a sphere outside law. But customary law, as we have seen in the cases highlighted in previous chapters, while appearing to the British as 'grounded in immemorial usage and unalterable custom' did not necessarily conform to these definitions (Derrett, 1961, p. 20).

To say that the legal practices present in India lacked a particular kind of sophistication present only in modern, industrial societies would be incorrect. Durkheim's descriptions of evolutionary higher legal systems have features in common with informal legal systems in India. Durkheim's conclusions may not be universally applicable; however, his arguments hold significant value in giving a social basis to law, and in doing so, 'some kind of primacy to law as a social variable' (Baxi, 1986, p. 1), indicating that social diversity also entails legal diversity and law cannot always be considered an exclusive domain. Later scholars such as Galanter (1989) furthered this connection, arguing that an approach across disciplines, which encourages the study of law in its social context, 'tries to appreciate the distinctiveness of law against the background of larger patterns of social behaviour rather than as something autonomous and self-contained' (p. 298).

Moreover, most of modern Western scholarship on anthropology and law saw law as fundamentally bound to the very idea of being human. Law became an important parameter to distinguish between human and non-human (or even inhuman, requiring the historical reform and elimination of certain 'inhuman' and baser aspects of law). In the words of John Comaroff, 'Not only did much of modernist Western thought owe its understanding of the social to one or another version of contract theory, but it rested on the implicit truth that *homo sapiens* was, everywhere, *homo juralis*' (Comaroff and Comaroff, 2009, p. 31). Modern legal systems, as Galanter (1968) mentions, were also characterized by 'uniform territorial rules based on universalistic norms, which apportion rights and obligations as incidents of specific transactions, rather than of fixed statuses. These rules are administered by a hierarchy of courts, staffed by professionals, organised bureaucratically and employing rational procedures' (p. 66).

These moves established two mutually agreed conceptions about law and society—(*i*) law was functionally implicated in indicating what the nature and condition of society it inhabited was (even if it indicated a split from its social environment) and (*ii*) law, or a philosophical understanding of it, was fundamental to being human, and thereby fundamental to human society.

Yogendra Singh (1988) carries the analogy of law as an index of social conditions further by suggesting that law can be viewed 'as an indicator of the nature of societal complexity' (Y. Singh, 1988, p. 45). If law is the organizing principle in society—the framework on which social order is achieved—and points to the level of complexity present in a society, what, then, takes place in those nations or communities where the relationship between law and society is diminished? A diminishment or transformation of the relationship between law and society can be understood through two aspects—(*i*) when foreign dominion attempts to replace and transform indigenous traditions and (*ii*) when modern nations deliberately retain the incongruity between formal governing systems and local realities by retaining two incompatible belief systems at both levels—which distances national law from the nation it is intended for.

Merry (1988) argues that for the new nation states of the mid-twentieth century, law was believed to be a modernizing tool. According to this understanding, it was only natural that a modern legal system (based on Galanter's description) should be in place in a nation state travelling towards modernity. However, Merry also notes how this vision has deviated far from the ideal it envisioned. Citing a study by Pool and Starr (1974), Merry writes how massive law reforms in Turkish society resulted in very little on-ground change. Local order persisted in its pre-reform form in villages. Moreover, Moore (1973) proposes the idea of a 'semi-autonomous social field', irreducible to one single social group, one where 'the outside legal system penetrates the field but does not dominate it; there is room for resistance and autonomy' (Merry, 1988, p. 878). This, Merry uses as a possible explanation for why in Turkey 'vast majority of the Turkish population continued to follow customs incompatible with the new codes' (Merry, 1988, p. 880), demonstrating that 'social arrangements are often effectively stronger than the new laws', which may often be alien to the societies on whom they are imposed (Moore, 1973, p. 723).

These have been the main questions defining our research. Through British incursion into Indian laws, we have tried to show how Indian traditions were often replaced and transformed. In uncritically accepting several British concepts, concepts alien to Indian society, the Independent Indian nation state also furthered the distance between law and society. The indigenous legal system in India, scholars such as Singh argue, was not amenable to homogenization and was characterized by what could be called an 'inter-structural autonomy', where a series of hierarchical orders ensured fairly significant autonomy at the lowest levels and minimal intervention at the highest (Y. Singh, 1973). Groups at the local level had 'their own judicial processes through panchayats, community leadership of elders, or the intervention of the chief of the dominant local caste' (Y. Singh, 1988, p. 46). Additionally, those villages that did not have a clear dominant caste, as discussed in Chapter 3, found themselves in a state of near perpetual conflict with shifting and changing bodies for settlement of disputes (Cohn, 1965). Singh also goes on to state that 'depending upon the exigency of circumstances, local priests and community leaders always had the right to new interpretation of legal codes' (Y. Singh, 1988, p. 46).

Much like Cohn (1965) and Béteille (1965), Singh argues that were we to look systemically at the Indian legal system at the local level, we would find several structural incompatibilities with the formal state law. Both Cohn (1965) and Singh (1988) claim that indigenous processes of settling disputes 'acted in harmony with the cultural ethos' (Y. Singh, 1988, p. 47). Singh goes on to add that the emphasis on community (contrary to Western individual equality before law) ensured that 'the resultant legal process was oriented more to "adjustment" than "judgement"' (Y. Singh, 1988, p. 47).

Rural populations, marginal jatis, minority religions, and geographically less accessible communities rely in varying degrees on the informal legal system for everyday disputes. Information based on the People of India survey conducted between 1979 and 1984 showed that most Indian communities in rural areas preferred local means of dispute resolution before entering the formal legal system at all. The communities, broadly divided according to jatis, the lists of scheduled tribes and scheduled castes in India, and other religious and migrant groups, tended to rely on informal modes of dispute settlement either in place of or in addition to the formal state legal system (People of India Project Published Materials, 1979–84). Customary law in India holds a troubling position in the logic of the Indian state, where assimilation offends the cultural integrity of communities (Rajan, 2000), and recognition and integration are always partial projects. Rajan, in her paper on the uniform civil code's implications for women in India, notes that different communities follow different rationales to either oppose or support the uniform civil code in India. For several marginal communities, a uniform civil code is often opposed, keeping in mind that uniformity would invariably be a majoritarian rather than an equitable one. Moreover, communities in India also believe that uniformity comes at the cost of flattened cultural identities.

As discussed in previous parts, uniform rule of law was subverted several times in the colonial period by the British themselves (Kolsky, 2010; Singha, 1998). Other unificatory projects such as the mobilization of the public during India's freedom struggle, too, have been revealed to be partial in nature, involving only a small section of the population with access to English and all the privileges that came with it (Chatterjee, 1999). State attitudes and concerns regarding indigenous Indian communities, too, have been inconsistent and subject to easy shifts in policy. Early European anthropologists when encountering tribal cultures outside of Europe viewed them as lawless primitives better left in isolation. Later missionary movements through early and late nineteenth-century Empire viewed them as unenlightened albeit lawful communities, which had a proliferation of arbitrary rules and traditions to which they were blindly bound (Malinowski, 1924), and intervened in eliminating those forced traditions that could be considered inhuman. The period of late colonialism, realizing that attitudes of laissez faire as well as attitudes of focused intervention had both caused extensive damage, established protectorates and reserves, thereby deepening the isolation of tribes and similar 'jungle' communities and preventing organic interaction between tribal populations and the mainstream population, often at the cost of undoing historical continuities that had already existed between tribal and non-tribal groups in India. However, despite all the changes in consideration regarding treatment of indigenous Indian traditions, particularly, law, indigenous Indian society, in whatever form, was consistently viewed as modern Europe's premodern ancestor.

It is Malinowski who can arguably be credited with first articulating that pre-industrial societies too had their own sophisticated systems of law and order. While much of European scholarship focused on defining tribal societies in terms of ideas of the group and the community, as opposed to Western individuality, Malinowski argued that legal realities in these communities could not be identified by such terms of reference; they needed to be seen in the perspective of their own operation, in terms of 'concrete fact', not solely through their opposition or relation to Western realities. Ownership, then, in the tribes of the Trobriand Islands was not so much based on 'communism' (in opposition to capitalism) or such terminologies other theorists tended to use, but, much like in developed societies, it was 'the sum of duties, privileges, and mutualities, which bind the joint owners to the object and to each other' (Malinowski, 1924, p. 9). Pre-industrial legal frameworks of ownership, in this case, were not so different from developed notions of rights and obligations. However, these frameworks were different in noted and important ways as well, and the focus on difference allowed for incompatible state systems to be imposed on to native fabric. Given India's colonial past and post-colonial continuation of several structures with little change, distance between the state and the non-state legal systems, and a misfit between law and society, is but a natural outcome. Greater integration, argues Baxi (1976), is required to ensure that the state and the non-state legal systems take *both* the broad domains of law into consideration, while administering justice and maintaining social order.

The 2016 report titled 'Synergy between Tribal Justice System and Regular Justice System of the Country', by the Parliamentary Standing Committee on Personnel, Public Grievances, Law, and Justice, highlights some of these confusions in legally pluralistic societies. The report outlines the constitutional provisions extended to tribes under scheduled areas, and then goes on to collate comments and depositions by several departments of the state such as the Department of Justice and the Ministry of Tribal Affairs, as well as suggestions by state governments and tribal advisory councils and other stakeholders.

What these notes highlight, however, is that despite the hierarchy in justice delivery outlined by the Constitution of India, several communities continue to rely solely on their traditional legal orders, either through state-sanctioned tribal justice systems or through informal and non-state legal mechanisms based on tribal customary law. While those under scheduled areas and other special provisions benefit from the continuation of their customary practices, those falling outside these definitions do not. (Department-Related Parliamentary Standing Committee on Personnel, Public Grievances, Law, and Justice, 2016).

According to the report, the nodal ministry for tribes in India, the Ministry of Tribal Affairs, claimed its scope of operation was restricted to areas under the Fifth Schedule, automatically excluding Sixth Schedule tribes. This is important in that it shows that the primary, nodal ministry for regulating tribal affairs itself restricts its scope to only a part of all the tribal communities of the country. Additionally, to check misuse, the ministry suggested, it needed to be brought into consonance with the formal legal system.

The committee received comments from state governments of Meghalaya, Mizoram, Tripura, Nagaland, Manipur, Sikkim, and Arunachal Pradesh. States whose areas fell under the schedules noted the presence of state-sanctioned tribal justice systems based on the practice of customary law. In addition to the presence of tribal justice systems, the states also noted variously successful/unsuccessful attempts at codifying the diverse customary legal practices of the communities. The tribal justice systems in these areas, according to official specifications, act within the purviews of customary laws, but are also bound hierarchically to the state legal system, where decisions of tribal councils can be appealed at higher courts of law.

In Sikkim and Manipur, which do not fall under the scheme of scheduled areas, the state governments cited no recognized tribal justice system while also acknowledging the presence of a diverse set of customary laws, which may influence the lives of the people. While the Tripura government suggested greater uniformity could be achieved by codifying customary laws, and retaining those in adherence with general principles of natural justice, and rejecting those offensive to it, the state government of Nagaland highlighted the impossibilities of codification given the immense diversity of customary laws among tribes. The Arunachal Pradesh government cited lack of access to justice, lower costs, participatory nature of dispute-resolution processes, and democratic proceedings, among others, as reasons for the persistence of tribal justice systems. These examples of the ways in which operations of tribal justice systems in Arunachal Pradesh differ from state mechanisms of law and order are similar to aspects of the lok adalat examined in greater detail in previous chapters. Both the stated systems of non-state law are characterized by lower costs, greater accessibility, and participatory proceedings. Further research into comparisons between the two systems can reveal whether they share more such aspects in common with each other.

Tribal representatives from the Singpho community (located mostly in Assam and Arunachal Pradesh) echoed the Arunachal Pradesh state government's deposition, stating that customary ways deliver justice in more accurate and amicable ways, and disputes in rare and exceptional cases reach the formal law and order mechanisms of the state, further reinforcing the community's independence from the state legal system.

Most of the recommendations of the committee, however, were unidirectional, involving greater cooperation from tribal councils and representatives than from their mainstream, official counterparts. Training and capacity-building programmes have been suggested for customary judicial officers. However, there are no suggestions for simultaneous such programmes for *state* officers to train them in tribal and/or customary law even at the rudimentary level to make processes better integrated.

The committee in its final comment recommended the following:

> The Committee in its Twenty Sixth Report on Demands for Grants (2008–09) of Ministry of Law and Justice, presented to Parliament on 29th April, 2008 had recommended for establishing separate High Courts for North Eastern States which will in turn play the role of evolving codification of the tribal laws. It had felt that such a step would ensure that the judgements of the High Courts will be treated as precedents, which with passage of time, can evolve into written law. The interpretations given to the existing uncodified rules/laws by the High Courts, can in future, be consolidated and this will result in codified laws and uniformity of judgements. This Committee now reiterates that all the North-Eastern States should have separate High Courts and independent Judicial Academy should be established in every State to fulfil the real goal of synchronisation of Tribal Justice system with the National mainstream of unitary Judicial system which is the architecture of Indian Constitution. (Department-Related Parliamentary Standing Committee on Personnel, Public Grievances, Law, and Justice, 2016, p. 25)

Considering that the Committee had made this recommendation nearly a decade before this last report, codification of customary law by a state authority to *create* judgments which would act as precedent has been an ongoing consideration for the Indian state.

These high courts, as envisioned by the committee, will perform the parallel tasks of codifying all customary law for the purposes of adjudication while creating a compendium of precedents on cases decided according to customary law to slowly make the precedents the primary source for future judgments, over time, with the aim of making tribal systems of law and order obsolete and give to the state its primacy in all matters of settlement of disputes. While the committee's projected aim has been one to integrate the state and the tribal justice systems, the suggestions are oriented more towards displacing traditional justice systems by incorporating them within the rubric of the state common law system—a project of assimilation rather than synergy and integration.

Broad Implications of This Research

Re-evaluating the Classification of India as a Common Law System

As stated in previous chapters, there are several approaches employed by comparatists to classify different jurisdictions into different parent legal families or family trees. India has conventionally been understood as a common law jurisdiction primarily owing to its colonial legal heritage. However, this may not be the case; one, notwithstanding India has many features of a common law system, such as a case-based system of law, hierarchical doctrine of precedent, typical categories and concepts of law, and most distinctively no substantial or structural public/private law distinction, it also has major features closely associated with other legal families, such as the Codes and a general proclivity to compile and codify (civil law system) (David and Brierley, 1985) personal laws being governed by Hindu, Islamic, and customary legal systems, operation of indigenous tribal legal systems in several areas, and the voluntarily imported features from non–common law jurisdictions in the Indian Constitution. As a result, the state legal system is a vibrant mix of several parallel operations, influences, importations, and mutations of features that originate in non–common law jurisdictions. However, it is to be remembered that all this is still within the domain of the *state* legal system. The state legal system, in several cases, accounts for the operation of other legal systems, and as a result it may be termed as a *mixed legal system.*

This brings us to the second point, as to why India might not neatly fit into the category of a common law system. In the context of non-state legal systems, a very small quantum of legal discourse has given due credit to such legal systems. This includes the observance of laws, rules, norms, settlement of disputes, adjudication of claims, and so on outside the realm of the state altogether. In addition to the application of Hindu law in state courts, or the interpretation of Islamic Sharia law by state's judges, law continues to operate outside the ambit of the state. Law operating outside the realm of the state entails several informal mechanisms of applying customary or traditional law and settling disputes. Religion-based, caste-based, village-based, tribe-based, trade/profession-based legal orders are not operative in India only at the periphery of the state legal system, but evidence clearly shows that they exist on the very centre-stage of Indian society, that is, these informal community-based systems are the first resort for most Indians who attach more legitimacy to these systems rather than the state system, thereby indicating that the state legal system itself may sometimes be at the periphery of Indian society (Mendelsohn, 2014).

Conceptualizing Legal Systems Differently

A vast amount of jurisprudence surrounds the idea and concept of 'legal systems'. Many scholars have tried to define it and spell out its basic features. Dam (2005) argues how legal systems are seen as *structures* in most Western jurisdictions, which operate over a large range of aspects of an individual's life; this range is highly comprehensive in many jurisdictions. However, in the case of tribal communities, a legal system is so intrinsic to the culture of that community on the whole that it is less of an independent 'structure' but more of a 'process' that is linked to a range of aspects of an individual's or group's life. Dam thus proposes a process-oriented approach rather than a structure-oriented approach. This approach will ensure that legal systems that do not resemble the state legal system in its comprehensive scope, formal institutions, complex and detailed laws and rules, and so on will also be termed as 'legal systems'. They will not be robbed of this status merely because they are traditional, simple, informal, comprising non-institutional mechanisms for dispute settlement, and so on. In this respect, the 'legal system' is more a process of applying commonly cherished values of social conduct and control within the larger context of culture rather than a stand-alone structure with legal rules and how they operate procedurally in the legal institutions.

Future of the Postcolonial Penchant for Uniformalization

There are several ways in which the Indian state has tried to uniformalize (and continues to do so) the plethora of laws and legal orders that exist in India. May it be in the form of legislation, executive action, or judicial interpretation, the state has been engaged in a constant quest for gaining superiority over all other legal systems. For instance, Article 44 of the Indian Constitution lays down an aspirational goal for having a uniform civil code in place, in the nature of a common criminal code. Many scholars have questioned the viability of this endeavour, so much so to call it unenforceable (Menski, 2008).

As indicated in this volume, there is enough evidence to suggest that India has a socio-cultural and religious plurality that is arguably unparalleled in any other single jurisdiction. There is also no ambiguity over the fact that the *state* and those who serve it recognize and acknowledge that this plurality is more than just socio-cultural/ religious/ethnic; it also implies 'legal plurality' where communities have their own laws and means of application and dispute settlement. Yet, uniformalization has more to do with increased state control rather than a lack of knowledge of the hard facts. The state's obsession with positivism coupled with its incessant need to control the lives of its populace may be a result of the colonial obsession to do the same; however, the British cannot be incriminated at every juncture in the postcolonial context. Indian governments have erroneously compared India with other lego-centric Western legal systems where populations are more homogenous and the state does control every detail of an individual's life (Menski, 2008). Hence, a similar expectation is created here at home. The debate around the uniform civil code has been driven sporadically by politicians and judges alike; however, considering India's long-standing experience with pluralism, the realization of a uniform civil code is a distant dream. Diversity is always natural while uniformity is always forced (K.S. Singh, 2014).

Constitutionally Recognized Heterogeneity

In this book, we focused on legal heterogeneity based on an underlying basis of socio-cultural/religious/ethnic heterogeneity. The Indian Constitution too recognizes and accommodates legal heterogeneity in varied other forms, oftentimes based on other set of factors. For instance, the federal system can be considered proof of heterogeneity owing to recognized differences such as geographical, historical, social, cultural, linguistic, and other differences. States are not treated equally in matters of administration, resource allocation, and, in effect, even legal matters (such as in implementation of certain laws and policies). The Constitution takes a step forward in imposing special obligations to protect cultural and linguistic minorities and tribal populations within states (K.S. Singh, 2014). However, protectionist measures, often tend to view its beneficiaries from a charitable model, reiterating the inequities which Parmar (2011) noted in her study of the tribal representative's treatment by other members of the Constituent Assembly.

The Constitution also lays down special provisions for protection of minorities and other citizens for conserving a distinct language, script, or culture. Socio-economically backward classes such as Scheduled Tribes and Scheduled Castes and, aside from these categories, women and children receive benefits and protection in the Constitution. Singh explains how all these other provisions of the Constitution establish that

> while the Constitution in its Preamble assures the unity and integrity of the nation, it also endorses, preserves and supports its plurality. Even the goal of national unity stated in the Preamble and considered by Granville Austin as one of the three strands of the seamless web in the Constitution is strengthened rather than weakened by its due recognition of pluralism. (Y. Singh, 2014, p. vii)

However, constitutional ideals are often hard to recognize, and conservation of cultures often comes at the risk of deepening the distance between mainstream Indians and minority groups.

The Indian Legal System and International Pressures

In the wake of universalization of human rights and a global concern for human dignity, one can gauge a gradual increase in the responsiveness of international law towards the demands for individual freedom (Tesón, 2015). However, alongside this movement, certain state practices reflecting cultural particularities have created a tension between international human rights standards, on the one hand, and national sovereignty, on the other. This tension is manifested in international deliberations when governments point in the direction of national cultural traditions to justify failures to comply with international law (Zalaquett, 1983). The concept of cultural relativism is highly pertinent for this study, especially when the international perspective is taken into consideration. Implications as to positive international law making the same error as national positive law makes while ignoring the plurality and relativism is to be considered and further researched upon. Can we draw a parallel in this respect? On the one hand, the state lays down Part III, which has a qualifying threshold for customs and usages, while, on the other, personal laws are allowed to derogate some of the *universal inalienable* rights enshrined in Part III. While personal laws were allowed to stand outside the realm of Article 13, it is still a matter of on-going controversy. Similarly, nations that cite cultural relativism as an opposing force against the 'universality' of human rights are although 'allowed' to continue certain actions in derogation of the Universal Declaration of Human Rights, it is not without ample debate and criticism.

The second parallel that may be drawn is that just as the theory of cultural relativism has several different meanings, so is the case with legal pluralism vis-à-vis the extent and scope of state power and control (Tesón, 2015). However, at the core, both these approaches, which are indubitably linked, challenge the viability of a uniform straight-jacket standard for all peoples that share varied cultures, histories, ethnicities, values, and so on. This further escalates into a distant goal of properly determining the existence and scope of certain civil and political rights enjoyed by individuals in any given society (either at the community or the state level). A central tenet of relativists and pluralists alike is substantive human rights standards or application of uniform state law (that may be based on such human rights principles) vary among different cultures and resultantly reflect idiosyncrasies within a given construct. Hence, tolerance and respect for self-determination has to be equally cherished alongside positive international human rights literature such that the rights enshrined in black letter are read to mean different things for different nations (or communities within nations). This sentiment has developed over the years with respect to international covenants on the rights of indigenous peoples, starting out from the ILO Convention No. 107 in 1957 all the way up to Convention No. 169 in 1989, and the International Declaration on the Rights of Indigenous Peoples, 2007.

Appendix I

Index of Cases Illustrating Judicial Engagement with Customary Law in India

The following index contains a description of the case analysis done as a means of gauging the nature of judicial engagement with customary law. Under the broader theme of the state's engagement with customary law and non-state legal systems and traditions, it becomes imperative to study cases that involve a question of custom, personal law, or any other legal aspect that draws its origin from a source other than the state. Such cases stand as instances where two different legal systems, traditions, or, more broadly, legal *values* come in conflict with each other. Here, the term 'conflict' includes a wide range of situations. Chief among them is one wherein the constitutionality of any custom is challenged, that is, any custom or tradition is made to stand the test of the Constitution, which is the primal founding document of the state polity. Such conflict may result in one system overpowering the other by striking down the latter's validity and legitimacy; it may result in a confluence of two systems, where one incorporates features of the other within its fold and functioning; and it may also result in a complete avoidance of the conflict altogether, where each system/tradition is allowed to operate in its own right.

The following index is illustrative of the instances where the state legal system has encountered other parallel legal systems and traditions. It is by no means exhaustive. Cases in this list have marked this journey in the postcolonial era, and are considered landmark or watershed cases owing to their precedential value for future judgments. These cases are cited repeatedly in the courts of law even today as not only indicators of the *existence* of other legal systems and traditions in India, but also as qualitative assessments of one of the ways in which the state *deals* or *engages* with legal plurality extant within its jurisdiction. However, cases only chronicle one side of the story, that is, they are able to only shed light on instances where the *state* has engaged with other systems through its judicial institutions and not the other way around. Engagement in the true sense ought to include the hundreds and thousands of instances where *other prevailing systems and traditions* engage with the state: may it be in the everyday lives of individuals who attach greater legitimacy to their traditional system over and above the normative laws of the state, may it be in traditional legal institutions and fora that apply traditional norms, social norms, and laws of the community to any given dispute over and above the laws of the state, may it be in self-governing organizations that maintain social control via traditional mechanisms other than the state's. This entire plethora of human legalistic activity ought to be relevant for the purpose of 'engagement', and yet the cases argued in Supreme Court and high courts comprise only one (albeit highly significant) chapter of this large narrative.

While studying these cases, the ratio decidendi that stands as a precedent for future cases has been considered alongside the obiter dicta, both of which are highly useful in a study such as this. Reading these judgments in toto has helped us not only ascertain the final result of a conflict between two systems, but also understand the reasoning employed and the general psyche of the judges while engaging with non-state law and non-state legal systems. In some of these cases, while the judges have extensively reasoned the need for intervention by the state in matters of personal laws in pursuance of gender equality and women empowerment (as obiter), they have ultimately refrained from actually doing so (as ratio); in other cases, while judges have expressed the dangers and difficulties in uniformalizing laws for all communities through the imposition of state law (as

Table A1.1 Judicial Engagement with Customary Law

S. No.	Case Name	Citation	Subject Matter	Brief Facts	Judicial Reasoning
1.	*State of Bombay v. Narasu Appa Mali*	AIR 1952 Bom 84	Constitutionality of marriage and divorce law.	The accused person was guilty of entering into a bigamous marriage. He argued that some provisions of the Bombay Prevention of Hindu Bigamous Marriages Act, 1946, were in contravention to the custom of bigamy (within his specific sect of Hindus).	The court upheld the constitutionality of the Act. The state had the power to hold any custom unconstitutional under Article13. However, personal laws are not within the ambit of this Article. If they were so, there would be no need for Articles 17 and 35(3).
2.	*Ram Prasad v. State of Uttar Pradesh*	AIR 1957 All 411	Constitutionality of marriage and divorce law.	The petitioner in this case challenged certain provisions of the Hindu Marriage Act, 1955, that prohibited bigamy. He alleged that the Hindu religion required a man to have a son without whom he could not attain *moksha*. In order to get a son, he may be permitted to marry a second wife (with the permission of the first). This, he argued, was his fundamental right under Article 25.	The court dismissed the petition, stating that, one, there was no such custom or mandatory requirement within the Hindu religion. Furthermore, his right to bigamy was not included within the scope of Article 25 considering it was a *practice* and not *faith* itself.

Table A1.1 (Cont'd)

S. No.	Case Name	Citation	Subject Matter	Brief Facts	Judicial Reasoning
3.	*Gazula Dasaratha Rama Rao v. State of Andhra Pradesh*	AIR 1961 SC 564	Constitutionality of a village custom.	Appointment of a village chief (in Peravalipalem village) according to the village's custom that succession shall be hereditary. This was secured by the Madras Hereditary Village-Offices Act, 1895, whereby the British allowed for the hereditary succession with some exceptions. The petitioner in this case has challenged the validity of this Act against Articles 14 and 15.	Custom and Act was held unconstitutional. This case reiterated the *Narasu* ratio that customs could be declared unconstitutional under Article 13. If the *Narasu* case set the tone for dealing with cases challenging personal laws, then this case was among the first that delved into customs having the force of law and how they either ought to be allowed or disallowed.
4.	*Sant Ram v. Labh Singh*	AIR 1965 SC 312	Law of pre-emption in sale of property.	During the sale of property, the appellant contended that there is a law of pre-emption based on vicinage in the particular village community.	The appeal was disallowed on the basis that such a custom stands against Article 19(1)(f) (then in force). This is because if a valid agreement to sell any property had been concluded, then it had to honour in spite of any such prevailing custom. Thus, such custom was struck down as per Article 13.

| 5. | *Sheikriyammada Nalla Koya v. Administrator* | AIR 1967 Ker 259 | Law of testamentary succession that goes against prevailing custom. | In a will, one deceased person laid down certain specifications and conditions regarding how property should be divested. Some parts of this testament went against the prevailing custom within the community. | The administrator who executed the will did not recognize certain clauses regarding partition of *tarwad* property (Hindu undivided family), as this went against the prevailing custom within this island (Lakshadweep) community).[1] There was no concept of partition within this tribal community prior to this case. The plaintiff (also a member of the tribe) claimed that Article 19(1)(f) guaranteed the right to hold property and no custom could completely disallow partition of tarwad property. The Kerala High Court ruled in favour of the plaintiff going into the reasoning that membership to a tribe could not be coercive, and that if members wish to hold individual property then customs preventing the same should be struck down. |

(Contd)

Table AI.1 (Cont'd)

S. No.	Case Name	Citation	Subject Matter	Brief Facts	Judicial Reasoning
6.	*Swaraj Garg* v. *K.M. Garg*	AIR 1978 Delhi 296	Restitution of conjugal rights.	The petitioner applied for restitution of conjugal rights with his salaried wife, who did not return to his house. This question was considered on the basis of personal law and constitutional law.	The Hon'ble Delhi High Court ruled that the wife need not stay exclusively at her husband's place if there was no prior consensus to that regard and even if any personal law warranted that. The court further noted that Article 14 of the Constitution guarantees equality before law and equal protection of the law to the husband and the wife. Any law which would give the exclusive right to the husband to decide upon the place of the matrimonial home without considering the needs and aspirations of the wife would be contrary to Article 14 and unconstitutional for that reason. This case is cited as an example of where a court suggests that uncodified personal laws are subject to the Constitution.

| 7. | Krishna Singh v. Mathura Ahir | AIR 1980 SC 707 | Validity of Hindu custom of Sudras being incapable of holding a religious office for a particular sect. | The respondent (original plaintiff) filed a suit for declaration of title over management and right to collect rent at the Garwaghat Math. The petitioner alleged that being a Sudra, the respondent was incapable of holding such a position, owing to customs of the Sant Math Sampradaya. This is a very important case; facts are more complicated than as stated above. | The court dismissed the petition. The court reasoned on the lines of the custom itself, and hardly touched upon the question of violation of fundamental rights or social exclusion of Sudras. The court established how there was no bar against Sudras holding the position of manager of math. Herein the court looked into the ceremonies that initiated a member into a math, if such ceremonies were performed in the case of the petitioner, then it was proof that this member held a valid position according to the custom itself. |
| 8. | Reynold Rajamani v. Union of India | (1982) 2 SCC 474 | Interpretation of Christian divorce laws. | The issue as to whether divorce by means of mutual consent could be read together into the provisions of Section 10 of the Indian Divorce Act, 1869, | The Hon'ble Supreme Court considered the issue as to whether mutual consent can be read as a ground of divorce in the provisions of the Indian |

(Contd)

Table AI.1 (Cont'd)

S. No.	Case Name	Citation	Subject Matter	Brief Facts	Judicial Reasoning
				though not expressly provided in the statute.	Divorce Act, 1869. The Hon'ble Court held that the grounds for divorce were stipulated in Section 10 of the Indian Divorce Act, 1869, and since 'mutual consent' was not specified therein, the Hon'ble Court could not add that ground via its judgment.
9.	*Mohammed Ahmed Khan v. Shah Bano Begum*	AIR 1985 SC 945	Question of whether maintenance had to be provided for a Muslim woman under a secular law like Code of Criminal Procedure, 1973, contrary to the position under Islamic law where	Appeals were filed by the petitioner Mohd Ahmed Khan against the decision of the Madhya Pradesh High Court. The appellant, who had divorced his wife, Shah Bano, aged 62 years, mother of 5 children, refused to provide maintenance beyond the iddat period. The wife asked for further maintenance to sustain herself under Section 125 of CrPC, 1973.	The Hon'ble Supreme Court in its 5-judge-bench judgment pronounced that there was no conflict between the provisions of Section 125 of the Code and those of Muslim personal law on the question of a Muslim husband's obligation to provide maintenance for his divorced wife who is unable to maintain herself. The Hon'ble Court held that the provisions of the Code

were secular in nature, and applicable to all citizens irrespective of their religion and that those provisions expressly dealt with vagrancy and destitution where maintenance was inadequate and ordered the petitioner to pay Rs 10,000 as maintenance to his wife. This judgment generated a lot of controversy and criticism as it was considered by many as a judicial overstep into matters of personal law, which they considered their sole right to manage.

maintenance had to be provided only during the *iddat* period.[2]

| 10. | *Maharshi Avdesh v. Union of India* | 1994 Supp (1) SCC 713 | Constitutionality of Muslim Women (Protection of Rights on Divorce) Act, 1986, challenged. | Constitutionality of Muslim Women (Protection of Rights on Divorce) Act, 1986, challenged in the writ petition, along with praying for issuance of writ of mandamus for enacting the uniform civil code. | The Hon'ble Supreme Court held that these are all matters for legislature and that the court cannot legislate in these matters. The writ petition was dismissed accordingly and the court refused to grant any relief. |

(Cont'd)

Table A1.1   *(Cont'd)*

S. No.	Case Name	Citation	Subject Matter	Brief Facts	Judicial Reasoning
11.	*Amini E.J. v. Union of India*	AIR 1995 Ker 252	Constitutionality of marriage and divorce law.	Constitutionality of Section 10 of the Indian Divorce Act was challenged by the petitioners who were 2 Christian women. Section 10 (at the time this case was being heard, prior to the 2001 Amendment) did not provide for adultery by husband as an independent ground for divorce.	The court held that Section 10 was unconstitutional and urged the legislature to make reforms. This judgment is particularly interesting because for the first time the court broke away from the trend of judicial restraint towards personal laws and customs. However, the *Amini E.J.* judgment stands per incurium in the sphere of constitutionality of personal laws, because cases after it slid back into the trend of judicial restraint.
12.	*Mary Sonia Zacharia v. Union of India*	1995 (1) Ker LT 644 (FB)	Constitutionality of marriage and divorce law.	Constitutionality of Section 10 of the Indian Divorce Act, 1869, was challenged by the petitioners who were Christian women. Section 10, prior to the 2001 Amendment did not provide	The court followed the principle that to remove the arbitrariness or unconstitutionality of a provision of law, which can be done by severing the offending

No.	Case	Citation	Issue	Facts	Decision
				for adultery by husband as an independent ground for divorce (similar to the *Amini E.J.* case).	portions and saving the beneficial portions. The court, thus, struck down the provision as violative of Articles 14, 15, and 21. The differentiation provided between the husband and wife with respect to the grounds for dissolution of marriage was condemned by the court.
13.	*Smt. Sarla Mudgal v. Union of India*	(1995) 3 SCC 635	Validity of second marriage under Hindu law if one of the parties converts to a different religion.	Four petitions were clubbed together:The facts of the first petition were that one Jeetender Mathur, a Hindu, had embraced Islam to marry another woman, leaving his first wife, and later he reconverted back to Hinduism, leaving his second wife, a Muslim, stranded and deprived of her marital rights and maintenance.Similar facts were presented in the other petitions. The court was asked to consider	In a landmark judgment, the Hon'ble Supreme Court ushered in the immediate need for the implementation of the uniform civil code as per Article 44 of the Constitution. The court reasoned that the conversion of one or both the Hindu spouses to a different religion did not dissolve the marriage. It furthered this by stating that Hindu law placed strict emphasis on monogamy

(Cont'd)

Table A1.1 (Cont'd)

S. No.	Case Name	Citation	Subject Matter	Brief Facts	Judicial Reasoning
				whether a Hindu man married under Hindu law by embracing Islam could solemnize a second marriage and also whether the apostate husband would be guilty of the offence of bigamy under Section 494 of the Indian Penal Code.	and that neither of the spouses could solemnize a second marriage without dissolving the first, and if anybody did so, that person would be liable for punishment of the offence of bigamy under Section 494 of the Indian Penal Code. The Hon'ble Court also stated that polygamy can be superseded by the state, as it cannot be considered a customary right. The personal law operated under the *authority* of the legislation and not under religion.
14.	*Madhu Kishwar & ors v. State of Bihar & ors*	1996 (5) SCC 125	Constitutionaliy of laws of intestate succession.	The provisions of the Chota Nagpur Tenancy Act, 1908, that provide for only male heirs as capable of inheriting family propery were challenged by the petitioner as discriminatory	The court did not entertain the petition and urged the legislature to amend the law. The court reasoned that such matters involved policy and governance questions, which

				against women. This Act was enacted by the Bihar Legislative Assembly in order to spell out the laws of landlord and tenant among members of the tribal community residing in the Chota Nagpur region.	the judiciary ought not get into. This case marks the dichotomy between the position of law in the *Narasu* and the *Gazula* cases, and also marks the beginning of judicial restraint in matters of personal law and customs and usages.
15.	*Masilamani Mudaliar* v. *Idol of Sri Swanathaswami*	(1996) 8 SCC 525	Interpretation of Section 14 of the Hindu Succession Act, 1956.	The petitioner (widow) in the instant case challenged the limited estate of a widow as being violative of her fundamental rights.	While the Supreme Court has observed in the above-mentioned cases that the personal laws cannot be tested upon the touchstone of Part III of the Constitution, the same court has made exceptions and thus created an anomaly of judicial precedents. The Hon'ble Supreme Court held that the concept of restrictive or limited widow's estate under Section 14(1) of the Hindu Succession Act, 1956, was violative of Articles 14 and 15. The law

(Contd)

Table AI.1   *(Cont'd)*

S. No.	Case Name	Citation	Subject Matter	Brief Facts	Judicial Reasoning
16.	*Ahmedabad Women Action Group & ors v. Union of India*	AIR 1997, 3 SCC 573	Constitutionality of several personal laws (statutes).	The petitioners filed 3 separate writ petitions challenging the validity of certain personal laws such as the Hindu Marriage Act, 1955, Hindu Succession Act, 1956, and the Protection of Rights on Divorce Act, 1986, and so on, on the basis that they discriminate on the grounds of sex (Articles 14 and 15).	should not be permitted to discriminate against women in holding property under the law. The court declined to entertain the writ petitions on the grounds that the matter involved a policy question that was not appropriate for the judiciary to look into. Here it cited the *Madhu Kishwar* judgment, which dealt with customs and not personal laws. Its conclusion that personal laws do not fall within the scope of Article 13 was in line with *Narasu*. However, scholars argued that both the *Narasu* and *Ahmedabad Women Action* cases made erroneous interpretations of Article 13 (thereby stating that personal laws did in fact fall within the ambit of Article13)

No.	Case	Citation	Subject	Challenge	Holding
17.	*P.E. Mathew v. Union of India*	AIR 1999 Ker 345	Constitutionality of marriage and divorce law.	Constitutionality of Section 17 of the Indian Divorce Act, 1986, was challenged by the petitioner.	In this case, the court ought to have adopted the same approach as in *Amini E.J.* but it did not do so stating that changing personal laws would be a legislative action that involved questions of public policy and governance. It cited *Ahmedabad Action and Madhu Kishwar* for justifying the same.
18.	*Githa Hariharan & anr v. Reserve Bank of India*	AIR 1999 SC 1149	Constitutionality of the laws of minority and guardianship.	Constitutionality of Section 6 (a) of the Hindu Minority and Guardianship Act, 1956, and Section 19 (a) of the Guardians and Wards Act, 1890, was challenged by the petitioner.	The court held that the mother of a child could be its 'natural guardian' given the fact that Hindu law mandated that only the father could act as natural guardian of the child under the Hindu Minority and Guardianship Act, 1956. The court did not strike down any provision but tried to harmoniously interpret them with the Constitution. Hence, it read into the term 'after' in Section 6 so as to save it from unconstitutionality.

(Cont'd)

Table A1.1 (Cont'd)

S. No.	Case Name	Citation	Subject Matter	Brief Facts	Judicial Reasoning
19.	*Daniel Latif v. Union of India*	(2001) 7 SCC 740	Constitutionality of Muslim Women (Protection of Rights on Divorce) Act, 1986, challenged.	The petitioner alleged that the Act was discriminatory and violative of Article 14 and Article 21 as it excluded the Muslim women from the purview of Section 125 of the Code of Criminal Procedure, 1973, with no valid justification.	The court upheld the constitutionality of the Act as well as the women's right to have a fair and reasonable settlement along with other reliefs such as return of valuables and mehr. While upholding the constitutional validity of the Act, the Hon'ble Court affirmed that the Act had substituted the earlier right of recurrent maintenance under Section 125 of the Code of Criminal Procedure, 1973, with a new right of a lump sum provision to be made and paid to the woman soon after her divorce, within the iddat period. If the husband failed to make the payment, the Muslim woman had the right to appeal to a magistrate's court.

20.	*John Vallamattom & anr v. Union of India*	AIR 2003 SC 2902	Constitutionality of testamentary succession law challenged.	Constitutionality of Section 118 of the Indian Succession Act, 1925, challenged.	The Hon'ble Supreme Court held that Section 118 of the Indian Succession Act, 1925, which put several unreasonable conditions for testamentary disposition of property for Christians only as against people from other religions. The Hon'ble Court cited *D.S. Nakara v. Union of India* (1983) 1 SCC305 stating that Article 14 forbids class legislation but permits reasonable classification for twin tests of classification. The court then proceeded to strike down the section as violative of Article 14.
21.	*Javed & anr v. State of Haryana*	(2003) 8 SCC 369	Constitutionality of the provisions of Haryana Panchayati Raj Act, 1994, challenged.	The petitioner had challenged the provision in the Act that barred people from holding the specific positions in panchayat who had more than 2 children as violative of Articles 14, 21, and 25 of the Constitution of India.	The court held that the provision was neither arbitrary nor unreasonable. The disqualification contained a laudable socio-economic policy for population control and was not violative of Article 14.

(Cont'd)

Table AI.1 (Cont'd)

S. No.	Case Name	Citation	Subject Matter	Brief Facts	Judicial Reasoning
					Further, the court observed that nowhere in Islam was it mandated that there was a specific mandate to procreate with all the 4 wives and even having 4 wives did not necessarily mean that one needed to have more than 2 children. Hence, nowhere a personal right to practise and profess one's religion was hampered.
23.	*Seema v. Ashwani Kumar*	(2005) 4 SCC 443	Issue arose with respect to mandatory registration of marriages.	The question of compulsory registration of marriages was brought into consideration before the Hon'ble Court and the court considered the question as to whether it could direct compulsory registration of marriages all over the country.	The Hon'ble Supreme Court in its landmark judgment ordered the central Government to issue directions to various states and union territories to authorize individuals to keep a record of marriages so that they can be kept as evidence in different proceedings if and when the necessity arises.

23.	*Ewanlangki-i-Rymbai v. Jaintia Hills District Council*	(2006) 4 SCC 748	Election dispute in the Jaintia Hills region.	A member of the tribe married a Christian woman, who later stood for Jaintia Hills Tribal Council elections. The Jaintia Hills Act debars any person who is not a member of the tribe to hold certain positions (one of which is in contention in this case). The petitioner claims that this provision is against Articles 14 and 15.	The Kerala High Court, where this petition was initially filed, ruled against the petitioner stating that the tribe itself has the power to determine rules of membership and mere marriage may not be sufficient to forge a new identity within tribal groups. The bar against non-tribals contesting elections is not in violation of the Constitution, as tribal autonomy is also a constitutional goal. The Supreme Court concurred with the high court.
24.	*Vishwa Lochan Madan v. Union of India*	(2014) 7 SCC 707	Legality of fatwas and Dar-ul-Qazas/Nizam-e-Qazas.	The petitioner, a Delhi-based lawyer, had approached the Supreme Court by way of a public interest litigation alleging that the Muslim clerics had set up Sharia courts all over the country, rendering judgments	The Hon'ble Supreme Court in its judgment held that such Dar-ul-Qazas and such courts may have laudable objectives; however, they have no legal status and are not part of the corpus juris of the state. As for

(Cont'd)

Table A1.1 (Cont'd)

S. No.	Case Name	Citation	Subject Matter	Brief Facts	Judicial Reasoning
				in the form of fatwas, which comprised a parallel judicial system in the country.	the fatwas, the court said that these have no legal value and it was unto the discretion of the persons to obey, defy, or simply ignore them. Any forceful imposition of the fatwas would be illegal and dealt in accordance with the law.
25.	*Shayara Bano v. Union of India*	Writ Petition (Civil) No. 118 of 2016	Constitutional validity of Triple Talaq.	The petitioner, a divorced Muslim woman, had approached the court through a PIL to adjudicate regarding the constitutional validity of Triple Talaq.	The 5-judge bench of the Supreme Court held Triple Talaq to be constitutionally invalid by a majority of 3:2. The majority's view was that Triple Talaq was not a custom and its validity was to be tested on the ground of reasonableness. By contrast, the minority held Triple Talaq to be valid customary law of Muslims belonging to the Hanafi School.

Source: Authors.

[1] Under a matrilineal society, where mother is the head of the family or clan, a family consisting of all children either male or female descending from a common ancestress is called a tarward (*Kalyani* v. *Narayanan*, AIR 1980 SC 1173 [1177]).

[2] The 'iddat period' in the case of a divorced woman means: (*i*) three menstrual courses after the date of divorce, if she is subject to menstruation; (*ii*) three lunar months after her divorce, if she is not subject to menstruation; and (*iii*) if she is enceinte at the time of her divorce, the period between the divorce and the delivery of her child or the termination of her pregnancy, whichever is earlier (Section 2 in The Muslim Women [Protection of Rights on Divorce] Act, 1986).

obiter), they have gone ahead and done just that by striking down certain customary practices and applying state law. Thus, the last column of Table AI.1 not only indicates what was held in the case, but also includes a brief description of the judicial reasoning employed in order to reach this point.

The sequence in this index is arranged chronologically and does not indicate the significance or importance of judgments in terms of their precedential value.

Appendix II

State Profiles Indicating Reliance on Traditional, Non-state Legal Systems

While beginning the study, we thought it necessary to refer to latest data on prevalence of preference on non-state legal systems in India. The AnSI's People of India project (1985–90) was suited to our purpose, since, unlike other large-scale surveys, it recorded certain social-anthropological parameters such as kinship, inheritance patterns, and social organization and maintenance of social order in communities in India, and was the latest, consolidated information on the same. While current statistics may have changed given the changed socio-economic scenario of the nation, the Project is important to understand that despite the operation of the Indian common law system for over three decades, a significant portion of people preferred traditional, informal systems of law and order.

In arriving at a list of communities in India, the Project not only referred to the existing lists and schedules currently in use in government and administrative endeavours, but also referred to anthropological information regarding castes and tribes in India, coming to a consolidated number of 4,635 communities after conducting preliminary pilots. The entire list can be found on AnSI's website. The

Project has been heavily critiqued by social scientists, considering it perpetuates the ordering and organization of 'difference'—something which the Census of India and other such large-scale state surveys have repeatedly been accused of doing (Jenkins, 2003). Counting and taxonomies have been critiqued, especially due to their nature of enabling targeted attacks on communities, such as the manipulation of electoral rolls to target the Sikh community in Delhi during the 1984 riots.

However, for this study, the published findings of the survey have been read to note the prevalence of dependency on what is considered the non-state legal system to answer our greater questions on India's legal reality. To this end, and in keeping with research norms, we have generated state profiles, along with state-specific charts, to show the degree of reliance on non-state legal systems by communities in the states of Andhra Pradesh and Telangana, Assam, Delhi, Gujarat, and Himachal Pradesh. The materials were reviewed keeping in mind broad geographical divisions of north, south, east, and west, and Delhi was chosen as an urban representation.

The Project distinguishes between several institutions of dispute settlement, namely:

1. Statutory Village Bodies: These are the state-recognized gram panchayats, which were institutionalized in independent India. Statutory village bodies, as per government orders, must demonstrate cross-community representation and adequate diversity. However, such diversity is often contested, considered traditional panchayats were almost always composed of dominant male members of communities.

2. Heterogeneous Village Panchayats: These are the panchayats in villages or areas were a statutory body either does not exist, or exists but performs limited administrative and welfare functions. Most instances of statutory gram panchayats are but a formalized and recognized version of erstwhile heterogeneous village panchayats. Heterogeneous village panchayats usually demonstrate inter-caste alliances. However, representation of lower castes is marginal.

3. Traditional Caste/Community Councils: These are intra-caste/community councils that deal with matters within the

community. Inter-caste disputes are usually referred to either the heterogeneous village panchayats or the council of the dominant community of the region. Examples of these are *jamat, jati panch, kula panchayat, biradari panchayat,* and so on.

4. Other Informal Village/Community Councils: These are councils in villages and communities that are not based either on the principle of a formal panchayat or caste affiliation. These councils, composed largely of village elders and other sources of wisdom, such as the deity's oracle, the priest, and so on, usually operate either in the absence of or alongside the other forms of councils and bodies outlined above. While it is stated that these councils do not affiliate on the basis of caste, they are predominantly composed of male members of the dominant caste or jati in the village.

5. Associations and *Sangh*s: These are non-legal bodies with little say in matters of social order. They are usually trade-, religion-, and community-based informal organizations that focus mainly on cultural preservation and related community activities. Trade associations and sanghs sometimes operate in the domain of economic semi-legality in terms of setting prices and other such market considerations.

Of the associations, bodies, and councils listed above, heterogeneous village panchayats, traditional caste/community councils, and informal village/community councils fall in the domain of the non-state legal system. Published materials of the Project were reviewed to note which community reported reliance on one or more of these bodies.

However, it is important to note that these definitions of councils and bodies are not rigid. Some communities report jamats and panchs that exercise what can be considered adjudicative powers, while other appropriate the organization and the duties closer to the associations and sanghs. Moreover, synergies of a different kind can be noted when influential members of society—leaders of caste councils formed of members of dominant castes, priests, and other dominant members—find representation in statutory bodies as well (the Pajiara community, highlighted in Chapter 3, can be one such example of this). Caste/community councils, in some cases, are not much differentiated from village panchayats, even in multi-caste villages where while the village may be heterogeneous, the panchayat may not and comprise only of dominant caste members. Moreover, in a few cases, samajs and sanghs venture into what can be considered domains of law and order when they officiate divorce and other such settlement proceedings.

General trends extracted from the reports show:

1. Of over 1,000 communities reviewed by us, over 700 report some level of reliance on traditional caste or village councils—approximately 70 per cent of the communities reviewed in our sample. While more updated empirical research may show results which are in disagreement with these findings, this approximation is telling since it demonstrates a picture of independent India not all may be aware of. Further, deeper research is required to assess the contemporary viability of these numbers, and what they entail for the continued identification of India as a common law country with one state legal system. It should be noted that the distribution of such communities is not even across the states surveyed. Some states, such as Andhra Pradesh, demonstrate significantly higher prevalence of reliance on non-state legal systems (nearly two-thirds). However, other states, such as Himachal Pradesh (a little more than one-third) and Delhi (approximately half), show lower degrees of reliance of communities on non-state legal systems. Considerations such as social and economic development, rural–urban distribution, and access to institutions and mechanisms of the state legal system, among others, need to be taken into consideration while examining prevalence in greater detail.

2. Most communities demonstrate reliance on mixed legal traditions—where the traditional councils handle marriage, divorce, and other such domains governing sexuality and sexual relationships (and sometimes by association, rape), the statutory councils handle administrative and welfare duties, and the law and order mechanisms handle 'serious' crimes such as murder and assault.

3. Non-legal practices such as child marriage, dowry, and child labour continue to prevail, according to the findings of the

survey. While these may not all be indicators of lack of legal obedience, they too can be read as the failure of the state legal system to penetrate to Indian society or its distance and lack of alignment with social realities of the people.

4. Property rights for women exist in an extremely small percentage of the communities reviewed. The national percentage of communities practising male equigeniture (transfer of property to male members of the family) was, at the time of the survey, noted to be 79.4 per cent, while 72.2 per cent of communities surveyed have self-reported the status of women to be lower than that of men.

5. Penalties levied by traditional organizations are usually in the form of fines and compensation or, in extreme cases, excommunication, which is largely reversible. There are no reported instances of capital punishment or confinement. Community members also report avoiding state legal systems due to harsh, irreversible punishments, and fixed and permanently binding judgments. Deeper inquiry into the institutions and process of law and order can indicate whether the redressal mechanisms of the state are greatly incongruent with traditional methods.

Andhra Pradesh and Telangana

General Trends

1. Of the communities surveyed, *all* are monogamous and patriarchal.

2. The Project has surveyed 389 communities in Andhra Pradesh.

3. Of all the surveyed communities, 360 communities (92.54 per cent) follow the inheritance rule of male equigeniture. Only 19 (0.05 per cent) communities give women a share in ancestral property.

4. Child labour has been reported to exist in 205 (52.71 per cent) communities.

5. Within the social organization of tribes in Andhra Pradesh, widow remarriage is permitted in all communities. Moreover, widows do not experience diminished status as is the case in Hindu communities.

6. Trading and artisan communities often have community associations which exercise power in some aspects of social transactions—mainly economic activity.

Overview of Report

Out of 389, 253 (65.04 per cent, nearly two-thirds) communities report the existence of traditional caste councils, while 57 still rely on traditional heterogeneous village councils. Traditional councils usually monitor the domains of kinship—marriage, divorce, and so on. Kinship also includes ensuring the perpetuation of the clan, and, therefore, reproductive and sexual relations (in some cases, rape as well) are also monitored by the traditional councils. Both customary councils and state systems monitor property. Homicide, murder, and serious crimes are often the domain of the state legal system. However, the Kondh traditional councils exercise complete social control and handle murder cases as well.

Traditional councils exercise significant social control. Statutory panchayats, though widespread, deal mostly with welfare and development initiatives, leaving most adjudicating power in the hands of the traditional caste, community, and village councils. Reliance on police and courts of law for maintaining social control, although reported, is not widespread.

Puberty restrictions on menstruating women are widespread among most communities and universal in tribal communities. This consists of a period of pollution where the girl is secluded in one part of the house and not allowed cohabit, cook, go near the hearth, touch stored grain or seed, or participate in any religious or cultural activities.

Table AII.1 gives some details about non-state legal practices in Andhra Pradesh and Telangana. The number of communities in the table is fewer than the total number of communities enumerated by the Project as having traditional councils, as subdivisions of some communities (for example, the Yerukula have several subdivisions) have been subsumed under the main community name.

Assam

Table AII.1 Communities in Andhra Pradesh and Telangana with Reported Reliance on Non-state Legal Systems

1.	Adi Dravida	An informal council formed of community elders handle disputes over land, water, family issues, adultery, and rape.
2.	Agnikula Kshatriya	In single-caste villages, the *kula panchayat* (caste panchayat) decides social and economic disputes. In multi-caste villages, heterogeneous panchayats perform the same role. Regional community associations (registered societies) handle welfare and development issues.
3.	Aguru	The traditional council (*kula sangham*) is presided over by the headman (*kula pedda*), assisted by village elders. The *pedda naidu* (regional council chief) handles disputes relating to several villages. The decision of the regional caste association—the *sangha nayakudu*—is binding. Defaulters are fined.
4.	Aiyarakulu	The community panchayat exists alongside the heterogeneous village panchayat, and a statutory gram panchayat. A community association at the regional level looks after welfare and development.
5.	Andh	The community panchayat exists alongside the heterogeneous village panchayat, and a statutory gram panchayat. A community association at the regional level looks after welfare and development.
6.	Arab	A traditional association called the Al-Jamaitual-Arabia exists in Hyderabad to exercise social control. Domestic quarrels and property disputes are handled by this association. Islamic law is followed for inheritance and marriage.
7.	Arakala	The Arakala have an informal kula panchayat for social control. It deals with cases of theft and adultery, among others. Offenders are excommunicated.

(Cont'd)

Table AII.1   *(Cont'd)*

8.	Are-Bondili/ Bommalatavallu	Traditional kula panchayats composed of community elders maintain social order. Zonal councils maintain territorial integrity (Are-Bondilis are a nomadic group that camp on government wasteland). Traditional councils can punish offences through excommunication and imposing physical punishment and fines. Statutory councils look after welfare and development.
9.	Are Kapu	Rural areas have kula panchayats to administer justice, while in urban areas they have been replaced by welfare-oriented kula sanghams.
10.	Are Katika	While there are no traditional panchayats to maintain social control, informal community associations settle disputes, regulate prices (the Are Katikas are traditional butchers and meat sellers), marriage, and welfare activities.
11.	Arundhatiya/ Arunthatiyar/ Arunthathiyar/ Arundhatiyar	Inter-community disputes are handled by the kula panchayat. Heterogeneous village panchayats also administer social control. The kula panchayat handles cases of adultery, divorce, widow remarriage, and family disputes. Physical and cash punishments, based on the nature of the dispute, are imposed. The decisions of the kula panchayat are binding.
12.	Atar/Gandhodi Saibulu	The local jamath looks after welfare, spreads the teachings of Islam, and acts as a divorce court.
13.	Attar Saibulu	The local jamath looks after welfare, spreads the teachings of Islam, and acts as a divorce court.
14.	Bagatha	The Bagatha have local, regional, and village councils. The local tribal council (kula kattu/ kula panchayat) deals with political matters at the village level. Regional councils oversee a region comprising of 20–70 continuous villages. A village council (*voorukattu*) handles disputes between different clans in the village. Common punitive measures include expulsion from the tribe, imposition of fines, and expiation feasts. Common offences include

homicide, incest, witchcraft, sorcery, adultery, bodily injury, and prohibited sexual relations.

15. Baita Kammara — A community panchayat settles disputes relating to property, adultery, theft, and so on. For matters like divorce, courts of law are approached.

16. Balasanthu/ Balasanthosha — The kula panchayat regulates marriages and settles intra-community disputes.

17. Balija/Setti Balija — Kula panchayats settle conflicts in rural areas, kula sanghams perform the same functions in urban areas. Kula sanghams also handle inter-community disputes. Most of the cases are solved by these bodies without going to court.

18. Balija/Vada Balija/Voda Balija — The kula panchayat has full jurisdiction over inter-family relationships and matters concerning marriage and social control.

19. Banda/Bander/ Lander — The Banda headman (kula pedda), assisted by village elders, resolves disputes at the village level. The second level of dispute management is at the regional level—disputes that are not favourably resolved by the kula pedda are taken to the *kula guruvu* (regional head of the community). Offences are penalized by heavy fines, which are distributed evenly to all present.

20. Bandollu — A traditional kula panchayat officiates matters relating to marriages, rituals, and special occasions.

21. Banjara/ Mathura Banjara — A community panchayat exists to settle cases like adultery, rape, and elopement. However, the head (*naik*) acts as a link with official (state) agencies.

22. Banjara Sikh — Banjara Sikhs live in their traditional settlements called *tanda*. The tanda has a traditional council with a hereditary headman to settle local and regional disputes.

23. Bariki — A traditional caste panchayat exists to settle common disputes such as adultery, theft, widow remarriage, and so on. Punitive fines are paid in either cash or kind.

(Cont'd)

Table AII.1   (Cont'd)

24.	Bavuri	A traditional kula panchayat settles disputes over theft, adultery, land disputes, and cases of divorce, while a kula sangham handles welfare and development issues. Each village has a headman, who is second in authority to a regional head—a *behara* for every group of villages (*mutah*)
25.	Budaga Jangam/ Beda Jangam	The traditional kula panchayat handles cases of divorce, adultery, and breach of cultural norms. Statutory panchayats exist to monitor welfare and development.
26.	Bestha/Bestar	Traditional councils are largely defunct, and most villages rely on statutory panchayats for law and order. However, community councils still exist in some areas, and look after marriage and divorce proceedings, elopement, and minor crimes.
27.	Bhondari	A traditional community council resolves caste-related disputes.
28.	Bindla	A kula panchayat settles intra- and inter-community disputes.
29.	Bohara	Every Bohra settlement (*mohalla*) refers to a jamath (association) for social order.
30.	Bolla	The Bolla caste panchayat deals with cases related to elopement, adultery, land and water disputes, and theft.
31.	Bondili/Bondil	Elected community councils settle local and regional disputes.
32.	Borewale	A local jamath settles cases of small disputes and petty thefts.
33.	Boya/Chaduru Boya	The caste council settles petty crimes. In places, where a traditional caste panchayat is absent, the village priest settles disputes.
34.	Boya/Pedda Boya	Previously recorded as a criminal tribe, the Pedda Boyas rely on a clan subgroup called *kavali doralu* to settle disputes. The kavali doralu act as arbitrators when disputes arise among community members.

35.	Boya/Bedar	Most disputes are settled using traditional systems. The headman (dora) settles all disputes along with the counsel of village elders. Caste associations are found at the village, mandal, district, and state levels. Regionally, the Boyas all come under an association for the entire state of Andhra Pradesh.
36.	Buddabukkala	A traditional community panchayat maintains social control using punitive measures such as fines and social boycott for offenders.
37.	Budubudikki/ Are Budbudikke	Kula panchayats comprising of village elders settle disputes such as adultery and rape. A rapist has to marry the victim under the Marumanuvu system. Accused persons dip their fingers in hot oil to prove their innocence according to the *deva sathyam* custom (trial by ordeal in which the truth is revealed in front of god when the accused undergoes trial).
38.	Budubudikka/ Ganta Budbudikke	The community panchayat settles issues such as divorce, remarriage, adultery, and so on. Violators are tried and punished by the panchayat.
39.	Byagara	The traditional caste council—the kula panchayat—settles disputes such as adultery, elopement, divorce, deviation from caste norms, and so on.
40.	Chakketakare	A traditional jamath handles community issues and organizes cultural affairs.
41.	Chalavadi	Kula panchayats handle minor disputes and the headman (kula pedda) officiates marriages.
42.	Chamadollu	The kula panchayat is active in some villages. Most villages have fishing associations to regulate their traditional economy.
43.	Chamar	A traditional caste panchayat decides disputes such as divorce, widow remarriage, adultery, theft, and other family issues. Kula sanghams also exist at the regional level.

(Cont'd)

Table AII.1   *(Cont'd)*

44.	Chembadi	Traditional caste councils play a great role in social control handling disputes of various issues. Statutory gram panchayats are present as well, and resorting to justice through courts has also been reported.
45.	Chenchu	Each village refers to an elder called *peddamanchi* to be the final word in all disputes. Occasionally, the peddamanchi is assisted by a group of 5–6 village elders.
46.	Chippollu/Mera	The kula panchayat settles inter- and intra-community disputes. A regional sangham exists as well.
47.	Christians	Christians in Andhra Pradesh often have parish councils and 'congregational panchayats' to settle disputes. Communal boycott is observed for questionable behaviour.
48.	Chundollu	The kula panchayat settles marriage disputes, divorce cases, adultery, property disputes, and so on. Statutory formal panchayats exist as well to handle welfare and development related matters.
49.	Dakkal/ Dakkala/ Dakkaliga	Kula panchayats exist to settle disputes relating to adultery, elopement, theft, and so on. Dakkalas reside in the peripheries of villages and have no active part or presence in the statutory bodies or heterogeneous panchayats of the village.
50.	Dammali	A traditional council comprising of village elders congregates to settle social and economic disputes.
51.	Dandasi	Dandasis rely heavily on their kula panchayats for social control. Groups of villages fall under a headman, *behara*, at the regional level. Their participation in statutory panchayats is limited.
52.	Dasari	Dasaris have kula panchayats at the village level. Unresolved cases are brought to

gurus at their community seats—Kanchi, Tirumala, Karmadai, and Penugonda. Gurus in consultation with the caste councils give the final verdict on cases relating to insult, elopement, adultery, and theft.

53.	Devanga	Kula panchayats exist to maintain social control and handle cases of divorce, widow remarriage, theft, and loss of property.
54.	Devara	Regional kula panchayats exist with community councils comprising of elders in every village to handle issues regarding social control. Statutory gram panchayats focusing on welfare and development exist as well.
55.	Didoyi	An informal village council maintains law and order at the village level. All offences are brought to the notice of the council and matters such as theft, adultery, land, and property disputes are settled by the council. A thief is required to recompense the victims depending on the nature of theft; if a man marries a lower caste woman, he is excommunicated; and accepting cooked food from a lower group is a punishable offence. Statutory village panchayats are reported to exist in some villages.
56.	Dombara	A community council exists at the village level to settle disputes.
57.	Dudekula/ Panjukutti	Kula jamaths exist to maintain social order and statutory panchayats handle welfare and development.
58.	Ekere	Traditional kula panchayats handle cases relating to internal conflicts, communal tensions, property disputes, inter-caste marriages, and so on. State courts are also accessed.
59.	Pala Ekiri	Traditional councils exist at village and regional levels and judge offences such as adultery, prostitution, land disputes, disrespect of traditional norms, sexual violations, and theft.

(Cont'd)

Table AII.1   *(Cont'd)*

60.	Faqir/Fhakir Budbudki	Marriage and death rituals are handled by the jamath. Defaulters are punished with cash fines. Statutory panchayats also exist at village levels.
61.	Gadaba	The kula panchayat plays an important role in social control. Offenders are fined for cases such as theft, adultery and marriage after divorce.
62.	Gandalla	Kula panchayats maintain social control and handle cases of adultery, elopement, divorce, and theft, and property disputes. However, these have been waning in influence since the advent of statutory bodies.
63.	Gandla/Ganuga/ Tilakula	A traditional kutam or kula panchayat, headed by a *chetty* (clan or council chief), meets to settle disputes such as adultery, rape, divorce, theft, quarrels, and conflicts. Disputes are often referred to the police and the courts, based on the discretion of the caste councils.
64.	Gangireddula	A nomadic community, Gangureddulas reside in hutments only during the months of November and December, and this is when their panchayats convene. The kula panchayat handles a manner of cases such as elopement, divorce, property disputes, quarrels, and conflicts. The decision of the panchayat is final, and offenders are excommunicated.
65.	Gantasayebulu	A traditional panchayat settles disputes, punishes offenders, and rewards good behaviour.
66.	Godagali	Kula panchayats exist at local and village levels, and settle cases of divorce, minor disputes, and cases of elopement. Community norm violators are fined.
67.	Godari	A caste panchayat settles petty disputes and divorce cases.
68.	Golla/Pedditi Golla	A council of community elders maintains social control, and a statutory village panchayat takes care of welfare and development.

69.	Yerragolla	The Yeragollas have an elaborate system of social control. A woman suspected of infidelity is first made to enter a temporary kitchen set-up and decorated for the purpose of the trial. The woman is supposed to fast for three days before her trial. On the day of the trial, a betel leaf is immersed in a pot of boiling ghee, and the suspect has to retrieve it using her bare fingers. In case the fingers are burnt or scarred, the woman is proclaimed guilty, and the husband has the right to divorce her. A community of village elders maintain social control.
70.	Gond	A traditional village council, headed by a srapatlal, exists to maintain social control. The council's functions are defined and their decisions are binding. Inter-village councils called *raya Sabha*s settle disputes among villages and maintain unity among Gonds and other hill tribal settlements.
71.	Gosangi	Traditional caste panchayats headed by a *peddaiah* settle disputes such as adultery, rape, and violation of traditional norms. Statutory village panchayats deal with welfare and development.
72.	Goudu	A traditional council called *pradhano* exists to handle issues pertaining to divorce, marriage alliances, pre-marital and extra-marital sexual relations, property issues, and so on. Offenders are fined.
73.	Gowda	Traditional community councils handle cases of theft, adultery, and land and water disputes, and offenders are fined.
74.	Guddi Eluguvallu	A traditional jamath headed by a *khazi* handles social problems such as divorce, remarriage, and inter-caste marriage (in the case of the last, the offender is excommunicated). Statutory panchayats deal with welfare and development.

(Cont'd)

Table AII.1 (Cont'd)

75.	Gudia/Gudiya	Community councils comprising of village elders decide divorce cases and fine offenders for violating community norms.
76.	Gurika/ Palaguriki	Community associations handle both welfare and development projects, as well as internal disputes, property disputes, and cases of theft.
77.	Hajam/Nai/ Navind	A traditional jamath attends to marriage and death ceremonies, and regulates religious issues. Defaulters are punished with cash fines.
78.	Hatagar/Hatgar/ Hatagara	A traditional caste council headed by a peddamandhi officiates in marriage and death rituals, solves disputes, and punishes defaulters.
79.	Irani	The Irani jamath headed by a sardar settles cases such as adultery, rape, elopement, and theft. Offenders can be punished with social boycott and excommunication. A statutory panchayat exists to implement welfare and development activities.
80.	Irla	The kula panchayat settles cases of adultery, theft, divorce, rape, and elopement. Punishments are imposed in accordance with the nature of the crime.
81.	Jaggali	The kula panchayat decides cases of theft, adultery, divorce, rape, and quarrels. Offenders have to pay fines to aggrieved parties.
82.	Jalakaduguvallu	A traditional caste council deals with issues like adultery and elopement. Fines and social boycott are usual punishments.
83.	Jalari/Pallae	Traditional village councils maintain law and order along with statutory bodies.
84.	Jambuvulu/ Jambavulu/Adi Jambavulu	A traditional caste panchayat exerts full power to decide disputes on widow remarriage, divorce, adultery, and theft. The caste panchayat also looks after welfare and development. Inter-caste unions are punished with excommunication.

85.	Jandra	A strong traditional caste panchayat handles cases of adultery, elopement, and theft. Inter-caste unions are punished with excommunication.
86.	Jangam/Jangama	The traditional panchayat settles issues regarding adultery, divorce, and elopement. They handle welfare and development along with statutory panchayats. Police and courts of law are also approached to settle disputes.
87.	Jatapu/Jatapu Dora	The traditional village council headed by a *havanthy* or *dora* settles all disputes and is empowered to fine an offender.
88.	Jogi/Jugi	A community council maintains social control and oversees social welfare. Defaulters may be punished with fines.
89.	Kachi/Kashi	Community councils exist at village and regional levels. The latter serves as a higher appellate authority. The decisions of the councils are binding. Adultery, elopement, and pre-marital sexual relations are punishable offences.
90.	Kaikalolan	A kula panchayat headed by the kula pedda settles family quarrels and adultery cases, and conducts marriage and death rituals.
91.	Kalinga/Kalinji	Community elders form the traditional council and settle divorce disputes and conduct marriage alliances.
92.	Kamatamollu	A traditional kula panchayat comprising of village elders settles disputes. Cases related to inter-caste marriages, divorce, adultery, family issues, and disrespect to traditional norms are settled by this council. Offenders are fined or excommunicated based on the severity of the offence. The formal legal system is approached for cases of theft, rape, and murder. Statutory panchayats handle welfare and development.
93.	Kammara/Ozulu	A traditional tribal council assists in the settlement of disputes such as adultery,

(Cont'd)

Table AII.1   (Cont'd)

		elopement, and violation of tribal norms. With the advent of the statutory panchayats, council members are often elected as gram panchayat members as well.
94.	Kampo	A village caste panchayat with a hereditary head, who comes under a regional head settle social disputes. The headmen have the authority to fine offenders and excommunicate them should their crimes warrant such punitive measures.
95.	Kanchari	A traditional kula panchayat comprising of village elders settles conflicts, quarrels, and various disputes. Divorce and inter-caste marriages are prohibited.
96.	Kandara/ Kandra/Kondara	A traditional kula panchayat settles disputes and protects traditional customs and norms.
97.	Kapu/Munnuru Kapu	Munnuru Kapus do not have a traditional council of their own. However, they approach the traditional heterogeneous village councils to settle their disputes. Courts of law are approached as well. And the statutory gram panchayat handles welfare and development.
98.	Karnibhakthulu	Community councils manage social control. They mainly look after community welfare, and settle inter- and intra-community disputes and divorce cases.
99.	Katikapala/ Katipapala	Community elders—kulam peddulu— maintain social order in the community. They settle cases of adultery, remarriage, divorce, and petty quarrels.
100.	Khatika	Village elders resolve intra-community disputes. Statutory panchayats implement development programmes.
101.	Khatik/Khatik Muslim/Kasab	Community elders convene to solve intra-community disputes. District and regional associations exist to promote the general

		welfare of the community and statutory panchayats take care of planning and implementing development activities.
102.	Kolam	Kolams live in exclusive settlements, each of which is controlled by the village headman. Disputes such as marital maladjustments, adultery, theft, and quarrels are settled by the headman in consultation with the village priest. Cases of murder are reported to the police.
103.	Kommu Dasari	Traditional caste councils maintain social order and handle cases of adultery, theft, and insult to the traditional panchayat.
104.	Kommula	A caste panchayat decides offences such as adultery, rape, elopement, and disputes over land and water. Punishments include fines and social boycott. Statutory panchayats handle welfare and development.
105.	Konda Dora	A hereditary head of the entire society—the *koya konda*—wields both secular and religious power. At the village level, a kula panchayat headed by a naidu settles disputes such as divorce, adultery, theft, and so on. Regional heads—*muttadaris*—collect land revenue for prescribed areas called *muttas*. After the advent of statutory bodies, the traditional functionaries are often re-elected into the state bodies.
106.	Konda Kammara	Each village has its traditional council to maintain social order where punishments are decided for various offences and disputes are settled. Punitive measures include social boycott and excommunication.
107.	Konda Kapu/ Kondakapu	Both kula panchayats and statutory panchayats exist—while the former maintains social control and settles disputes, the latter handles welfare and development.
108.	Konda Reddi/ Hill Reddi	Every Konda Reddi village has a headman (*pedda kapu*) who consults with heads of families to settle disputes. Majority opinion is held as binding. Cases of incest, adultery,

(Cont'd)

Table AII.1 (Cont'd)

		elopement, divorce, land disputes, and theft are dealt with the village council. The kula pedda, the community leader, is the highest level of social control. Inter-village disputes are referred to the kula pedda whose decision is final.
109.	Kondh/Kond/ Kandha	Every Kondh settlement has its own traditional council which exercises complete social control. Cases of adultery, incest, violation of traditional norms, murder, elopement, quarrels, and property disputes are all decided by the council.
110.	Koracha	A kula panchayat of community elders, along with heads of families, settles disputes after taking oaths in the name of caste deities. Adultery, disrespect to traditional norms, and inter-caste marriages with lower castes are punishable offences.
111.	Koshtha/Koshta/ Koshti	A traditional jati panchayat settles family disputes and divorce cases. Matters that are unresolved by the jati panchayat are referred to the traditional heterogeneous village panchayat. Statutory panchayats handle welfare and development.
112.	Kotia/Kotiya	Kotias have tribal councils for social control. The councils handle cases of adultery, theft, elopement, and land and water disputes. The guilty can be made to pay cash fines and are socially boycotted and excommunicated for severe offences.
113.	Koya/ Koya Dora	A traditional village council maintains social order and handles cases of adultery, rape, theft, elopement, and violation of traditional norms. Punishments include cash fines, social boycott, and excommunication.
114.	Koya/Konda Rajulu	A traditional tribal panchayat deals with offences such as adultery, rape, and elopement. Cash fines are imposed and excommunication is also reported to take place. Statutory bodies handle welfare and development.

115.	Koya/Racha Koya	Traditional kula panchayats exist at the village level and settle issues such as divorce and inter-tribal marriages. A regional traditional council called a *samuthu* handles inter-village disputes. Cash fines and social boycott are among the forms of punishment.
116.	Kulia	The Kulia have their own kula panchayat to regulate social, religious, and occupational activities and settle disputes. The decision of the kula panchayat is binding.
117.	Kummara/ Kumbara/ Kummari	A traditional kula panchayat settles various inter- and intra-family disputes pertaining to property, personal behaviour, and so on. A statutory village panchayat handles welfare and development.
118.	Kurahina Setty/ Kurni	The traditional kula panchayat resolves disputes such as divorce, property issues, and inter-caste marriages.
119.	Kurakula	A kula panchayat settles disputes within the community as well as negotiates among communities. Cash fines or excommunication are usual punishments, depending on the severity of the offence.
120.	Kuruma/Kuruba	A traditional caste panchayat settles inter- and intra-community disputes. Statutory panchayats implement welfare and development activities.
121.	Labbai/Labbi	A traditional jamath handles social issues and religious affairs. Property affairs, however, are left to the state legal system.
122.	Madiga/ Baineedu	A traditional caste council manages cases related to adultery, theft, divorce, quarrels, and division of property. Statutory panchayats implement welfare and development activities.
123.	Madiga Christian	Madiga Christians have a traditional panchayat to settle disputes. Statutory panchayats implement welfare and development activities.
124.	Madiga Mashten/	A traditional caste panchayat, headed by a guru, maintains social order. Social boycott,

(Cont'd)

Table AII.1 *(Cont'd)*

	Madiga Mashteen	excommunication, and cash fines are some of the punishments, and the guru's decision is final.
125.	Mahar	A traditional caste panchayat comprising of community elders settles cases of adultery, rape, elopement, and other disputes. Community elders are also represented in the statutory village bodies, which largely look after welfare and development.
126.	Majjula	A traditional kula panchayat deals with cases of adultery, disputes over land and water, and divorce. Punishments include fines and excommunication. Kula panchayat members are often re-elected into statutory bodies.
127.	Mala/Asadhi Mala	A traditional caste panchayat comprising of community elders maintains social control. Statutory panchayats implement welfare and development activities.
128.	Mala Christian	A traditional caste panchayat settles cases of adultery, rape, elopement, disputes over land and water, theft, disrespect to traditional norms, and other disputes. Statutory panchayats implement welfare and development activities.
129.	Mala Dasari	A traditional caste council headed by an elderly and experienced member called the *pina pedda* controls social behaviour in a village.
130.	Mala Jangam	A kula panchayat along with the statutory village panchayat maintains social order. Common cases include rape, adultery, elopement, disputes over land and water, and so on. The guilty are fined.
131.	Mala Masti	A traditional caste panchayat comprising elders of the community settles disputes. The panchayat, however, does not take punitive measures. Statutory panchayats implement welfare and development activities.

132.	Mala Sale/ Netkani/ Nethakani	A traditional caste panchayat settles interpersonal and inter-family disputes, and decides divorce proceedings. Statutory panchayats implement welfare and development activities.
133.	Mali	A traditional kula panchayat arranges marriage alliances and solves petty problems such as theft, misbehaviour, and so on. Inter-community marriages are a serious offence. Malis are represented in statutory bodies as well.
134.	Malis	A traditional kula panchayat comprising of village elders decides cases relating to divorce, adultery, elopement, disputes over land and water, theft, and so on. Inter-community marriages are punished with excommunication and cash fines are imposed for other offences.
135.	Mang	Rigid social control is exercised by the hereditary caste head—the *pedda mathar*. Those who fail to abide by the pedda mathar's decision are excommunicated.
136.	Manne	Kula panchayats exist in every village, dealing with cases of adultery, violation of caste norms, divorce, and elopement. Property disputes are often settled help of rich, upper-caste agriculturists. Statutory panchayats implement welfare and development activities.
137.	Manne Dora/ Manna Dora/ Manna Dhora	A traditional tribal panchayat exercises social control over community members, and handles cases related to divorce, elopement, adultery, theft, disrespect to traditional norms, and so on. Inter-community marriages are punished with excommunication.
138.	Matangi	A traditional kula panchayat maintains social order and settles disputes in the community. Individual villages have village councils represented in the community by one elderly member. Statutory panchayats implement welfare and development activities.

(Contd)

Table AII.1 *(Cont'd)*

139.	Medari/ Mahendar/ Meda/Madari	A post-Independence association of bamboo planters and basket makers exists to regulate economic affairs of the community and sustain their traditional occupation.
140.	Mehadi/Mehdi	A traditional jamath headed by a *peshimam* maintains social order. Defaulters are punished with cash fines. Statutory panchayats implement welfare and development activities.
141.	Matha Ayyalvar/ Mithula Ayyavarlu	Kula panchayats exist at the regional level. Individual villages are headed by the kula peddalu, who decide cases concerning marriage, adultery, divorce, breach of caste norms, and so on. Statutory panchayats implement welfare and development activities.
142.	Muchi	The traditional panchayat settles disputes such as divorce, widow remarriage, adultery, theft, and other family issues. All members of the community are called on to solve disputes. Guilty are punished with fines.
143.	Mudiraj	Kula panchayats maintain social order by solving inter-community, intra- and inter-family disputes and settling divorce cases. Statutory panchayats implement welfare and development activities.
144.	Mulia	Kula panchayats exist for every two to three villages and settle cases of adultery, elopement, and disrespect to traditional norms. Guilty are punished with fines. Inter-caste marriages are punished with excommunication.
145.	Musti Chenchu	A community council headed by the kula pedda settles offences such as elopement, divorce, theft, and so on.
146.	Nagavamsam/ Nagavasam	The traditional kula panchayat is the chief agency of social control. Courts of law are largely avoided
147.	Nakkala/ Narikorava	A traditional caste panchayat maintains social order and deals with issues such as adultery,

rape, elopement, disrespect to traditional norms, insults to the council, and so on. Statutory panchayats implement welfare and development activities.

148.	Neo-Buddhist/ Nav Buddhist	A regional council called a *sanghamulu* provides moral guidance and settles disputes.
149.	Nethagiri	Village-level kula panchayats maintain social control. There are detailed procedures to verify guilt or innocence in criminal cases. In case the dispute is unresolved at the level of the community council, the heterogeneous panchayat (composed predominantly of upper caste members) of the village is approached. While statutory panchayats exist, they are largely secondary, and the traditional councils' decisions are binding.
150.	Neyyala	Traditional kula panchayats assist in regulating marriage alliances, performance of rituals, solving family and property disputes, divorce, and inter-community quarrels.
151.	Nhavi	A traditional council settles disputes among members of the community. One of its functions is to regulate marriage and enforce endogamy to ensure ethnic identity.
152.	Oddar/Odde	The Oddar community panchayat maintains law and order and settles disputes. Punishments include cash fines.
153.	Ontari	A traditional caste panchayat settles communal disputes and issues relating to land and water. Punishments include cash fines and physical punishment.
154.	Padigarajulu/ Padigi Rajulu	A traditional community panchayat deals with offences such as rape, adultery, elopement, and disrespect to traditional norms. Statutory panchayats implement welfare and development activities.
155.	Pagativeshagallu	A kula panchayat oversees marriage, remarriage, and divorce proceedings.

(Cont'd)

Table AII.1   (*Cont'd*)

156.	Paky	The kula panchayat, an informal body for social control, deals with adultery, elopement, and divorce. Punishments include cash fines.
157.	Paky/Thoti	The Thotis have a traditional kula panchayat for social control, which oversees issues such as divorce and remarriage. Statutory panchayats implement welfare and development activities.
158.	Pambala	Traditional kula panchayats resolve issues including conflicts, quarrels, adultery, divorce, theft, and elopement. Punishments include fines and social boycott.
159.	Pamidi/Paidi	A traditional caste panchayat enforces social order and manages inter-community problems, divorce cases, marital alliances, and cases of adultery and theft. Punishments include cash fines.
160.	Pardhan	A traditional formal social council maintains social control at the village level. A religious head acts as the community leader. Adultery and commensal relations with lower castes are punished with excommunication, and re-admittance takes place only after elaborate purification rituals.
161.	Pardhi	Traditional councils, headed by a sardar, exist at the village level and manage issues such as family disputes, property cases, divorce, and adultery.
162.	Pariki Muggula	A traditional kula panchayat handles cases of adultery, elopement, theft, remarriage, bride price, and inter-caste marriage. Punishments include cash fines and physical punishments.
163.	Paroja/Parja/ Porja	All tribe subgroups have headmen who solve minor disputes and levy punitive fines.
164.	Pathan	A traditional jamath looks after community welfare, and settles cases of divorce, property division, and familial problems. Statutory panchayats implement welfare and development activities.

165.	Patra/Patra Thanti	A traditional kula panchayat governs some aspects of social control, such as extra-marital relations. Offenders are made to pay cash fines.
166.	Pitchiguntla/ Pichchiguntala	A traditional community council maintains social control. Statutory panchayats implement welfare and development activities.
167.	Pondara	A kula panchayat comprising three village elders settles divorce cases, property disputes, and helps in fixing marriage alliances.
168.	Qureshi/ Kureshi/ Khureshi	The community council called the jamath deals with cases of divorce, adultery, theft, disrespect to traditional norms, and insults to community elders. Defaulters are punished with fines. In cases of disobedience of the jamath's ruling, the offenders face complete social and religious boycott, including inability to avail of mosques and burial places.
169.	Rajannalu	Traditional village councils, headed by the kula pedda, resolve community disputes and fine offenders. Disregard of council judgement leads to social and community boycott and excommunication.
170.	Rajput/Rajput Bondili	Community elders help maintain social and economic order.
171.	Rama Jogula/ Rama Jogulu	Traditional kula panchayats resolve issues related to divorce, elopement, adultery, theft, and property. The offices of the community heads are hereditary, and disputes are fined differentially according to the degree of offence.
172.	Ravulo/Ravulu	The Ravulus have traditional kula panchayats at the village level. Punitive measures are rare, with offenders usually getting away with warnings, and a stress on amicably resolving disputes.
173.	Reddi Dora/ Reddy Dora	The Reddy Dora kula panchayat, headed by the kula pedda, deals with cases such as theft, incest, property and family disputes. The council represents the tribe in inter-tribal disputes as well. Offenders are fined and, in rare cases, socially boycotted.

(Cont'd)

Table AII.1   *(Cont'd)*

174.	Reddika	Reddika kula panchayats exist at the village level. Villages are subdivided into thirty-house clusters, called *doddi*s, and a representative from each doddi is selected for membership in the kula panchayat. The council mediates in issues of rape, adultery, religious conversions, divorce, theft, and other cases. Women marrying into lower castes are excommunicated. Men marrying into lower castes are readmitted after expiatory feasts. Offenders are usually fined.
175.	Reddy/Desai Reddy	The Reddy community head is the *pattapu desai reddy*, who also heads other communities such as the Moras Kapu, Musugu Kapu, Kotha Devara Kapu, and Palakapu. The community council comprises the community head, the village headman (*gowda*), the family head (*yajman*), and the community elders (*devara peddalu*). All crimes and offences such as adultery, rape, elopement, disputes over land and water, disrespect to traditional norms, insult and theft are brought to the pattapu desai reddy, who, with the assistance of the other members, pronounces judgement, and offenders are fined or excommunicated. Formal statutory panchayats implement welfare and development activities.
176.	Reddy/Ganjam Reddy	Traditional community councils, called *chavidi*s, settle matters such as rape, elopement, adultery, land disputes, and so on. The head of the council is called the kula pedda and is assisted in all matters by the *chinna pedda*.
177.	Reddy/Gone Reddy	The village council comprising of community elders assist in resolving disputes.
178.	Reddy/Illela Reddy	Community elders assist in resolving disputes. Statutory panchayats take care of welfare and development.

179.	Reddy/ Nanikonda Reddy	Community elders are the first level of dispute resolution. Failing acceptable judgement, disputes are referred to the police and courts of law.
180.	Reddy/Paala Kapu	Land and water disputes are resolved by traditional councils. Criminal offences are referred to the state legal system, and statutory panchayats plan and implement welfare and development activities.
181.	Reddy/Panta Kapu/Panta Reddy	Traditional panchayats exist in some villages to settle disputes regarding loss of property or damage to crops. Statutory panchayats plan and implement welfare and development activities.
182.	Reddy/Pedakanti Kapu/Pedakanti Reddy	Traditional panchayats, oriented towards amicable settlement of disputes, exist to maintain social order. Statutory panchayats plan and implement welfare and development activities.
183.	Reddy/Rayalama Kapu	Traditional community councils are headed by the *peddamunshulu*, and while they exercise no punitive power, the councils' verdicts are respected. Statutory panchayats plan and implement welfare and development activities.
184.	Reddy/ Sugamanchi Reddy	The kula panchayat, assisted by the community elders, settles disputes over land and water and disrespect to traditional norms. Statutory panchayats plan and implement welfare and development activities.
185.	Relli	The caste panchayat, headed by the kula pedda, regulates social behaviour. Disputes such as elopement and divorce are handled by the panchayat, and offenders are usually fined.
186.	Rona	Traditional tribal panchayats settle disputes on matters of adultery, elopement, disrespect to traditional norms, insult to the traditional panchayat, theft, and so on. Statutory panchayats plan and implement welfare and development activities.

(Cont'd)

Table AII.1 *(Cont'd)*

187.	Sakala Budbudike	Kula panchayats impose fines and physical punishment in cases of adultery, rape, and theft. The guilty must prove their innocence by the means of *deva sakshyam* (where the accused must dip their fingers in hot oil). Liquor is provided as compensation for breaking community norms and rules.
188.	Sakunapakshollu	Kula panchayats enforce social norms and handle issues such as divorce, adultery, rape, theft, and so on. Cash fines are issued to the guilty, and in severe cases, excommunication and social boycott is practiced as well. Statutory panchayats plan and implement welfare and development activities.
189.	Salapu	Kula panchayats headed by a *senapathi* exist to maintain social order and handle offences such as adultery, rape, and elopement. The hereditary senapathi fixes the amount of fines offenders have to pay, and in extreme cases, offenders and often their families are boycotted. Expiatory feasts are also a way of compensating for breaking social rules. Statutory panchayats plan and implement welfare and development activities.
190.	Samayavallu	Traditional kula panchayats adjudicate disputes between families, and settle cases of adultery, rape, molestation, cruelty, divorce, and so on.
191.	Saora	The village headman, *gamong*, is in charge of social order. The gamong, along with the religious head, *bhuyya*, and the heads of the families, settles disputes that may arise. Statutory panchayats plan and implement welfare and development activities.
192.	Saradagallu	Cases of divorce and maladjustment are settled by the traditional kula panchayat. In cases of adultery or premarital sexual relations, the offender is often encouraged to either wed

or maintain the woman concerned, in case he is already married. Violating the rule of endogamy leads to excommunication. Punitive feasts are also practised as means of retribution for wrongdoing.

193.	Sarangulu	A kula sangham deals with cases of adultery, theft, divorce, and disputes over land and property, and has powers to excommunicate offenders.
194.	Satpurohitulu/ Kamma Brahmans	A traditional community council settles disputes such as divorce, widow remarriage, adultery, theft, and other such problems.
195.	Segedi/Srisayana	Traditional kula panchayats consisting of village elders exercise social control and settle cases of adultery, elopement, land and water disputes, and theft. Fines are levied on the guilty.
196.	Senapathi	Groups of families, or *undi*, are headed by one headman, *pedda*, and it is these kin groups which exercise social control.
197.	Shaik/Sheikh	Traditional jamaths maintain social and religious order, and have the power to impose cash fines on offenders.
198.	Siddi	The community head, the *ameer*, meets with members of the council, or the *risala*, to settle issues of rape, adultery, divorce, theft, and petty quarrels. Only the ameer has the right to speak on social norms, rules, and values.
199.	Sikligar/ Saiqulgar/ Shikalgar/ Sigligar Sikh	An informal sabha settles matters such as quarrels and divorce. Matters are settled before five witnesses, or *panchpyare*. The punishment of offences such as murder is excommunication, or *tuntagerna*, and fines are imposed for lesser crimes. Statutory panchayats plan and implement welfare and development activities.
200.	Sudugadu Siddha	All disputes are brought to the head of the community council. Adultery, divorce, theft, beating—these are some of the common offences which the council settles.

(Cont'd)

Table AII.1 *(Cont'd)*

201.	Sugali	The Sugali tribal council, headed by elders (naiks), has the final say in offences such as adultery, rape, elopement, theft, breach of traditional norms, and so on. Offenders are usually punished with cash fines or, in extreme cases, social boycott.
202.	Sunar	The Sunar traditional council, called the *malav*, enforces social norms for the community. Offences relating to family and kin relations, as well as those of sexual nature, are settled by the council. The guilty are punished with fines.
203.	Sundi/Sondi	The kula panchayat intervenes in offences such as rape, theft, and divorce.
204.	Syed/Saiyed/ Sayyad/Mushaik	The community council, called the *jamabandi*, settles cases of divorce and adultery. Offenders are fined, and the amount collected is redirected into social welfare activities.
205.	Telukula	Telukula kula panchayats are hereditary, and play a role in maintaining social order.
206.	Thirugatigantla	Traditional community councils intervene in matters of divorce and adultery.
207.	Thogataveera Kshatriya	All community disputes are brought before the traditional panchayat. Statutory panchayats plan and implement welfare and development activities.
208.	Tolakari	Kula panchayats headed by the kula pedda and assisted by community elders maintain social order. Issues such as theft, elopement, insults, and adultery, are settled by the *kula panchayat*.
209.	Uppara	Uppara members take their disputes to traditional heterogeneous village panchayats for settlement. Cases such as adultery and land and water disputes are settled by the panchayat.
210.	Valmiki	The head of the tribe, assisted by the panchayat, handles matters relating to divorce, adultery, and theft. Cash fines are imposed on

the guilty. Tribal heads often hold positions in the statutory village panchayats as well. The state legal system is referred to when the judgement of the headman and the panchayat are seen to be unsatisfactory.

211.	Valmiki Christians	The kula panchayat composed of three to four members, or kula peddalu, settles matters of divorce, adultery, and theft. Cash fines are imposed in cases of theft. In cases of adultery, if a married woman wishes to divorce her husband, the new husband must pay compensation. Compensation and expiatory feasts with liquor are also some of the punitive measures.
212.	Vanjari	A hereditary kula panchayat maintains social order and settles inter- and intra-family disputes, cases of theft, divorce, and elopement.
213.	Veera Musti/ Veera Mushti	Kula panchayats at the regional level settle cases of adultery, theft, rape, and so on. Offenders are fined.
214.	Vipravinodulu	Traditional caste councils intervene in matters of adultery and theft, to name a few. Inter-caste marriages are punished with excommunication. Statutory panchayats plan and implement welfare and development activities.
215.	Viswabrahman	Traditional councils regulate religious and social order, fix marriage alliances, and settle divorce and separation cases. Offenders are excommunicated.
216.	Vokkaliga/ Morasu/Moras Kapu	(Ref. #176 in this table: Desai Reddy) The Desai Reddy, arbitrates matters in the Moras Kapu community, assisted by the village headman, or *yejaman*. Offences such as adultery, elopement, land disputes, property divisions, and water disputes are referred to the council. Cash punishments are imposed. Statutory panchayats plan and implement welfare and development activities.

(Cont'd)

Table AII.1 (Cont'd)

217.	Vysya/Vaishya/ Kalinga Komati	A traditional kula panchayat settles disputes, and fines are imposed on the guilty. Excommunication, too, is practised.
218.	Vysya/Vaishya/ Trivarnika	The Sri Trivarnika Vaishnava Yethi Raja Seva Samithi handles both welfare and social order. Instead of going to courts, the *samithi* handles disputes, quarrels, and family issues. The judgement of the samithi is binding.
219.	Yadava/Golla	Traditional kula panchayats settle disputes related to marriage, property, and divorce, among others.
220.	Yanadi/Challa Yanadi	Challa Yanadis seldom approach courts or other apparatuses of the state legal system, and their disputes are settled by the traditional *kula panchayats* headed by a *maistri* and two community elders. All disputes of the community are settled by the panchayat, and fines imposed according to the nature of the crime.
221.	Yata	The kula panchayat is the chief agency of social control. Cases of divorce and separation are handled by the council, and offences punished with cash fines, the money acquired from which is used for social welfare activities.
222.	Yatagiri	Adultery, thefts, and other disputes are handled by the traditional kula panchayat headed by the *pina pedda*. Offences are punished with cash fines, the money acquired from which is used for social welfare activities.
223.	Yatla	The traditional kula panchayat settles disputes related to adultery, theft, divorce, and so on. Cash fines are imposed on offenders.
224.	Yerukula	A powerful traditional council, the *beromanosom*, exercises control over offences. The council, with assistance from village elders, adjudicates occupational and connubial offences. The maximum penalty levied is

		excommunication, which can be taken care of by giving an expiatory feast after a purification ceremony. Traditional trials such as *agnipariksha* (trial by fire) have been reported. Statutory panchayats are present in some regions, and plan and implement welfare and development activities.
225.	Yite	Yites are itinerant acrobatic performers, moving from village to village. Loss of traditional occupation means that several of their numbers now work as seasonal labour. A community panchayat exists to settle disputes and take care of welfare activities.

Source: Authors (based on *People of India: Andhra Pradesh*, Vol. XIII, Parts I, II, III, general editor, K.S. Singh; editors, D.L. Prasada, N.V.K. Rao, S. Yaseen Saheb. New Delhi: Affiliated East-West Press, 2003).

General Trends

1. Assam has mix of both ethnic (tribal) groups and of 'functional' castes/ communities.
2. Geographically the state's population can be divided into the plains and hill, with a majority residing in the Brahmaputra and the Barak Valleys, with only eighteen reported communities inhabiting the hilly areas.
3. In total, the Project has studied 114 communities of Assam.
4. Assam is linguistically heterogeneous with as many as 45 languages spoken by its communities.
5. Regarding the inheritance of property, male equigeniture is the rule (99.86 per cent). Matriliny (acknowledging descent from the mother's side of the family) is observed only among the Garo and Jaintia. Dimisa Kachari is the unique case of bilateral or double descent system, recognizing both the father's and the mother's lineages.
6. Most of the communities are monogamous and prefer adult marriage.

Overview of Report

Of the 114 communities in the two volumes analysed, 66 communities (57.88 per cent, approximately) rely significantly on traditional councils. Traditional village administration is generally conducted by elder members of the community known as *goanbura*. The traditional council primarily deals with petty offences, in most cases described as matrimonial issues, rape, and theft. Councils also monitor day-to-day village welfare. It is also observed that the traditional councils of few communities also take charge of serious offences such as murder. The community, in a sitting, considers the aspects of the crime and decides whether or not the matter should be referred to the state legal system. Forms of punishment generally include fines and excommunication in the severest of cases. The traditional councils in Assam, for the most part, act as first level arbitrators, deciding whether the offence should enter the register of the state legal system at all.

All 66 communities reported here predominantly rely on their customary councils for social control. However, the report also observes that there is general decline in the importance of traditional council in Assam. Of the communities not included in this count, there are few who have a defunct traditional council. For instance, the survey reports that after Independence, the Kachari Dimisa community became politically active, and with introduction of the District Council, the traditional council slowly lost importance. At present, their legal and administrative issues are looked after by the official district council. Table AII.2 gives more details about communities relying on non-state legal practices in Assam.

Table AII.2 Communities in Assam with Reported Reliance on Non-state Legal Systems

S. No.	Community	Comments
1.	Kharia	There is no traditional council. But in tea industry, elderly influential people act as *chowkidar* and exercise social control. They also look over minor disputes and crimes.
2.	Khasi Bhoi	Previously social control was maintained by the *gaonbura*. Post-Independence the *gaon panchayat* looks after the village administration and crimes.

S. No.	Community	Comments
		The *raja* (chief) is the head of the panchayat. Punishment is imposed in cash or kind or through excommunication.
3.	Khasi Lyngum	Social control is exercised by the village council, comprising of president and secretary appointed by the community. The government also appoints an elderly person from the community as gaonbura (headman). Prior to Independence they had a separate traditional council called *nava*.
4.	Kshatriya	A traditional council with a headman known as *metabor* maintains social order. The council looks into all development related aspects of the community as well as crimes. Local disputes are solved under the leadership of metabor. Punishments include cash fines and beating up the culprit, tonsuring of head, and excommunication. From time to time, the traditional council also submits a memorandum to the central government and the state governments.
5.	Kuki	The traditional council is known as *hausa semang pachong*. All posts in the council are ascribed and follow male primogeniture. The council punishes a person for committing offences such as adultery, rape, elopement, theft, and murder.
6.	Kurmi	There is a traditional panchayat for every Kurmi village. The panchayat comprises eleven members. The traditional panchayat decides major social offences. Punishments are imposed in the form of fines, followed by excommunication in event of failure to comply.
7.	Lalung/Tiwa	The group of elders is the highest authority of the village. Once they become a member of the traditional council, they remain a member till they are able to work. Primary functions are the settlement of disputes, to look after the general welfare, to inflict punishment upon the offenders and maintaining law and order in the village

(Cont'd)

Table AII.2   *(Cont'd)*

S. No.	Community	Comments
8.	Mali/ Phul Mali/ Malakar	The traditional council is not homogenous—it comprises the members of Mali community as well as elder members of other communities of the village. Besides other developmental activities, the council has other functions such as disposal of petty cases and enforcement of codes of social and religious conduct.
9.	Manipuri (subdivided as (*i*) Meitei, and (*ii*) Bishnupriya)	Bishnupriyas do not have a traditional council. Meiteis have a separate traditional council called the *khuntinba*. The khuntinba looks into criminal matters such as encroachment of land, water, violation of traditional norms, adultery, rape, and theft.
10.	Mann	The Mann does not have a separate traditional council. However, matters are referred to the traditional, heterogeneous village panchayat.
11.	Mishing	A traditional council headed by a gaonbura (elderly village head) exists to maintain social order. The traditional council looks into petty offences. At present, the importance of traditional council has diminished, community members prefer to take their disputes to higher government authorities.
12.	Moran	There is a traditional council to decide trivial issues. Criminal cases of serious nature are reported to the courts of law.
13.	Mukhi	The Mukhi community has a traditional caste panchayat as well as statutory gram panchayat. The statutory panchayat looks into administrative matters. Offences are dealt by caste panchayat of the concerned village
14.	Munda	The traditional political and administrative unit is known as *parha*—it comprises ten or more villages. The head of the parha is known as raja. The parha is also the unit of social order. At present, relevance of the traditional council has gone down.

S. No.	Community	Comments
15.	Mushahar	A traditional council exists for disposing both civil and criminal cases. The elder member is known as *foudari*. Each member of the community has to report matters of death, birth, marriage, and criminal matters to foudari.
16.	Kabui/ Rongmei	They have traditional council known as *paikai*. All disputes of a Rongmei village are settled by this traditional council. Punishments are mostly inflicted for breach of social customs.
17.	Konyak	The traditional council consist of headman and his assistant. The post of the headman is hereditary. All community disputes are referred to the headman. Punishment is imposed only in form of fines.
18.	Rengama	The traditional council has two heads—one selected by the villagers, and another selected by the district council known as *sarkari gaonbura*. The sarkari gaonbura acts as a liaison agent between the government and villagers.
19.	Naga/Sema	The traditional council looks into only minor disputes. Major criminal cases are reported to higher legal authorities. The traditional council is slowly being replaced with statutory village panchayat; nevertheless, their authority is still recognized.
20.	Naga/Zemi	A distinct village council named *nieu-ndui* adjudicates on matters of social order. The body is represented by village headman, village priest, and two representatives from the youth dormitory. Functions include dealing with disputes and divorce cases, punishing the offenders, and allotment of lands.
21.	Namosudra	They refer the matters to the village council with an attempt to resolve all their disputes within the village.

(Cont'd)

Table AII.2   *(Cont'd)*

S. No.	Community	Comments
22.	Nocte	No separate traditional council exists for the community. All disputes are referred to the village heterogeneous traditional council. Matters are referred to civil courts only when the village council is not able to resolve them.
23.	Rabha	They have a separate traditional council. A person well conversant in the social norms is nominated as the head of the council. The council decides all matters of common concerns. Even after the introduction of Panchayati Raj bodies, the traditional council has not lost its functions. The statutory panchayat hardly has any impact on the organization or social life of Rabha villages.
24.	Rajbanshi	The traditional caste council is known as *gaonlia mel*. It consists of elderly members from all communities inhabiting the locality. The community council has limited functions, such as the settlement of petty disputes, and can make decisions on the code of social conduct, adultery and divorce, and similar matters.
25.	Rangidhoba	In keeping with the tradition there is a distinct community council. The community council looks after all internal disputes. Nowadays, people do not attach much importance to the traditional council and prefer to go to the court for settlement of any kind of dispute.
26.	Ravidas	The village-level council is known as the *samaj*. The samaj decides intra-community disputes and criminal offences such as exogamy and rape. The guilty are punished through excommunication.
27.	Riang	The traditional village administration is conducted by the *chaudhury* (headman). The headman decides civil and criminal cases at the village level. The decision of the village council is binding. They discourage the parties from taking the cases to higher authorities.

S. No.	Community	Comments
28.	Santal	They have a homogenous association known as the *santal panchayat*, which administers the rites and rituals of the community. The position of the headman is hereditary. The Santal communities living in the tea gardens do not have a separate traditional council, they refer their matters to the tea garden labour union.
29.	Sutradhar	The traditional council decides all disputes relating to the social and religious matters. All other disputes are referred to the statutory gram panchayat.
30.	Singhpo	They have a village council known as *shalang*, whose main functions are to settle disputes between members of the community, to look after village development, to inflict punishment upon the offenders, and to maintain law and order. Criminal cases are, however, reported to the court for adjudication.
31.	Tai Pake	The community possesses an elaborate code of traditional law and justice called the *tamachat*. While deciding cases, the congregation of village elders refer to this code. All matters are decided by the community council. The statutory village panchayat looks after the village welfare.
32.	Tantubay	In cases of intra-community disputes where a person is found to commit offence such as rape, adultery, elopement, theft or defying any traditional norms, the community council looks into the matter. In such cases, community worship of Satyanarayan is organized, and the convicted person has to bear the expenses of the rituals. Inter-community disputes are referred to the village council of the other party.
33.	Teli	The caste council is known as *teli samaj*. They look into the law-and-order issues. Encroachment upon property, theft, and sexual offences are punished by the council.

(Cont'd)

Table AII.2   (Cont'd)

S. No.	Community	Comments
34.	Thengal	The traditional village council is headed by gaonbura (headman) appointed by the villagers. Village councils settle cases such as theft, rape, encroachment, and so on. More serious offences are referred to the block development officer and courts.
35.	Tripuria	The traditional council is two tiered. The upper tier is a regional council consisting of several villages. The lower tier belongs to individual villages. The officials are selected by a voice vote. The village council decides all criminal cases, except murder. Murder is reported to police authorities.
36.	Turung	Social control is exercised by the *meregdingla* (the village headman). He is assisted by the council of village elders. The headman performs socio-religious functions, and also inflicts punishment upon the offenders where found guilty.
37.	Ahom	They have a traditional administrative system, looked after by noble clansmen known as *borghain*. At present, panchayat systems have been introduced to these communities, yet in matters of dispute at the village level, settlements are carried out according to the traditional justice system.
38.	Aiton	There is a traditional council in each of the Aiton village. The office of the headman is a hereditary position. The headman performs religious activities, and also takes account of land disputes, family disputes, and quarrelling. Statutory panchayats do not exist. Changes in mechanisms of social control brought about by the post-Independence regime are not significant in this community.
39.	Assamese Brahman	A traditional caste council known as *gaonalia* is found among the community. However, their role is limited to the matters of petty disputes only. Major disputes are settled in district courts.

S. No.	Community	Comments
40.	Assamese Muslim	Gaon managing committees exist, which deal exclusively with the issues relating to the slums in the village. The committee mostly settles interpersonal and household disputes.
41.	Assamese Sikh	They have their own *aanchalik* committee whose main function is to settle land disputes, theft cases in agricultural matters, family disputes, and any disputes regarding customary laws.
42.	Bania	They have a traditional caste council consisting of members of Bania community and elders of other communities of the village. The council settles disputes relating to socio-religious matters. In case of criminal allegations, formal proceedings take place. Guilty parties are punished in cash or kind, after due consideration of evidence. Cases of very serious nature, such as murder, are referred to appropriate court.
43.	Baroi	They have traditional councils to look into socio-economic disputes. At present, most of the other matters are referred to the statutory village panchayat or civil courts.
44.	Basphor	Only civil disputes are submitted to the caste panchayat. Divorce is allowed only with the sanction of caste panchayat.
45.	Bhangi	They have their own caste council but the effectiveness of the council has deteriorated to a considerable extent. Minor cases such as theft, divorce, and so on are settled by them while major cases are referred to the court.
46.	Bhuyan	They generally decide all internal disputes within the village, led by their village council. They prefer amicable settlement of disputes. If they fail, cases are referred to the district court.
47.	Bilaspuri	They resolve their internal disputes by referring them to the village council. When there is a dispute between two or more villages, then matter

(Cont'd)

Table AII.2 (*Cont'd*)

S. No.	Community	Comments
		is referred to the *aanchalikpanchayat* (statutory body).
48.	Chakma	There is a traditional council in each Chakma village. The office of the head of the council is hereditary. Cases of theft, adultery, elopement, and rape are reported to the traditional council. Forms of punishment include both cash and kind.
49.	Chutiya	They have a traditional council but the headman of the council is also a representative of the state government. He is appointed by the deputy commissioner of the district. Family disputes are brought to the traditional council for amicable settlement.
50.	Deori	The traditional council, *mel*, plays an important role in the smooth functioning of welfare works and during their socio-religious festivals. They deliver judgments in case of any disputes and punish the offenders.
51.	Dowaniya	The community has its own traditional council, the members of which sit together to solve an issue along with the village headman. Village statutory panchayats are gradually replacing the traditional council, but the headman still controls socio-economic activities. The power to decide criminal cases has been taken away by the statutory panchayat.
52.	Ganak	Traditional panchayats known as mels decide all offences and crimes of the villagers. The offender is penalized in cash or kind, depending upon the nature of offence. In case the mel is unable to deicide a case, the matter is referred to court for adjudication.
53.	Halam	The community has its traditional council and this council is a two-tier one. The village level council functions as a coordinating and judicial body to regulate the socio-economic life of the

S. No.	Community	Comments
		villagers. Such a body may punish a person for committing crimes such as theft, fighting, and inflicting injuries on others, adultery, rape, bigamy, elopement, and disrespecting the council.
54.	Hajong	There is a state-level association of the community known as Assam Sate Hajong Welfare Association, which is responsible for the community development activities. Although they try to decide all their internal disputes through their traditional village council, in some cases people go to court for settlement of disputes.
55.	Jal Keot	Village councils locally known as *gaonliamels* exist among them, which consist of a presiding officer, a secretary, and a treasurer. The council decides petty disputes, and the members of the community accept and comply with its decision. The secretary maintains records of the cases tried in the gaonliamel, and the treasurer maintains the accounts of the funds.
56.	Jhalo-Malo	The community council is known as *hajar samiti*. It is entitled to fine an individual for theft, for drinking liquor, and for marriage with lower-caste groups. All other matters are taken care of by the statutory village panchayat.
57.	Jolha	In 1984, a regional association called the All Assam Muslim Tea and Ex-Tea Garden Mazdur Association was organized. It is a non-statutory organization responsible for the entire development of the community. In case of serious offences, the guilty person is fined and sometimes excommunicated, according to the nature of offence. The punishment is imposed either by the traditional council or by the mosque committee.
58.	Kachari/ Barman	The traditional village council is known as *khunang* and has both administrative and judicial powers. It has general responsibilities for maintaining law and order. They do not prefer to refer their disputes to the court.

(Cont'd)

Table AII.2   (Cont'd)

S. No.	Community	Comments
59.	Kachari/ Boro	The members of the traditional council are elected by voice votes. Both men and women appear before the council to state their case. Forms of punishment are social boycotts, cash, and kind. The council is also responsible for development activities.
60.	Kaibarta	Generally, they refer all their disputes to the traditional village council. If they fail, the case is referred to the civil court. If any dispute arises between two villages, the matter is settled peacefully by referring it to the elders of both villages. The guilty member is fined. The money collected is utilized for the maintenance of the prayer hall. Non-compliance leads to excommunication of the offender and their family.
61.	Kalita	The members of this community gather in a public place to discuss all matters of the village, including crimes. Guilty persons are generally punished by imposing fines. If a guilty person does not obey the verdict of the village body, then he or she may be socially boycotted. In cases where the traditional council fails to deliver justice, matters are referred to the judicial authority.
62.	Karbi	They have a three-tier traditional council—a council for the Karbi state, a council for all Karbi villages, and the local council for each village. All disputes are first referred to the local council; when they fail to settle the dispute, the matter is referred to the higher authorities.
63.	Kayastha	Kayastha traditional council comprises of elderly members of other communities of the village too. The body has limited functions—it disposes all disputes relating to socio-political and religious issues. It also decided matrimonial disputes. In serious cases if the village council fails to deliver justice, matters are referred to the judicial authority.

S. No.	Community	Comments
64.	Keot	There is traditional village council; however, the locals often prefer to go to the civil courts directly. According to them, the village mel's verdict always favours rich and literate parties.
65.	Khamati	Traditionally, the Khamati community was controlled by the chief king. Though at present they do not have a king, there is one hereditary village headman whom the community honours the most. Except for murder cases (which are very rare) the headman decides all disputes.
66.	Khamyang	Traditional village councils known as *tra* still control and manage the affairs of the village. The statutory village council introduced by the government of Assam has not affected the traditional method of social control. The headman of the community along with the village council settles all disputes—both civil and criminal. The headman's decision to impose fine or compensation is final and binding. There is no practice of referring a dispute to court.

Source: Authors (based on *People of India: Assam*, Vol. XV, Parts I and II, general editor: K.S. Singh; editors: B.K. Bardoloi and R.K. Athaparia [New Delhi: Cambridge University Press, 2009]).

Delhi

General Trends

1. At the time of documentation, Delhi had a part rural and part urban composition. Planned urban areas existed alongside smaller, territorially bound villages. Delhi still retains much of this character, with erstwhile artisanal and small-economy villages existing within the bounds of the city. In addition, Delhi's urban map consists of unplanned slums, unrecognized settlements, and official resettlement colonies, as well as refugee camps. All contribute to variations of legal systems leveraged to maintain social order.

2. This volume identifies and profiles 150 communities in Delhi. The last such record was the 1912 *Gazetteer of Delhi*, which recorded only 20.
3. Most communities profiled in the volume follow a combination of traditional social control systems and state legal systems to maintain social order.
4. Of the 150 communities profiled, only 47 (less than a third) communities give inheritance rights to women, and a significant number give only partial rights (either less than male offspring, or only in the absence of sons). However, this is a much better representation compared to other states profiled in this book.

Overview of Report

Delhi reports at least 75 communities (50 per cent of the communities covered in the survey) that rely on traditional caste and other informal councils in some measure to maintain social control. Most of these communities are located in Delhi's urban villages. Only thirteen communities rely predominantly on their traditional councils to maintain social control. Among these, the Singhiwala community panchayat, at the time of documentation, claimed to exercise absolute control, with the power to overturn court verdicts.

In cases where the state and non-state legal systems work together, there is a more or less clear division of responsibilities. Traditional councils usually handle disputes that are related to marital relations, adultery, and the upholding of traditional norms. In some cases, the councils also handle disputes related to thefts and rape. In most cases, it is the state administrative and legal systems that handle 'serious' cases of homicide and theft. In several cases, rather than take punitive measures themselves, the traditional councils judge whether offences are severe enough to be referred to either the police or the courts of law for punitive measures. Social control, in a number of cases, is exercised by associations—sanghas or sabhas or samajs. These are independently registered societies, different from statutory bodies and traditional caste and *biradari* panchayats. In some cases, the erstwhile traditional councils have been subsumed by these registered bodies. Table AII.3 contains greater details of such practices.

Table AII.3   Communities in Delhi with Reported Reliance on Non-state Legal Systems

S. No.	Community	Comments
1.	Agri	Powers of social control vested in traditional councils extend to 'irregular unions, illegal sexual intimacy, family quarrels, and community transgressions' (p. 22). Cases of thefts, homicide, and divorce are the domain of the state legal system.
2.	Aheria	Powers of social control vested in traditional councils extend to thefts and adultery. Rest of the disputes are the domain of the state legal system.
3.	Ahir	Informal council composed of village elders settle minor community disputes. Majority of social order is the domain of the state legal system.
4.	Anglo-Indian	The church handles dissolution of marriages. Divorce is not recognized, and annulments are approved and implemented by the church councils. Rest of the disputes are the domain of the state legal system.
5.	Arain	The local *anjuman-qaum-arain* (community council of Arains) handles all intra-community disputes. However, the authority of the anjuman has been waning in light of presence and acceptance of state legal systems.
6.	Baha'i	Social order in Baha'i is maintained by their three-level institution—the local spiritual assembly, superseded by the national spiritual assembly, coming under the Universal House of Justice. The local spiritual assembly is the primary adjudicator of social control. The assembly handles offences related to sex, economy, society, and religion. For the first three, the assembly is advisory in nature, people to follow the law of the land.
7.	Bairwa	The Delhi Bairwa Maha Sabha handles minor disputes, takes welfare measures, and looks after community upliftment. The sabha has incorporated the traditional caste panchayat. Cases of thefts, homicide, and divorce are the domain of the state legal system.

(Cont'd)

Table AII.3 *(Cont'd)*

S. No.	Community	Comments
8.	Bajania Nat	The Bajania Nats rely almost entirely on their traditional *biradari* panchayats, which handle cases of divorce, custody and maintenance of children, rape, theft, and disrespect of traditional norms. The statutory panchayat handles the planning and implementation of welfare and development projects.
9.	Balmiki	Powers of social control vested in traditional councils extend to settling matrimonial disputes, quarrels, and property disputes. 'Serious' offences are the domain of the state legal system.
10.	Banjara	Each settlement relies on an informal body of elders to settle minor disputes. The caste panchayat, now within the Banjara Samaj Seva Sangh, is the second level of social control. 'Serious' offences are the domain of the state legal system.
11.	Bansphor/ Banswal	Powers of social control vested in traditional councils extend to settling matrimonial disputes, quarrels, and property disputes. 'Serious' offences and inter-community disputes are the domain of the state legal system.
12.	Bauria	Powers of social control vested in traditional councils extend to cases of adultery, elopement, theft, and breach of customary norms.
13.	Bazigar	Bazigars rely predominantly on the Bazigar Samaj to settle all disputes and quarrels within the community. It is in rare cases that the police or the courts of law are approached.
14.	Bene Israel	A ten-member synagogue quorum determines cases relating to maintenance of social order. However, other administrative and judicial systems are equally relied on.
15.	Bhanbhunja	Powers of social control vested in traditional council—the Kashyap Rajput Sabha—extends to cases of family disputes, divorce, and welfare.

S. No.	Community	Comments
16.	Chhipi	Villages in Delhi with Chhipi presence usually follow a combination of state and non-state legal systems—traditional caste councils and statutory panchayats—to exercise social control. Welfare measures are handled by the Namdev Mission and the Rohilla Tank Shatrya Maha Sabha.
17.	Christians	Crimes such as sexual offences, disrespect of social norms and sacred laws, heresy, and disobedience of church edicts are punished by social boycott or excommunication by the church councils.
18.	Dafali	Powers of social control vested in traditional councils extend to cases of adultery, theft, and divorce. 'Serious' offences are the domain of the state legal system.
19.	Dhaiya	Caste panchayats maintain all social control. Infarctions are punished by levying cash fines, physical punishments, and social boycott.
20.	Dhanak	Caste panchayats are complex and exist on several levels. However, powers of social control vested in traditional councils extend to cases of matrimonial and property disputes. They are punished by cash fines and excommunication. In addition, Dhanaks also have an Akhil Bhartiya Dhanak Mahasabha, which handles social welfare and community upliftment.
21.	Dhariwal	The Jain sabha and its Hindu counterpart exercise social control to a limited degree. The state legal system is also followed.
22.	Dhobi	The biradari panchayats maintain social order. Symbolic as well as compensatory fines are levied for offences. In severe cases, members are also excommunicated. Among the Muslim dhobis, Islamic law is used to negotiate marriage and divorce transactions. 'The Dhobis rarely, if ever, go to a court of law' (People of India, Delhi, p. 189).
23.	Dom	Powers of social control vested in traditional councils extend to property, illegal matrimony

(Cont'd)

Table AII.3   (*Cont'd*)

S. No.	Community	Comments
		alliances, minor quarrels, and so on. 'Serious' offences such as robbery, theft, and homicide are the domain of the state legal system.
24.	Fakir	The traditional council of the fakirs handles cases related to land disputes and theft, while the masjid panchayat regulates marital disputes among Muslim fakirs. 'Serious' offences such as murders are the domain of the state legal system.
25.	Gaddi Muslim	Traditional panchayat regulates the observance of traditional norms. For other matters, the state legal system is relied on.
26.	Gaduliya Lohar	Traditional caste panchayats exert social control in all matters. 'No Lohar disputes go to the police or to the courts' (p. 215). Those refusing to follow the panchayat's verdict are excommunicated (panchayats regulate traditional norms, marital unions, and violence during drinking).
27.	Gharami	The traditional council exists to maintain social cohesion. Its punitive powers, however, are now diluted. The caste sabha mostly deals with marital problems and cases of divorce.
28.	Ghasiara	Powers of social control vested in traditional councils extend to matrimonial and other inter-community disputes. Property disputes and 'serious' offences such as robbery, theft, and homicide are the domain of the state legal system.
29.	Ghosi	The traditional council exists to adjudicate social irregularities, and the punishment is through social boycott or excommunication. The state laws and regulations are also followed.
30.	Giarah	Powers of social control vested in informal councils (registered societies which incorporate the erstwhile caste councils) extend to cases concerning property, marital disputes, minor quarrels, welfare, and social upliftment. 'Serious' offences such as theft and homicide are the domain of the state legal system.

S. No.	Community	Comments
31.	Gujaratis	The Gujarati Samaj negotiates minor disputes. 'Serious' offences are the domain of the state legal system.
32.	Jat	Powers of social control vested in caste panchayats extend to property, marital disputes, minor quarrels, adultery, and domestic disputes. In villages, the statutory bodies handle of welfare disbursements and development programmes.
33.	Jogi	Caste panchayats, with hereditary chieftainships and power to impose fines and excommunication, exist to maintain social order. The impact of the state legal system is minimal.
34.	Julaha	Village elders form an informal council to settle minor everyday intra-community disputes. Inter-community offences and those of a serious nature and general law and order are maintained through state systems such as courts of law and the police.
35.	Kabutari Nat	Inter-community social, legal, and economic conflicts are resolved by the caste panchayats. The local level panchayats handle issues of elopement, theft, marital disputes, disrespect of traditional norms, and insults to the traditional council. The main caste panchayat for the community is located in Alwar, Rajasthan. Punishments include cash fines and excommunication on refusal to comply with panchayat's verdict.
36.	Kachhi	Social reform and welfare measures are managed by the Kachhi registered society—the Nav Yuval Shakya Biradari Sudhar Samiti. The samiti occasionally negotiates minor issues relating to marital disputes, property disputes, and so on. Divorce and 'serious' offences such as theft and homicide are the domain of the state legal system.
37.	Kalander	A strong traditional caste panchayat maintains all social order, and punishments are in the form of cash fines and excommunication. Offences include disrespect of traditional norms, insulting the traditional council, gambling, theft, and so on.

(Cont'd)

Table AII.3   *(Cont'd)*

S. No.	Community	Comments
38.	Kandera	Caste panchayats, with hereditary chieftainships and power to impose fines and excommunication, exist to maintain all social order.
39.	Kanmaelia	Traditional caste panchayats handle most issues relating to social order. Islamic law is used to negotiate marriage and divorce transactions.
40.	Asthana/ Kayastha	Registered and democratically elected associations exert punitive measures such as social boycott for defaulters of social norms. In general, law and order is maintained through courts of law and the police.
41.	Khandelwal	A reformist association—the Anuvrata Samiti—regulates social life. The samiti also carries out welfare activities. Offences handled by the samiti are theft and disrespect of social norms. In general, law and order is maintained through courts of law and the police.
42.	Khatbune	The traditional caste panchayat (Labana Sikh Panchayat) exercises social control and handle cases of adultery, rape, disrespect of traditional norms, insult to the traditional council, marital disputes, and divorce. Punishments levied are in the form of cash fines and excommunication. Their reliance on the state legal system is limited.
43.	Khatik	Powers of social control vested in traditional caste councils extend to minor disputes, endogamy, breaking of betrothals, and so on. 'Serious' offences such as theft, robberies, and homicide are the domain of the state legal system.
44.	Koli	A traditional panchayat consisting of community elders plays an important role in everyday settlement of disputes. Disputes handled are usually related to property, money transactions, and irregular unions, and disputes that threaten the integrity of the community. The panchayat can levy punitive measures such as cash fines and excommunication. However, recently, the

S. No.	Community	Comments
		authority of the panchayat has been waning under the promise of an equal treatment before law in the eyes of the state legal system.
45.	Kurmi	The informal panchayat deals with cases of adultery, rape, elopement, disrespect for traditional norms, insult to the traditional council, and marital disputes. The police and courts of law serve as the second level of regulation, where cases of non-compliance are handed over.
46.	Lodha	Powers of social control vested in informal councils extend to property, marital disputes, and minor quarrels. Divorce and 'serious' offences such as theft and homicide are the domain of the state legal system.
47.	Lohar	Powers of social control vested in informal caste councils extend to theft, marital disputes, minor quarrels, welfare, adultery, rape, disrespect for traditional norms, and insult to the traditional council. The police and courts of law serve as the second level of regulation, where cases of non-compliance are handed over.
49.	Machhi	Powers of social control vested in biradari panchayats extend to adultery, rape, and disrespect to traditional norms. Islamic law is used to negotiate marriage and divorce transactions.
50.	Mahapatra	Mahapatras have official trade unions which have punitive powers to ensure professional integrity is maintained. Offenders are either boycotted by the community, or made to pay cash fines.
51.	Maithil Brahmans	The Maithil Association, a registered body, implements welfare programmes and maintains a small degree of social control by exercising powers of levying fines and social boycott on offenders.
52.	Mallah	Powers of social control vested in community panchayats extend to cases of minor disputes, social irregularities, and welfare activities. In general, law and order is maintained through courts of law and the police.

(Cont'd)

Table AII.3   (*Cont'd*)

S. No.	Community	Comments
53.	Mathur Chaturvedi	Powers of social control vested in the community sabha extend to maintaining the integrity and purity of the community. In general, law and order is maintained through courts of law and the police
54.	Mazbi	An informal biradari panchayat exists to settle cases on marital disputes and divorces. The council, however, has no punitive or rewarding powers. In general, law and order is maintained through courts of law and the police.
55.	Meena	Powers of social control vested in the caste panchayat extend to cases of adultery, dissolution of marriage, disrespect to the traditional norms, and can be punished through levying fines or through social boycott. The police and courts of law serve as the second level of regulation, where cases of non-compliance are handed over.
56.	Mohial	A caste sabha exists to maintain social cohesion of the community. Punitive measures include social boycott. In general, law and order is maintained through courts of law and the police.
57.	Musalman Rajput	Powers of social control vested in the caste panchayat extend to cases of adultery, rape, dissolution of marriage, disrespect to the traditional norms, and disputes over land and water. These can be punished through levying cash fines. The police and courts of law serve as the second level of regulation, where cases of non-compliance are handed over.
58.	Nalband	'Social Control is fully regulated by their traditional *biradari*' (p. 511), headed by a *sulemani* (chief). Only in cases where the biradari is unequipped to deal are the police and the courts approached.
59.	Naqqal	The dargah has a community panchayat to punish infarctions such as adultery and disrespect to traditional norms. Marriage, divorce, and inheritance are regulated by Islamic law.

S. No.	Community	Comments
60.	Naribat	Powers vested in the traditional caste panchayat extend to regulating disputes over property, matrimonial disputes, minor quarrels, rape, and adultery. The police and courts of law handle cases such as robberies and homicides.
61.	Nayak	Powers vested in the traditional caste council extend to cases of adultery, rape, and disrespect of traditional norms. The panchayat hands the offender over to the police and the courts of law for punishment.
62.	Odh	The traditional caste panchayat settles intra-community disputes and exercises social control. The police and courts of law serve as the second level of regulation, where those cases that have failed proper resolution at the hands of the panchayat are handed over.
63.	Pattharkat	Powers vested in the traditional caste panchayat extend to cases of adultery, rape, theft, insult to the traditional panchayat, marriage, and divorce. Punishments include cash fines and excommunication. For social control, the caste panchayat is relied on more than the state legal system.
64.	Patwa	Powers vested in the traditional caste panchayat (now a registered society called the Patwa Vaishya Mahasabha) extend to regulating and negotiating minor disputes. The panchayat does not hold punitive powers, but decides on cases to be taken to the police or the courts of law.
65.	Perna	Powers vested in the traditional biradari panchayat extend to rendering physical punishment and imposing fines for infarctions such as adultery and disrespect for traditional norms. A statutory village panchayat for the block within which the Pernas reside exists as well. However, Pernas have not been reported to be members of this panchayat.

(Cont'd)

Table AII.3   *(Cont'd)*

S. No.	Community	Comments
66.	Raigar	Powers vested in the traditional caste panchayat extend to adjudicating on marital disputes, cases of illicit sexual relations, and money transactions. Registered societies implement community welfare programmes.
67.	Saini/Sayani	The traditional caste panchayat, now incorporated within a registered society (All India Saini Sabha), handles minor disputes related to property and marriage, apart from its usual welfare activities. Sabha decisions are meant to be taken seriously, and families may be excommunicated on failing to follow a decision. In general, law and order is maintained through courts of law and the police.
68.	Sansi	Powers vested in the traditional caste panchayat extend to adjudicating marital and property disputes and upholding traditional norms. Punishments include cash fines, physical punishment, and excommunication.
69.	Sapera	Here, the traditional caste panchayat, which used to handle divorce, elopement, and marital disputes, has now given way to a more informal community council of elders, which settles minor disputes. In general, law and order is maintained through courts of law and the police.
70.	Shaikh Abbasi	Powers vested in the informal caste panchayat extend to adjudicating cases of adultery, minor domestic and property disputes, and minor thefts. In general, law and order is maintained through courts of law and the police.
71.	Sikligar	Powers vested in the informal caste panchayat extend to handling minor cases such as marital and property disputes. The panchayat does not practice any punitive measures—the objective is to reconcile the disputing parties.
72.	Singhiwala	Powers vested in the traditional council extends to all forms of social control. The council has the power to impose fines and social boycott. The

S. No.	Community	Comments
		panchayat's decision is binding. Even those cases that get referred to courts have no power unless ratified by the panchayat.
73.	Sunar	The traditional caste council, now incorporated within two registered societies, handles minor disputes related to property and marriage, apart from its usual welfare activities. In general, law and order is maintained through courts of law and the police.
74.	Teli	The traditional council composed of elders of the community handle minor disputes. In general, law and order is maintained through courts of law and the police.
75.	Tibetan	Tibetans in Delhi are concentrated mainly in two refugee colonies. The colonies have their own panchayat empowered to impose fines and physical punishment for offences such as adultery, elopement, and theft.

Source: Authors (based on *People of India: Delhi*, Vol. XX, general editor: K.S. Singh; editors: T.K. Ghosh and Surendra Nath [New Delhi: Manohar Publications, 1996]).

Gujarat

General Trends

1. The state of Gujarat demonstrates significant heterogeneity and high levels of syncretism due to various sects of different religions residing within the same state boundary. Communities are largely referred to as *nyatis* or 'occupational groups'.
2. In total, 289 communities have been profiled in the report.
3. Child labour, as well as bonded labour, in three communities, had been noted at the time of the survey.
4. Much like other states, male equigeniture is the rule, with 258 of the communities reporting this inheritance pattern. Nearly all (288) communities recognize descent in the male line, according to which the eldest son also becomes the head of the household.

5. Only 54 communities at the time reported women as having relatively 'equal' status, usually referring to equal opportunity in education and household matters. Political representation of women in Gujarat, much like national trends, is reported to be extremely low.

Overview of Report

The volume of Gujarat reports widespread prevalence of traditional councils—be it caste councils, traditional panchayats, or other forms of community councils. Of the communities profiled, 245 report reliance on some mode of traditional dispute settlement or the other. Gujarat also reports a large number of pastoral and nomadic communities, which, due to the nature of their occupation, remain predominantly outside the state legal system. Community councils which show affiliation based on jati are called *jati panchs*. In Muslim communities, jamats play an equivalent role. Community councils ensure social norms are followed, and infringements are usually punished by compensation or ostracization. Several communities report the presence of a *police patel*, a state-appointed headman belonging to the community, who works in collaboration with community councils.

While most communities rely on their traditional councils for marriage, divorce, and related issues, communities have been reported which do not have favourable attitudes towards the incursion of the state legal system into their practices. For example, the Gallaria community considers its own traditional council as the primary institution of adjudication. If at all cases in the community reach the state legal system, they do so only on the counsel of the traditional council, and members view modern state methods with mistrust. Communities lower in the social hierarchy report similar divisions as outlined in the introductory note—taking their disputes to members of the dominant castes, such as the Rajputs. Table AII.4 highlights some of the community legal practices of Gujarat. The number of communities highlighted in the table may differ from the total number of communities relying on non-state legal systems, since subdivisions and smaller groups within one community have been subsumed under the primary community name.

Table AII.4 Communities in Gujarat with Reported Reliance on Non-state Legal Systems

S. No.	Community	Comments
1.	Abdal	The traditional council, called the samaj, controls community affairs such as marriage, divorce, remarriage, and so on.
2.	Agaria	The Agaria jamat, consisting of community elders, settles various disputes such as divorce cases, and punishes accused members with cash fines. Statutory councils are also reported to exist.
3.	Agri	Traditional institutions of the *panch* settle disputes relating to divorce and marriage. The head of the panch is known as the *pramukh*. The panch can fine the guilty and impose social boycott. Statutory councils are also reported to exist.
4.	Ahir	A traditional council headed by a *patel* exists to regulate social affairs among some of the Ahir groups. Disputes regarding sharing of ancestral property, divorce, and regulation of water are managed by the council. Statutory councils take care of planning and implementation of welfare and development activities.
5.	Ansari	The Ansari community traces its origin from the state of Uttar Pradesh, and it is to the Uttar Pradesh jamat that the local elders refer their community disputes. Fines can be levied for misdemeanours such as consumption of alcohol, gambling, and prostitution. Not following the edicts of the jamat can lead to social boycott and excommunication. Statutory councils take care of planning and implementation of welfare and development activities.
6.	Arab	The Arab jamat handles and reviews the community's activities. Although the jamat keeps a close eye on members of the community, it does not have the power to impose punishments.

(Cont'd)

Table AII.4   *(Cont'd)*

S. No.	Community	Comments
7.	Attarwala	The jamat consists of one representative each from fourteen *khandan*s (families). Besides serving as an institution for social control, the jamat also works in the domain of social welfare, specifically, education and other community activities. The jamat does not have the power to impose punishments.
8.	Audichaya Brahman	Caste councils settle cases of divorce, remarriage, and other such disputes among community members. The state legal system is also approached for legal remedies. Statutory councils take care of planning and implementation of welfare and development activities.
9.	Bafan	The Bafan Nagiari Jamat settles disputes among members of the community.
10.	Bahurupi	A traditional caste council exists with the pramukh as its head. Every Bahurupi has to report to their pramukh about their movement, expenditure, and wayward members are punished with cash fines and social boycott.
11.	Bajania	The traditional council, panch, settles disputes related to marriage, divorce, and other quarrels between community members. Statutory councils take care of planning and implementation of welfare and development activities, and arbitrate inter-community disputes.
12.	Bamcha/ Bavcha/ Bavecha	The traditional caste council headed by the *mukha* maintains socio-cultural norms. Statutory councils take care of planning and implementation of welfare and development activities.
13.	Banjara	The traditional caste council headed by the pramukh handles matters related to adultery, elopement, rape, and theft. Statutory councils take care of planning and implementation of welfare and development activities. Banjara Muslims refer their disputes to their local jamat.

S. No.	Community	Comments
14.	Barda	Barda traditional caste councils are headed by a *mukhiya* or *pradhan* and deal with matters related to social issues, petty land disputes, and quarrels between members of the community. 'Serious' offences are dealt with using the state legal system. Cash fines and social boycotts are imposed on offenders. Statutory councils take care of planning and implementation of welfare and development activities.
15.	Baria	Barias have traditional caste councils called the *samaj panch*, which deal with cases of adultery, divorce, assault, and breaking of betrothals in the community. Statutory councils take care of planning and implementation of welfare and development activities.
16.	Barodia	Community panchayats headed by a patel handle family quarrels and other social and community disputes. While family quarrels are largely supposed to be settled within the family itself, in case they are taken to the panchayat, the decision of the patel is final and binding.
17.	Barot	Barot community elders use the means of negotiation and persuasion to settle community disputes. Statutory councils take care of planning and implementation of welfare and development activities.
18.	Bavri	Bavri community elders constitute the panch that deals with social and religious matters. Statutory councils take care of planning and implementation of welfare and development activities. Criminal and other major offences are redressed through the state legal system.
19.	Bawarchi	The Bawarchi registered jamat takes care of maintenance of socio-religious norms. However, the jamat has no punitive powers, and, at most, can pressure members of the community to comply. Statutory councils take care of planning

(Cont'd)

Table AII.4   *(Cont'd)*

S. No.	Community	Comments
		and implementation of welfare and development activities.
20.	Bhadbhunja/ Bharbhunja	The jamat maintains social order in the community, and levies cash fines on offenders.
21.	Bhambi	Bhambhi caste councils, panchs, maintain social order in the community, along with the statutory village panchayats. The panch looks after the welfare of community members and handles marriage disputes, property rights, and divorce cases.
22.	Bhand	The *jati panch*, or the traditional caste council, exists in some areas the community inhabits. A patel, or headman, is chosen from every group of 20–5 households. The council handles problems related to property, divorce, remarriage, and deviance from caste norms.
23.	Bhangi	Traditional caste councils exist to maintain social order, and the headman settles social disputes and maintains caste rules. Offenders are penalized by excommunication for short periods of time and are allowed re-entry into the community after payment of fines. Statutory councils take care of planning and implementation of welfare and development activities.
24.	Bharthari/ Barthari	Community councils comprising of elders maintain social order and handle disputes relating to divorce and remarriage. For criminal cases, law courts are approached. Statutory councils take care of planning and implementation of welfare and development activities.
25.	Bharwad	Traditional caste councils called *nyati panchayats* exist to maintain social order and handle disputes among community members, forcible abduction of girls, and dowry demands, among others. Local level issues are escalated to the

S. No.	Community	Comments
		main seat of the Bharwad community council at Rajkot, if the decisions of village-level authorities are considered insufficient. It is when the decisions at this level are also considered unsatisfactory then the members of the community approach the state legal system for redressal. Cash fines, after considering the economic condition of the offenders, are imposed. The power of the traditional panchayat has not declined even after the emergence of statutory bodies.
26.	Bhavasar	The Bhavasar community has a traditional council composed of community elders for the maintenance of social order. Criminal offences, however, are referred to the courts of law and other apparatuses of the state legal system. Statutory councils take care of planning and implementation of welfare and development activities.
27.	Bhil	At the village level, a council, or gaon panch, is headed by the patel, who is assisted by community elders, or *agewans*. At the regional level, one patel from each village acts as a representative. Village councils deal with smaller offences such as minor physical assault, illicit sexual relations, and material loss. These are usually punished with cash fines. Regional councils handle issues such as major injury, serious theft, incest, divorce, and so on, which are compensated with greater fines. Non-compliance with the orders of the councils is punished with excommunication. Statutory councils take care of planning and implementation of welfare and development activities.
28.	Bhisti	The community council, panch, is a powerful institution actively involved in the lifecycle of its members. Deviant members are punished with social boycott.

(Cont'd)

Table AII.4   (*Cont'd*)

S. No.	Community	Comments
29.	Bhoi	Bhoi traditional councils, the jati panchayats, look after cases of divorce, remarriage, and community rituals. Offenders are fined or excommunicated, depending on the severity of the offence.
30.	Bohra	The Bohra community and its several subgroups have organized jamats to take care of socio-religious affairs such as marriage, divorce, and other events. Deviance from community norms, in a number of cases, is punished with cash fines and social boycott.
31.	Borpi	The Borpis do not have their own traditional caste council, and refer their matters to the traditional, heterogeneous village panchayat headed by a patel from the Dhodia or Kokna community. The panchayat, comprised of village elders, handles cases of rape, adultery, elopement, and theft.
32.	Chakee	The Chakee jamat resolves marital disputes and handles cases related to divorce. Guilty members are required to host punitive feasts to redress their wrongdoing.
33.	Chamar	The Chamar caste council, called the nati panchayat, is headed by the *metar*. The caste council handles issues such as disrespect for traditional norms, insults to the traditional council, and violation of caste rules. Offenders are punished with cash fines, and in some cases, excommunication. Statutory councils take care of planning and implementation of welfare and development activities.
34.	Charan	A *nat panchayat* exists to maintain social order and resolve community disputes. Fines are imposed according to the nature of the crime. Compensation is given to aggrieved members. A traditional heterogeneous village panchayat, presided over by a *sarpanch*, also exists to maintain order.

S. No.	Community	Comments
35.	Choudhuri/ Choudhury	A community council, *the jati panchayat*, exists to maintain social order and resolve community disputes. Statutory councils take care of planning and implementation of welfare and development activities.
36.	Chunara	Community elders handle disputes and assist in maintaining social order.
37.	Dabgar	The caste council, panch, settles matters such as divorce and violations of caste norms. Offences, based on their severity, are punished with cash fines. Statutory councils take care of planning and implementation of welfare and development activities.
38.	Dafer	Dafers are itinerant agriculturalists without a stable community council. They live in small groups headed by *mukhia*s and are wary of approaching state apparatuses of law and order. The community is characterized by high degrees of conflict and factionalism.
39.	Damor	The headmen settle disputes with the help of the council of elders. Issues such as adultery, elopement, and theft, are handled by the council.
40.	Dangashia	Traditional jati panchs handle matters relating to remarriage, divorce, education of children, and property, and ensure caste discipline.
41.	Dasnami Bawa	Caste councils handle disputes between members of the community, divorce, and remarriage, and frame and regulate community rules and affairs.
42.	Depala	The Depala community council, headed by the jati pradhan, handles social matters.
43.	Dhed-Bawa/ Dhed	A council of elders headed by a pradhan looks after land and property disputes, and bride price, divorce, and remarriage matters.
44.	Dhobi	Dhobi Muslims have their own community organization called the jamat that handles all disputes. People disobeying the decisions of the

(Cont'd)

Table AII.4   *(Cont'd)*

S. No.	Community	Comments
		jamat can be punished. Statutory councils take care of planning and implementation of welfare and development activities.
45.	Dhodia	Dhodias are divided into clans, or *juts*, with a head, angewan. The angewan is assisted by community elders in settling disputes. Regional organizations, *chauras*, comprising 20–5 villages, also exist as the second level of dispute settlement.
46.	Dhuldhoya	Dhuldhoyas do not have their own traditional councils, but refer to other communities' jamats to conduct socio-religious affairs and settle disputes.
47.	Dubla	A traditional council, *nate panch*, headed by a *faliya patel*, handles social order and settles disputes. *Bar gram chaura* is another organization which takes care of inter- and intra-tribal disputes. Statutory councils take care of planning and implementation of welfare and development activities.
48.	Gadhai	Gadhai caste councils settle disputes and oversee welfare activities of the community. Disputed judgments of the council are taken to statutory bodies for redressal.
49.	Galiara	The Galiara traditional council is homogenous and settles disputes such as marital problems and divorce. Disregard for traditional norms is considered a serious offence. State legal apparatuses may be approached, but only at the discretion of the council members. Statutory councils take care of planning and implementation of welfare and development activities.
50.	Gamit	A council of elders, panch, settle cases related to adultery, divorce, breaking of engagement, and economic disputes.

S. No.	Community	Comments
51.	Gandhrav	The community council settles social disputes. Statutory councils take care of planning and implementation of welfare and development activities.
52.	Garmatang	The nat panch settles all village and family disputes, and is concerned with social welfare and upliftment of the community.
53.	Garo/Garoda	A community council, panch, handles social affairs and disputes. Offenders are punished with social ostracism. Statutory councils take care of planning and implementation of welfare and development activities.
54.	Garvi	A traditional caste panchayat called a *choubatia* maintains social order and is headed by a patel. The council settles quarrels relating to divorce and other cases. Statutory councils take care of planning and implementation of welfare and development activities.
55.	Ghanchi	An informal council of elders handles minor social disputes. Criminal cases are taken to the state legal system. Ghanchi Pnjaras have jamats for handling socio-religious affairs. Statutory councils take care of planning and implementation of welfare and development activities.
56.	Gihara	While there is no traditional council, the village head, *mukhia*, settles disputes within the community. Cash fines are imposed in case of deviance from traditional norms. Statutory bodies or courts are never visited. Adultery, rape, theft, and elopement are considered offences.
57.	Godha	Traditional caste councils settle disputes related to rape, elopement, and adultery. Statutory councils take care of planning and implementation of welfare and development activities.

(Cont'd)

Table AII.4   *(Cont'd)*

S. No.	Community	Comments
58.	Golarana	Village-level community councils enforce customary rules and maintain peace. Statutory councils take care of planning and implementation of welfare and development activities.
59.	Golsinghare	A caste council, panch, headed by an *adhyaksh*, settles social disputes. Cash fines and social boycott for deviation from caste norms and breach of marriage contracts, are usual punishments. Statutory councils take care of planning and implementation of welfare and development activities.
60.	Guggali Brahman	A caste association handles all social disputes internally, and they are never brought to public knowledge. Statutory councils take care of planning and implementation of welfare and development activities, and have no role in community affairs.
61.	Halaypotra	A caste council headed by a patel handles intra-community disputes. The community head, agayan, has the final say in all disputes. The council cannot impose punishments, and can only persuade members of the community to accept its verdict.
62.	Hati	A jati panch resolves community disputes.
63.	Hijra	Informal councils called *gurukuls* exist as the smallest unit for maintaining social order. These are headed by a guru. The organization and hierarchy of the councils parallels the state structure. Non-compliance with community rules can be punished with confinement, starvation, avoidance, neglience, torture, and excommunication.
64.	Humad	A traditional community council headed by a *seth* exercises social control. It looks after the maintenance of traditional norms

S. No.	Community	Comments
		and the settlement of minor disputes. Common punishments include cash fines, excommunication, and social boycott. Statutory councils take care of planning and implementation of welfare and development activities. Criminal offences are taken to the state legal system.
65.	Jalali	A jamat takes care of offences such as adultery, rape, divorce, property disputes, and disrespect to traditional norms. Guilty are penalized with cash fines.
66.	Jat (Muslim)	An informal council called the Kutchchi Jat Zamat maintains social order. A *karyavahi* committee convenes to punish offences, and defaulters have to pay cash fines, failing which they are socially boycotted. Remittance is allowed only after payment of further fines. Statutory councils take care of planning and implementation of welfare and development activities.
67.	Kadia	A council of elders helps maintain social order and resolves disputes related to marriage, death, and other domestic problems. Cash fines and excommunication are common punishments.
68.	Kamalia	An informal council of community elders handles intra-caste disputes. Statutory councils take care of planning and implementation of welfare and development activities.
69.	Kambodia Bhagat	An informal council of community elders handles intra-caste disputes. Statutory councils take care of planning and implementation of welfare and development activities.
70.	Kambasia	An informal council of community elders handles disputes such as infringement of community laws and social disputes between community members. Statutory councils take care of planning and implementation of welfare and development activities.

(Cont'd)

Table AII.4   *(Cont'd)*

S. No.	Community	Comments
71.	Kanphatia	An informal council of community elders convenes sporadically to handle community disputes. Statutory bodies play no role in community affairs.
72.	Kansaria	A council of elders, panch, headed by a patel, handle social affairs.
73.	Karadia Rajput	Traditional caste panchayats handle all caste matters and divorce cases. Statutory councils take care of planning and implementation of welfare and development activities.
74.	Kathodi/ Katkari	A council of village elders, presided over by a *mukhi*, handles matters pertaining to social order. Cases of divorce and illicit sexual relations are handled by the council. Statutory councils take care of planning and implementation of welfare and development activities.
75.	Ker	Caste councils at local and regional level exercise control over socio-religious affairs and have the power to impose cash fines and social boycott. Statutory councils take care of planning and implementation of welfare and development activities, and play no role in community affairs.
76.	Kharaua	Traditional caste panchayats handle socio-religious matters. Criminal offences are taken to the state legal system for redressal.
77.	Kharwa	All civil and criminal matters have to be brought to the traditional council, the panch. Approaching the state legal system is forbidden and the report goes on to say that often the police *refuse* to register Kharwa cases. The panch's verdict is final and binding. Exogamy is a punishable offence and can be punished by excommunication.
78.	Khaskeli	The Khaskeli do not have a council of their own, and refer matters to a local Sunni jamat. The jamat does not have punitive powers and

S. No.	Community	Comments
		can only persuade members to follow its edicts. Statutory councils take care of planning and implementation of welfare and development activities, and have no role in community affairs.
79.	Khatik	Village-level traditional councils exist to maintain social order. Next level of councils exist at the regional level. The edicts of the regional council can be challenged and disputes can be taken to the state legal system as well.
80.	Khatri	The Khatri jamat handles socio-religious affairs. However, it has no punitive powers and can only pressure members to follow its edicts.
81.	Kokna	Kokna jati panchayats maintain social order and handle cases pertaining to divorce. Statutory councils take care of planning and implementation of welfare and development activities.
82.	Koli	Some Koli subgroups have village and regional panchayats to maintain social order. The panchayats are composed of community elders, and the jati panch, at the level of the entire community, is the highest adjudicating authority. Divorce cases, breach of custom, and adultery are common cases handled by the traditional councils. Statutory councils take care of planning and implementation of welfare and development activities.
83.	Koshti	An informal council, samaj, takes care of issues such as divorce, marriage, and remarriage, and partakes in social and community reform.
84.	Kotwalia	An informal council of village elders settles local disputes.
85.	Kunbi	A traditional panchayat maintains social order and punishes offenders with cash fines and social boycott. Statutory councils take care of planning and implementation of welfare and development activities. In case members of the community find the panchayat's verdicts unfavourable, they take matters to the police and courts of law.

(Contd)

Table AII.4   (*Cont'd*)

S. No.	Community	Comments
86.	Labana	A village panch exists along with a higher, territorial *shahi panch*. These councils generally deal with divorce, remarriage, and adultery, and have the power to impose cash fines and ordain expiatory feasts. Money collected from fines is used for welfare activities. Statutory councils take care of planning and implementation of welfare and development activities.
87.	Lad Vania	Local and regional councils exist to handle community affairs and maintain social order. Disrespect for traditional norms results in social boycott.
88.	Lakhera	A caste panch maintains social order and looks at matters pertaining to local disputes and matrimonial problems. It has the power to levy cash fines. Crimes such as theft and murder are taken to the state legal system. Statutory councils take care of planning and implementation of welfare and development activities.
89.	Lamechu	A traditional council handles social affairs. Criminal offences are taken to the state legal system.
90.	Langha	The Langha jamat regulates community norms and endogamy. Exogamy is punished by excommunication. Statutory councils take care of criminal offences, and planning and implementation of welfare and development activities.
91.	Lodha	Caste councils comprising of five patels handle social disputes and divorce cases.
92.	Lohar	Traditional councils oversee family disputes, divorce, and marriage. Social boycott is awarded to those who commit rape, elopement, or adultery. Cash fines are also imposed for offences. In case of failure of traditional

S. No.	Community	Comments
		councils to settle disputes, the state legal system is approached. Statutory councils take care of criminal offences, and planning and implementation of welfare and development activities.
93.	Machiyar	The jamat handles all community disputes. In case of failure of traditional councils to settle disputes, the state legal system is approached.
94.	Madari	Madaris are an itinerant community. They have a traditional council for resolving social offences. Modes of punishment vary from an apology to the panch, to cash fines.
95.	Mahar	A council of elders, mandal, is headed by a *pramukh*. Mandals settle intra-community disputes pertaining to divorce and adultery. Fines are imposed on offenders.
96.	Mahyavanshi Vankar	Jati panchayats exist for the resolution of disputes in the community. Several levels of panchayats exist—at the level of the *tad* (a cluster of nine to ten villages), the *pargana*, and the nat (the entire community). Divorce, theft, and violation of community norms, are common matters handled by the councils. The nat can impose cash fines, and excommunicate offenders.
97.	Maiya	Village or caste elders settle community disputes.
98.	Maji Rana	Traditional councils deal with cases of family conflicts, divorce, theft, and other cases. Cash fines are imposed depending on the nature of the offence. Inter-community marriages are punished with excommunication.
99.	Makrani	The jamat maintains social order and punished offences with cash fines. In case of failure of traditional councils to settle disputes, the state legal system is approached.

(Cont'd)

Table AII.4 *(Cont'd)*

S. No.	Community	Comments
100.	Mandali	An informal caste council, jamat, maintains social order in matters relating to familial and marital domains. The body has the power to impose cash fines to offenders. Statutory councils take care of planning and implementation of welfare and development activities.
101.	Mangela	An informal community council comprising village elders handles issues related to divorce and physical assault. The study reports that those offenders who are reported to the police are nevertheless tried by the informal council as well. Cash fines are the preferred mode of punishment, and non-payment of fines can result in social boycott. Statutory councils take care of planning and implementation of welfare and development activities.
102.	Mang Kotwalia	A traditional panchayat headed by the patel takes cares of issues related to marriage and divorce and other problems of the community.
103.	Manihar	A community council exists, which is headed by the president, the *agresar*. An annual *mela*, fair, is held, where the members of the community convene and partake in social activities, and discuss and settle all community problems which may have taken place over the year. For urgent matters, meetings at short notice are often convened at the agresar's home.
104.	Mansoori	A traditional jamat composed of community elders settles disputes according to traditional norms and regulations, and punished offender with cash fines and excommunication. Statutory councils take care of planning and implementation of welfare and development activities.
105.	Maru Kumbhar	An informal council composed of community elders settles social disputes.

S. No.	Community	Comments
106.	Maru Vankar	Strong caste councils exist which enforce customary norms, and regulate matters related to marriage and divorce. Decisions are often reached in consultation with the heads of statutory bodies.
107.	Mewada	Community panchayats look after socio-religious affairs of the community. Punishments include cash fines, social boycott, and excommunication. Statutory councils take care of planning and implementation of welfare and development activities. Mewada Brahman communities report two levels of local councils, at the village and district levels. The village councils, *gnati panchayats*, handle everyday disputes. The district level bodies, *gol*, enforce customary norms in order to prevent infringement. Statutory councils take care of planning and implementation of welfare and development activities.
108.	Mir	Since the Mir does not have their own jamat, they associate themselves with other community jamats to enforce socio-religious order and settle cases related to marriage and divorce. Statutory councils and other state bodies have little involvement in the lives of Mirs.
109.	Mirasi	Traditional jamats headed by a pramukh handle social disputes. Divorce, adultery, rape, theft, and disrespect to social norms, are some of the common offences settled by the jamat. Punishments include cash fines and excommunication.
110.	Miyana	A traditional jamat presided over by a mukhi exercises social control. Offences such as theft or rape are punished with cash fines.
111.	Modh	Community councils at the village and the regional levels maintain social order.

(Cont'd)

Table AII.4   *(Cont'd)*

S. No.	Community	Comments
112.	Moghal	Since the community is not numerically significant, they do not have a pan-community council. However, they do have *mohalla jamat*s, or neighbourhood councils, which settle minor disputes and organizes welfare and cultural activities. Statutory councils and other state bodies have little involvement in the lives of the Mughals.
113.	Molesalam Girasia	Traditional panchayats maintain social order and punish minor infractions such as theft. Statutory councils and other state bodies have little involvement in the lives of the
114.	Multani	All Multani subgroups have their own jamats. A local caste council, called *sthanak jamat*, regulates matters related to marriage and divorce, and looks after the enforcement of customary norms. Unresolved matters can be taken to the state legal system for redressal.
115.	Narsingpura	The community council maintains social order and imposes punishments in the form of cash fines or social boycott. Statutory councils take care of planning and implementation of welfare and development activities.
116.	Nat/Nut/Nat Bajania	Strong traditional caste councils, panchs, exist at village and regional levels. All members are bound by the decisions of the council, and offenders are penalized. Marriage and divorce issues are settled by the panch.
117.	Natada	Traditional councils exist to solve inter-community disputes and other social problem. Offenders are punished with cash fines.
118.	Nayak (Muslim)	A jamat settles social disputes, and community members are obliged to follow its edicts. Punishments usually take the form of cash fines. Statutory councils take care of planning and implementation of welfare and development activities.

S. No.	Community	Comments
119.	Node	A jamat regulates all matters of socio-religious significance and imposes cash fines on those who violate community norms. Only when members of the community are dissatisfied with the rulings of the jamat, do they approach the police.
120.	Padamasali	A community council called the *nati panch* handles disputes. Heads of families are usually members of the nati panch.
121.	Padhar	At the village level, there is a headman, a *patel*, who exercises social as well as magico-religious control. The patel, along with the kotwal, comprise the territorial council, called the *bara gaon ni nyat*. At the level of the entire community, agwans, or clan leaders, are also included to form the samaj panch, which has the power to fine and punish those who offend community norms. Statutory councils take care of planning and implementation of welfare and development activities.
122.	Panar	The Panar community has a traditional *jamat* which handles matters such as adultery, rape, disputes over land and water, disrespect to traditional norms, theft, and divorce. Cash fines are common punishment. Inter-caste unions are punished with excommunication.
123.	Paradhi	A caste council called the *gnathi sabha* regulates social order. Offenders are usually punished with cash fines.
124.	Patanwadia	An informal council comprised of community elders manages everyday disputes. Statutory councils take care of planning and implementation of welfare and development activities.
125.	Patel	Community councils exist at the village level to exercise social control. Cash fines are usually imposed on offenders, and inter-caste

(Cont'd)

Table AII.4   *(Cont'd)*

S. No.	Community	Comments
		unions are punished with excommunication. Statutory councils take care of planning and implementation of welfare and development activities. Among Muslim Patels, the jamat exists to maintain socio-religious order. Offenders are usually punished with cash fines.
126.	Patelia	Village-level councils called nat panchs exist to handle disputes among community members, and conduct social welfare activities.
127.	Pathan	Traditional jamats maintain socio-religious order. Statutory councils take care of planning and implementation of welfare and development activities.
128.	Patni Vankar	A community panch manages social affairs and settles disputes related to divorce, remarriage, widow remarriage, and so on. Non-obedience of panch edicts are penalized and sometimes punished with social boycott.
129.	Patni Jamat	A traditional jamat maintains social order. Offenders are penalized with cash fines or excommunication. State legal apparatuses are seldom approached.
130.	Pinjara	A traditional jamat maintains social order. Offenders are penalized with cash fines. Statutory councils take care of planning and implementation of welfare and development activities.
131.	Pomla	Traditional caste panchayats headed by a mukhi convene to settle issues related to divorce, adultery, theft, and so on. Inter-caste marriages are punished with excommunication, other offences are punished with cash fines. Statutory councils take care of planning and implementation of welfare and development activities.

S. No.	Community	Comments
132.	Qureshi	A traditional jamat settles all family and community disputes. Offenders are punished with cash fines. People dissatisfied with the decisions of the council can elevate matters to the state legal system
133.	Regar	Informal councils comprising village elders maintain social control. Serious matters are elevated to the jati panch, a council at the level of the entire Regar community, located in Rajasthan.
134.	Rajput	Caste councils exist at the levels of the village, the *taluka*, and the district. The levels are hierarchically organized and dissatisfaction with the verdict of a hierarchically lower council can be elevated to the next level. Statutory councils take care of planning and implementation of welfare and development activities.
135.	Rangrez	A jamat headed by a pramukh maintains social order and settles disputes within the community.
136.	Raval	Traditional jati panchayats settle social disputes related to divorce, adultery, rape, theft, and so on. Cash fines and social boycott are common punishments. Statutory councils take care of planning and implementation of welfare and development activities.
137.	Raysipotra	Informal community councils comprising village elders settle disputes in collaboration with local Sunni jamats. Statutory councils take care of planning and implementation of welfare and development activities.
138.	Sadhu	Informal councils comprising community elders settle social disputes. Serious matters are often elevated to the state legal system. Statutory councils take care of planning and implementation of welfare and development activities.

(Cont'd)

Table AII.4 (Cont'd)

S. No.	Community	Comments
139.	Salat (Muslim)	A traditional jamat regulates socio-religious behaviour. Offences are usually punished with cash fines or social boycott. Statutory councils take care of planning and implementation of welfare and development activities.
140.	Salvi	A traditional caste council settles social disputes relating to marriage and divorce. Statutory councils take care of planning and implementation of welfare and development activities.
141.	Sanghar	Village heads called pramukhs together with regional heads called *jamothars* comprise the community council, or *gnath panchayat*. This council convenes to settles issues regarding sharing of resources such as water, and cases of disrespect to traditional norms. Statutory bodies play limited roles in their lives. Muslim Sanghars rely on jamats for the maintenance of socio-religious order.
142.	Sansi	A traditional council called the gnati panch maintains social order. Statutory councils take care of planning and implementation of welfare and development activities. Criminal cases are taken to courts of law.
143.	Sarania	Two levels of traditional council exist at the village and regional levels. Decisions of the lower level can be challenged at the next level.
144.	Sargara	Traditional councils headed by a panch maintain social order. All major and minor offences are dealt with by the council. Cash fines and social boycott are common punishments. Statutory councils take care of planning and implementation of welfare and development activities.
145.	Sheikh	Traditional jamats help regulate socio-religious order.

S. No.	Community	Comments
146.	Shenva	While the community has no organized caste councils, it takes matters requiring resolution to higher caste communities of the village. State legal apparatuses are seldom approached.
147.	Sikligar	Traditional councils comprising community elders settle disputes at both village and regional levels. Disputed decisions can be referred to the next level. Registering offences with the state legal system *before* the community panch is approached is a punishable offence. Offenders are punished with cash fines.
148.	Shravan	Traditional caste councils regulate the social lives of the people.
149.	Sindhi Luhana	Traditional caste councils settle all family and community disputes. Statutory councils take care of planning and implementation of welfare and development activities.
150.	Sipai Jamat	Traditional jamats maintain social order. Offenders are usually punished with cash fines or excommunication. Statutory councils take care of planning and implementation of welfare and development activities.
151.	Soni	Traditional councils called mandals handle social order and community welfare initiatives. Statutory councils take care of planning and implementation of welfare and development activities.
152.	Srimali	A traditional gnati panchayat maintains social order and conducts welfare initiatives. Serious offences are taken to the state legal system. Statutory councils take care of planning and implementation of welfare and development activities.
153.	Tai	A traditional jamat maintains socio-religious order and imposes cash fines on offenders.

(Cont'd)

Table AII.4 (*Cont'd*)

S. No.	Community	Comments
154.	Targalia	Traditional caste councils, panchs, maintain social order and punish offenders with penalties ranging from apologies to excommunication. Statutory councils take care of planning and implementation of welfare and development activities.
155.	Thakore	Traditional caste councils maintain social order and punish offenders with cash fines. Non-obedience of council edicts results in social boycott of the entire family of the offender. Inter-caste marriages are punished with excommunication.
156.	Theba	Community elders settle social disputes.
157.	Thori	Traditional caste councils maintain social order. Non-obedience of council edicts results in social boycott of the entire family of the offender.
158.	Tirgar	Regional level *pargana panchs* maintain social order. The verdict of the panch is final. Approaching state legal apparatuses without the consent of the panch is a punishable offence. Offenders are usually punished with cash fines.
159.	Turi	Community councils settle local disputes. Statutory councils take care of planning and implementation of welfare and development activities.
160.	Turk Jamat	Jamats regulate all socio-religious affairs. Cash fines are usual penalties. State legal apparatuses can be approached should members be dissatisfied with the decisions of the jamat. Statutory councils take care of planning and implementation of welfare and development activities.
161.	Vahivancha Charan Gadvi	Jati panchayats at the regional level convene to settle disputes regarding adultery, divorce, and rape, among others. Decisions of the jati panchayat are binding. Offenders are usually punished with cash fines or excommunication. Statutory councils take care of planning and implementation of welfare and development activities.

S. No.	Community	Comments
162.	Valand	Informal caste councils in villages with numerically significant community members maintain social order and settle disputes regarding property and handle cases of divorce.
163.	Vansphoda/ Bansphoda	Traditional councils headed by a patel maintain social order. Non-obedience of council edicts is punished with social boycott. Statutory councils take care of planning and implementation of welfare and development activities.
164.	Varli	A hereditary headman, mukhi, handles social disputes. He is usually assisted by community elders. Statutory councils take care of planning and implementation of welfare and development activities.
165.	Vayati	An informal council comprising community elders settles issues related to adultery, rape, theft, and elopement. Statutory councils take care of planning and implementation of welfare and development activities.
166.	Wagher	A community council, panch, regulates social order and handles disputes related to divorce, adultery, theft, and so on. Cash fines are imposed on offenders. Non-compliance with council edicts is punished with social boycott. Inter-caste marriages are punished with excommunication. Wagher Muslims have an equivalent jamat.
167.	Waghri	Minor disputes are handled by an informal council comprising community elders. Major offences are taken to state legal apparatuses.
168.	Wandharo	Community elders settle social disputes. Compromise is encouraged.

Source: Authors.

Himachal Pradesh

General Trends

1. Of the 116 communities profiled, 59 communities count dowry as an ongoing and socially necessary practice. Dowry, however, is claimed to be given mostly in kind. Most communities reported prior practice of bride price. Of those, 44 have reported a transition to dowry.
2. Nearly all communities show patrilocal residence (where the family resides in the paternal home), and most follow inheritance based on male equigeniture (where the property is divided equally among all sons). Only twelve communities give females the right to inherit property.
3. Child labour is prevalent mostly in pastoral communities.

Overview of Report

There is wide prevalence of traditional caste, community, and tribe councils of all the communities profiled, 37 of them rely in some measure on these councils for social control, either working alongside or largely ignoring the state legal system. Customary councils look after marital disputes and the enforcement and protection of traditional norms in most cases, and, in some, handle incest, theft, property disputes, and even rape. In communities where the customary councils practise greater power, the statutory bodies such as gram panchayats mostly handle implementation and monitoring of welfare activities of the state.

Himachal Pradesh (according to the communities surveyed) also reports significant incidence of division of conjugal rights—polyandry is practised in several societies, especially in Kinnaur and Spiti. Lineage, too, is sometimes matrilineal. However, there is low prevalence of education among girls.

Several villages follow a village deity (*deota*). The deota speaks through its oracle (*gur*), which is usually a man. Often, the gur, the traditional councils, and the statutory bodies work together to maintain social order. In several villages, the oracle has the ultimate decisive power. Going against the oracle is rare. And in some cases, the oracle, or the temple manager, is often the *pradhan* of the statutory body as well, replicating traditional and modern hierarchies. Himachal Pradesh, too, notes the presence of nomadic tribes and itinerant communities, which show minimal reliance on state legal systems either due to their culture of mobility and movement or through lack of access to facilities and institutions of the state legal system. Table AII.5 illustrates some of the customary and community-based legal practices in Himachal Pradesh at the time of the survey.

Table AII.5 Communities in Himachal Pradesh with Reported Reliance on Non-state Legal Systems

S. No.	Community	Comments
1.	Beda (Bodh)	Tribes that follow Buddhism are generally counted under Bodhs. Bodhs are mostly unaware of and have very little to do with the state legal system.
2.	Bhojki	Bhojkis are usually landless temple managers who rely more on their traditional councils for social control.
3.	Chuhra/Balmiki	Chuhras rely more on their traditional councils for social control.
4.	Dagi	Dagis rely more on their traditional councils for social control.
5.	Dosali	Dosalis' traditional occupation is making plates and cups from leaves. They have special forest rights. Statutory bodies are approached only after their traditional council is unable to resolve disputes.
6.	Gaddi Brahmans	Gaddi Brahmans rely more on their traditional councils for social control.
7.	Gaddi Rajput	Gaddi Rajputs rely more on their traditional councils for social control.
8.	Gaur Brahman	Gaur Brahmans rely more on their traditional councils for social control.

(Contd)

Table AII.5   (Cont'd)

S. No.	Community	Comments
9.	Gorkha	Gorkhas rely heavily on their traditional councils. However, the text is ambiguous about the extent of this reliance. Weightage on preferred means of settling disputes needs to be verified using other sources.
10.	Gujjar	The Muslim Gujjars in Himachal Pradesh are considered a Scheduled Tribe. They are a largely agricultural and pastoral community. They have special forest rights for grazing and foraging and have been allotted pastoral land. Nomadic Gujjars, due to their traditional occupation and lifestyle, are entirely outside the state system.
11.	Hadi	The Hadi traditional council had been defunct until very recently. However, it has seen a recent revival, mostly in order to mobilize scheduled caste status for the community.
12.	Hali	Halis rely more on their traditional councils for social control.
13.	Kanghigir	Kanghigirs rely more on their traditional councils for social control. Despite being economically linked to forest resources by virtue of their traditional occupations (Kanghigirs are traditional comb makers), this community does not enjoy special forest rights.
14.	Khampa	Khampas rely heavily on their traditional councils. However, the text is ambiguous about the extent of this reliance. Weightage on preferred means of settling disputes needs to be verified using other sources.
15.	Khasa	Khasas rely heavily on their traditional councils. However, the text is ambiguous about the extent of this reliance. Weightage on preferred means of settling disputes needs to be verified using other sources. Among the Khasas, the deota, or the village deity, is the presiding figure.

S. No.	Community	Comments
16.	Khatik	Khatiks rely more on their traditional councils for social control.
17.	Kinnaura	Kinnauras rely more on their traditional councils for social control.
18.	Mahajan	The Mahajan traditional council had been defunct until very recently. However, it has seen a recent revival mostly in the sphere of social reform.
19.	Malaneese	The Malaneese rely more on their traditional councils for social control. There is suspicion of state legal systems. Among the Malaneese, the deota is the presiding figure. They also claim an ancient parliamentary form of government—the *jayasthang*.
20.	Nalband	Nalbands rely more on their traditional councils for social control.
21.	Nar	Among the Nars, the deota is the presiding figure. The deota, speaking through the gur, or the oracle, collaborates with the traditional heterogeneous village panchayat to maintain order. The gur is instituted by the pradhan of the panchayat, and can be removed if unable to satisfactorily fulfil his duties.
22.	Nichar	Nichars rely heavily on their traditional councils. However, the text is ambiguous about the extent of this reliance. Weightage on preferred means of settling disputes needs to be verified using other sources.
23.	Noongar	Noongars rely more on their traditional councils for social control.
24.	Pajiara	Among the Pajiaras, the deota is the presiding figure. The deota, speaking through the gur, collaborates with the gram panchayat and the caste council to maintain order. *Pajiaras*, traditional temple managers, often themselves get elected into statutory bodies.

(Cont'd)

Table AII.5   *(Cont'd)*

S. No.	Community	Comments
25.	Pangwal Brahman	The Pangwal traditional councils work alongside the state legal system in maintaining law and order. Pangwal Brahmans enjoy special traditional rights over water. However, water rights are collective—about eight to ten households have special rights over one source.
26.	Pangwal Rajput	The Pangwal traditional councils work alongside the state legal system in maintaining law and order. Pangwal Rajputs enjoy customary forest and grazing land rights.
27.	Rawat	Muslim Rawats rely more on their traditional councils for social control.
28.	Rihara	Riharas rely more on their traditional councils for social control.
29.	Sanhai	Sanhais rely more on their traditional councils for social control.
30.	Sansi	Sansis rely heavily on their traditional councils. However, the text is ambiguous about the extent of this reliance. Weightage on preferred means of settling disputes needs to be verified using other sources.
31.	Sheikh	Sheiks rely more on their traditional councils for social control.
32.	Sikligar	Sikligars rely more on their traditional councils for social control.
33.	Sipi	The Sipi community rely more on their traditional councils for social control.
34.	Swangla	Swanglas rely more on their traditional councils for social control.
35.	Teli	Telis rely more on their traditional councils for social control.

S. No.	Community	Comments
36.	Vaish-Agarwal	Vaish-Agarwals rely more on their traditional councils for social control.
37.	Mahant	Mahants rely more on their traditional councils for social control.

Source: Authors (based on *People of India: Himachal Pradesh*, Vol. XXIV, general editor: K.S. Singh; editors: B.R. Sharma and A.R. Sankhyan [New Delhi: Manohar Publications, 1996]).

Bibliography

Acharyya, B.K. (1914). *Codification in British India.* Calcutta: S.K. Banerji.

Ackerman, B. (1993). *We the People* (Vol. I). Cambridge: Harvard University Press.

Agnes, F. (2008). 'Nation Building through the Enactment of the Hindu Code Bill: The Nehruvian Agenda' (Mimeographed). CSSSC Conference 'The Long 1950s'. Kolkata.

Ahmed, B. (1941). *The Administration of Justice in Medieval India.* Allahbad: The Allahabad Law Journal Press.

Aiyar, M.S. (2012). 'Local Government in Indian & China' [Comments]. *Brown Journal of World Affairs*, 8(1).

Alam, M. (2004). *The Languages of Political Islam, India 1200–1800.* New Delhi: Permanent Black.

Anthropological Survey of India (1996). *People of India: Delhi.* Vol. XX. General editor, K.S. Singh; editors, T.K. Ghosh and Surendra Nath. New Delhi: Manohar Publications.

———— (1996). *People of India: Himachal Pradesh*, Vol. XXIV. Edited by B.R. Sharma, A.R. Sankhyan, and K.S. Sharma. New Delhi: Manohar Publications.

———— (2003). *People of India: Andhra Pradesh*, Vol. XIII, Parts I, II, and III. General editor, K.S. Singh; editors, D.L. Prasada, N.V.K. Rao, and S. Yaseen Saheb. New Delhi: Affiliated East-West Press.

———— (2009). *People of India: Assam*, Vol. XV, Parts I and II. General editor, K.S. Singh; editors, B.K. Bardoloi and R.K. Athaparia. New Delhi: Cambridge University Press.

Arnold, D. (1994). 'The Colonial Prison: Power, Knowledge and Penology in 19th Century India'. In D. Arnold and D. Hardiman (eds), *Subaltern Studies VIII: Essays in Honour of Ranajit Guha*. New Delhi: Oxford University Press.

Arnot, Raymond H. (May 1907). 'The Judicial System of the British Colonies'. *The Yale Law Journal*, 16(7): 504–13.

Babbe, Paul T., Hon. T. Orth, and Charlie Wong (2016–17). 'The Honoré-Waldron Thesis: A Comparison of the Blend of Ideal-Typic Categories of Property in American, Chinese and Australian Land Law'. *Tulane Law Review*, 91: 740–88.

Bail, S. (2015). 'From Nyaya Panchayats to Gram Nyayalayas: The Indian State and Rural Justice'. *Socio-Legal Review*, 11.

Balakrishnan, C.J. (2008). 'An Overview of the Indian Justice Delivery Mechanism'. International Conference of the Presidents of the Supreme Courts of the World. Abu Dhabi.

Basu, D.D. (2002). *Durga Das Basu: Shorter Constitution of India*. Edited by Y.V. Chandrachud, V.R. Manohar, and B.P. Banerjee. Nagpur: Wadhwa Publications (13th Edition).

Baviskar, A. (2006). 'The Politics of Being "Indigenous"'. In B.G. Karlsson and T.B. Subba (eds), *Indigeneity in India*. London: Kegan Paul.

Baxi, U. (1976). 'From Takrar to Kara: The Lok Adalat at Rangpur'. *Journal of Constitutional and Parliamentary Studies*, 10.

———— (1986). *Towards a Sociology of Indian Law*. New Delhi: Satvahan Publications.

———— (1993). *Marx, Law, and Justice: Indian Perspectives*. Bombay: N.M. Tripathi; New Delhi: Lexis Nexis, Chapter 7.

———— (2003). 'The Colonial Heritage'. In P.L. Munday (ed.), *Comparative Legal Studies: Traditions and Transitions*. Cambridge: Cambridge University Press.

———— (2012). 'A Postcolonial Legality: A Postscript from India'. *Verfassung und Recht in Übersee/Law and Politics in Africa, Asia and Latin America*, 45(2).

———— (2016a). 'Towards an "Indian Legal Theory"'? *Indian Journal of Legal Theory*, 1.

———— (2016b). 'Demosprudence and Socially Responsible/Response-able Criticism: The NJAC Decision and Beyond: The Ninth Durga Das Basu Memorial Lecture WBNAJS, Kolkata'. *NUJS Law Review*, 9: 3–4.

———— (2017). 'Farewell to Adjudicatory Leadership? Some Thoughts on Dr. Anuj Bhuwania's "Courting the People: Public Interest Litigation in Post-Emergency India"—In Memoriam Justice Prafulchandra Natwarlal Bhagwati'. *Student Law Journal*, 4:1.

Baxi, U. and M. Galanter (1979). 'Panchayat Justice: An Indian Experiment in Legal Access'. *Access to Justice, Emerging Issues and Perspectives*, 3.

Beals, A. (1961). 'Cleavage and Internal Conflict: An Example from India'. *The Journal of Conflict Resolution*, 5.

Beals, A. and B. Siegal (1960). 'Pervasive Factionalism'. *American Anthropologist*, 62.

Benton, L. (2004). *Law and Colonial Cultures: Legal Regimes in World History.* New York: Cambridge University Press.

Benton, L. and Lisa Ford (2016). *Rage for Order: The British Empire and the Origins of International Law 1800—1850.* Cambridge: Harvard University Press.

Béteille, A. (1965). *Caste, Class and Power: Changing Patterns of Stratification in a Tanjore Village.* Berkeley: University of California Press.

———— (1986). 'The Concept of Tribe with Special Reference to India'. *European Journal of Sociology*, 27.

Bhabha, H.K. (1994). 'Of Mimicry and Man: The Ambivalence of Colonial Discourse'. In H.K. Bhabha (ed.), *The Location of Culture.* New York: Routledge.

Bhatia, H. (2001). *Mahrattas, Sikhs and Southern Sultans: Their Fight against the Foreign Power.* New Delhi: Deep and Deep Publications.

Bhuwania, A. (2017). *Courting the People: Public Interest Litigation in Post-Emergency India.* New York: Cambridge University Press.

Bilgrami, S.H. (1883). *Historical and Descriptive Sketch of His Highness, The Nizam's Dominions* (Vol. 1). Bombay: Times of India Steam Press.

Bodenheimer, E. (2011). *Jurisprudence: Philosophy & Method of Law.* New Delhi: Universal Law Publishing (7th Indian reprint).

Briggs, H. (1861). *The Nizam, His History and Relation with the British Government.* London: Bernard Quaritch.

Briggs, J. and J. Sharp (2004). 'Indigenous Knowledges and Development: A Postcolonial Caution'. *Third World Quarterly*, 25.

Butler, W. and V. Kudriavstev (1985). *Comparative Law & Legal System.* London: Oceana Publications.

Centre for Science and Environment (2008). *Rich Lands Poor People: Is Sustainable Mining Possible.* A citizen report. New Delhi: Centre for Science and Environment.

Community Forest Rights-Learning and Advocacy (CFR-LA). (2016). *Promise & Performance: Ten Years of the Forest Rights Act in India.* Citizens' Report on Promise and Performance of The Scheduled Tribes and Other Traditional Forest Dwellers (Recognition of Forest Rights) Act, 2006, after 10 Years of Its Enactment. Produced as Part of Community Forest Rights-Learning and Advocacy Process (CFR-LA), India (www.cfrla.org.in).

Canguilhem, G. (1991). *The Normal and the Pathological*. New York: Zone Books. Translation of *Le normal et le pathologique*.

Chakravarty-Kaul, M. (1996). *Common Lands and Customary Law: Institutional Change in North India Over the Past Two Centuries*. New Delhi: Oxford University Press.

Charles, M. (1835). *Report of the Select Committee of House of Commons* (Vol. III). London: J.L. Cox and Son.

Chatterjee, P. (1993). *The Nation and Its Fragments: Colonial and Postcolonial Histories*. Princeton: Princeton University Press.

———— (1999). 'Anderson's Utopia: Grounds of Comparison: Around the Work of Benedict Anderson'. *Diacritics*, 29(4).

———— (2011). *Lineages of Political Society*. New Delhi: Permanent Black.

Cohn, B. (1965). 'Anthropological Notes on Disputes and Law in India'. *American Anthropologist*, 67(6).

———— (1983). 'Representing Authority in Victorian India'. In E. Hobsbawm and T. Ranger (eds), *The Invention of Tradition*. Cambridge: Cambridge University Press.

———— (1996). *Colonialism and Its Forms of Knowledge*. Princeton: Princeton University Press.

Comaroff, J.L. and J. Comaroff (2009). 'Reflections on the Anthropology of Law, Governance, and Sovereignty'. In J. Eckert, F.V. Benda-Beckmann, and K.V. Benda-Beckmann (eds), *Rules of Law and Law of Ruling: On the Governance of Law*. Farnham: Ashgate.

Constituent Assembly of India Debates (1946–50). Retrieved from http://164.100.47.132/LssNew/cadebatefiles/cadebates.html.

de Cruz, P. (2008). *Comparative Law in a Changing World*. London: Routledge-Cavindish (3rd Edition).

Dam, S. (2006). 'Legal Systems as Cultural Rights: A Rights Based Approach to Traditional Legal Systems under the Indian Constitution'. *Indiana International & Comparative Law Review*, 16.

Dasgupta, S. (2014). 'A Language Which Is Foreign to Us: Continuties and Anxities in the Making of the Indian Constitution'. *Comparative Studies of South Asia, Africa and Middle East*.

Dash, T. and A. Kothari (2013). 'Forest Rights and Conservation in India'. In H. Jonas, S. Subramanian, and H. Jonas (eds), *The Right to Responsibility: Resisting and Engaging Development, Conservation, and the Law in Asia*. Kota Kinabalu, Malaysia: Natural Justice and United Nations University–Institute of Advanced Studies.

David, R. and J.E.C. Brierly (1985). *Major Legal Systems in the World Today*. London: Stevens and Sons.

Davis, D.R. (2010). *The Spirit of Hindu Law*. Cambridge: Cambridge University Press.

De, R. (2015). 'South Asian Legal Traditions'. In James D. Wright (Editor-in-Chief), *International Encyclopedia of the Social & Behavioral Sciences* (Vol. 23). Oxford: Elsevier (2nd edition).

Department-Related Parliamentary Standing Committee on Personnel, Public Grievances, Law, and Justice (2016). *80th Report*. Government of India.

Derrett, J.D. (1961). 'The Administration of Hindu Law by the British'. *Comparative Studies in Society and History*, 4.

——— (1968). *Religion, Law & the State of India*. London: Faber and Faber.

——— (1973). *History of Indian Law: (Dharmasastra)*. Leiden: Brill Publications.

Deshpande, V. (2006). 'Nature of the Indian Legal System'. In J. Minattur (ed.), *The Indian Legal System*. New Delhi: Indian Law Institute (2nd Edition).

Dirks, N. (1996). 'Foreword'. In B. Cohn, *Colonialism and Its Forms of Knowledge*. Princeton: Princeton University Press.

Donlan, S.P. (2015). 'Things Being Various: Normativity, Legality & State Legality'. In M.A. Heirbaut (ed.), *The Method & Culture of Comparative Law*. Portland: Hart Publishing.

Dumont, L. (1966). The 'Village Community' from Munro to Maine. *Contributions to Indian Sociology*, 67.

Durkheim, E. (1933). *The Division of Labour in Society*. Translated by G. Simpson. London: The Free Press.

Ehrlich, E. (2001). *Fundamental Principles of the Sociology of Law*. Translated by W. L. Moll. London: Transaction Publishers (Reprint of the 1936 Edition).

Eighth Law Commission of India. (1979). *Eightieth Report: Method of Appointment of Judges*. Ministry of Law, Government of India.

Elphinstone, M. (2011). *Report on the Territories Conquered from the Paishwa* (originally published in 1821). Cambridge: Cambridge University Press.

Fabian, J. (1983). *Time and the Other: How Anthropology Makes Its Object*. New York: Columbia University Press.

First Law Commission of India. (1958). *Fourteenth Report: Reform of Judicial Administration*. Ministry of Law, Government of India.

Galanter, M. (1964). 'Hindu Law and Development of Modern Indian Legal System' (Mimeo). Annual Meeting of American Political Science Association. Chicago.

——— (1966). 'The Modernization of Law'. In M. Weiner (ed.), *Modernization; the Dynamics of Growth*. New York: Basic Books.

————— (1968). 'The Displacement of Traditional Law in Modern India'. *Journal of Soical Issues*, 25(4).

————— (1972). 'The Aborted Restoration of "Indigenous" Law in India'. *Comparative Studies in Society & History*, 14.

————— (1981). 'Justice in Many Rooms: Courts, Private Ordering and Indigenous Law'. *Journal of Legal Pluralism*, 19.

————— (1989). *Law and Society in Modern India*. New Delhi: Oxford University Press.

Galanter, M. and J. Krishnan (2004). 'Bread for the Poor: Access to Justice and the Rights of the Needy in India'. *Hastings Law Journal*, 55.

Gardner, J. (2011). 'Can There Be a Written Constitution'. In L. Green and B. Leiter (eds), *Oxford Studies in Philosophy of Law* (Vol. 1). London: Oxford University Press.

George, J. and S. Sreekumar (1994). *Tribal Development Legislation and Enforcement*. New Delhi: Commonwealth Publishers.

Glenn, P. (2014). *Legal Traditions of the World*. New York: Oxford University Press (5th Edition).

Grigson, W. (1944). 'The Aboriginal in the Future India'. *Journal of Royal Anthropological Institute of Great Britain & Ireland*, 74(33).

Goudkamp, James (2017). 'Restating the Common Law? The Social Action, Responsibility and Heroism Act, 2015'. *Legal Studies*. DOI: 10.1111/lest.12158.

Guenther, A. (2006). 'Hanafi Fiqh in Mughal India: The Fatawa-i Alamgiri'. In R. Eaton (ed.), *India's Islamic Traditions: 711–1750*. New Delhi: Oxford University Press.

Gune, V.T. (1953). *The Judicial System of the Marathas: A Detailed Study of the Judicial Institutions in Maharashtra, from 1600–1818 A.D., Based on Original Decisions Called Mahzars, Nivadpatras, and Official Orders* (Vol. 12). Pune: Deccan College Postgraduate and Research Institute.

Halpérin, J.L. (2010). 'Western Legal Transplants and India'. *Jindal Global Law Review*, 2(1): 14.

Hardiman, D. (1987). *The Coming of the Devi: Adivasi Assertion in Western India*. Delhi: Oxford University Press.

Havell, E. (1918). *The History of Arayan Rule in India*. London: George G. Harrap and Co. Ltd.

Hooja, M. (2004). *Policies and Strategies for Tribal Development: Focus on the Central Tribal Belt*. New Delhi: Rawat Publications.

Jackson, P. (1999). *The Delhi Sultanate: A Political & Military History* (Cambridge Studies in Islamic Civilisation). Cambridge: Cambridge University Press.

Jaffe, J. (2014). 'Layering Law upon Custom: The British in Colonial West India'. *FIU Law Review*, 10: 85.

Jain, M.P. (2007). *Outlines of Indian Legal and Constitutional History*. Nagpur: Wadhwa and Co (6th Edition).

———. (2010). *Indian Constitutional Law*. New Delhi: Lexis Nexis Butterworths Wadhwa (6th Edition).

Jalal, Ayesha (2001). *Self and Sovereignty: Individual and Community in South Asian Islam since 1850*. New Delhi: Oxford University Press, pp. 150–3.

Jenkins, L.D. (2003). 'Another "People of India" Project: Colonial and National Anthropology'. *The Journal of Asian Studies*, 62(4): 1143.

Jois, M.R. (2010). *Legal and Constitutional History of India: Ancient Legal Judicial and Constitutional System*. New Delhi: Universal Law Publishing House.

Jones, Mary E. and Janki Nair (1998). *A Question of Silence: The Sexual Economies of Modern India*. New Delhi: Kali for Woman.

Kantowicz, H. (1937). Savigny & the Historical School of Law. *Law Quarterly Review*, 53: 326.

Kashyap, A. (1998). 'Parameters of Tribal Development: Some Key Conceptual Issues'. In V. Joshi and V. Joshi (eds), *Tribal Situation in India: Issues in Development*. Jaipur and New Delhi: Rawat Publishers.

Khare, A. (2012). 'Epilogue'. In R.A. Initiative (ed.), *Deeper Roots of Historical Injustice: Trends and Challenges in the Forests of India*. Rights and Resources Initiative.

Khare, R.S. (1972). 'Indigenous Culture and Lawyer's Law in India'. *Comparative Studies in Society and History*, 14(1): 71.

Klock, K. (2001). 'Notes & Comments, Resolution of Domestic Disputes Through Extra-Judicial Mechanisms in the United States and Asia: Neighbourhood Justice Centres, The Panchayat, and the Mahalla'. *Temple International & Comparative Law Journal*, 275.

Kolsky, E. (2010). *Colonial Justice in British India*. Cambridge: Cambridge University Press.

Kötz, H. and K. Zweigert (1992). *An Introduction to Comparative Law*. Translated by T. Weir. London: Oxford University Press (2nd Edition).

Kozlowski, Gregory C. (1985). *Muslim Endowments and Society in British India*. Cambridge: Cambridge University Press.

Kulshreshtha, V. (2005). *Landmarks in Indian Legal and Constitutional History*. New Delhi: Eastern Book Compnay.

Kumar, D. and M. Desai (1983). *The Cambridge Economic History of India* (Vol. II). Cambridge: Cambridge University Press.

Künkler, M. and Y. Sezgin (2016). 'The Unification of Law and the Postcolonial State: The Limits of State Monism in India and Indonesia'. *American Behavioral Scientist*, 60(8): 987.

Kurup, A. (2008–9). 'Tribal Law in India—How Decentralized Administration Is Extinguishing Tribal Rights and Why Autonomous Tribal Governments Are Better'. *Indigenous Law Journal*, 7: 87.

Lindsay, B. (1936). 'British Justice in India'. *The University of Toronto Law Journal*, 343.

Luhmann, Niklas (2014). *A Sociological Theory of Law*. Edited by Martin Albrow. London: Routledge.

Lundmark, T. (2012). *Charting the Divide Between Common and Civil Law*. London: Oxford University Press.

Maine, H.S. (1861). *Ancient Law: Its Connection with the Early History of Society, and Its Relation to Modern Ideas*. London: John Murray.

——— (1890). *Early Law and Custom*. London: John Murray.

Malaviya, H.D. (1956). 'Village Panchayat in India'. *Economic and Political Weekly*, 843.

Malinowski, B. (1924). *Crime and Custom in Savage Society* (Letter to the editor of *Nature*). Retrieved from https://wolnelektury.pl/katalog/lektura/crime-and-custom-in-savage-society.html.

Malmstrom, A. (1969). 'The System of Legal Systems, Notes on the Classification in Comparative Law'. *Scandinavian Studies in Law*, 13: 127.

Mani, L. (1989). 'Contentious Traditions: The Debate on Sati in Colonial India'. In K. Sangari and S. Vaid (eds), *Recasting Women: Essays in Colonial History*. New Delhi: Kali for Women.

Mantena, K. (2010). *Alibis of Empire: Henry Maine and the Ends of Liberal Imperialism*. Princeton: Princeton University Press.

Martin, J. (2011). 'Volunteer Police and the Production of Social Order in a Taiwanese Village'. *Taiwan in Comparative Perspective* 3: 33.

Matthai, J. (1915). *Village Government in British India*. London: Fisher Unwin.

Mendelsohn, O. (2014). 'How Indian Is Indian Law?' In O. Mendelsohn, *Law and Social Transformation in India*. New Delhi: Oxford University Press.

Menski, W. (2003). *Hindu Law: Beyond Tradition and Modernity*. London: Oxford University Press.

———. (2006). *Comparative Law in a Global Context*. Cambridge: Platinum Publishers (2nd Edition).

——— (2008). 'The Uniform Civil Code Debate in Indian Law: New Developments and Changing Agenda'. *German Law Journal*, 9(3): 211.

Merry, S. (1988). Legal Pluralism. *Law & Society Review*, 22.

Merryman, J.H. and R.P. Perdomo (2007). *The Civil Law Tradition*. Stanford: Stanford University Press.

Meschievitz, C.S. and M. Galanter (1982). 'In Search of Nyaya Panchayats: The Politics of a Moribund Institution'. *The Politics of Informal Justice*, 2: 47.

Miklian, J. (2009). 'The Purification Hunt: The Salwa Judum Counter-Insurgency in Chattisgarh, India'. *Dialectical Anthropology*, 33(3/4): 441.

Mill, J. (1848). *The History of British India*. London: James Madded.

Mishra, K. (2013). *Judicial Accountability*. New Delhi: Ocean Books.

Misra, K.P. (1964). 'Federal Judiciary in India: A Historical Retrospect'. *The Indian Journal of Political Science*, 25(3/4): 157.

Moncrieff, Abigail R. (2012). 'Common-Law Constitutionalism, the Constitutional Common Law, and the Validity of the Individual Mandate'. *Boston University Law Review*, 92: 1245.

Moncrieff-Smith, H. (1927). British India. *Journal of Comparative Legislation and International Law*, 9.

Monaghan, Henry P. (1975). 'The Foreword: Constitutional Common Law'. *Harvard Law Review*, 89(1): 1–45.

Moore, S. (1973). 'Law and Social Change: The Semi-Autonomous Social Field as an Appropriate Subject of Study'. *Law & Society Review*, 7.

Mukherjee, M. (2012). *India in the Shadows of Empire: A Legal and Political History 1774–1950*. New Delhi: Oxford University Press.

Munro, T. (1807). *Report of the Collector of the Ceded Districts 15th August 1807, on the Advantages and Disadvantages of the Zemindary Permanent Settlements and of the Ryotwar Settlements*. Papers Concerning Revenue, Administrative and Judicial Matters.

Murthy, H.S. (2010). *History of India*, Part 1. Lucknow: Eastern Book Company.

Nandy, A. (1983). *Intimate Enemy: Loss and Recovery of Self under Colonialism*. Delhi: Oxford University Press.

Nariman, F. (2006). *India's Legal System: Can It Be Saved?* New Delhi: Penguin.

Narwani, G. (2004). *Tribal Law in India*. New Delhi: Rawat Publications.

Nelken, D. (2008). 'Eugen Ehrlich, Living Law, and Plural Legalities'. *Theoretical Inquiries in Law*, 9(2): 443–71.

Nelken, D. (2009). 'Ehrlich's Legacies: Back to the Future in the Sociology of Law'. In M. Hertogh (ed.), *Living Law: Reconsidering Eugen Ehrlich*. Oxford and Portland: Hart Books.

Newbigin, Eleanor. 'Personal Law and Citizenship in India's Transition to Independence'. *Modern Asian Studies* 45(1): 7–32.

Örücü, E. (1996). 'Mixed and Mixing Systems: A Conceptual Search'. In E. Örücü, E. Attwooll, and S. Coyle (eds), *Studies in Legal Systems: Mixed and Mixing*. London: Kluwer Law International.

————. (2004a). 'Family Trees for Legal Systems: Towards a Contemporary Approach.' In M.V. Hoecke (ed.), *Epistemology and Methodology of Comparative Law*. Oregon: Hart Publishing.

————. (2004b). *The Enigma of Comparative Law*. Leiden/Boston: Martinus Nijhoff Publishers.

Padel, F. (1995). *The Sacrifice of Human Being: British Rule and the Konds of Orissa*. New Delhi: Oxford University Press.

Palmer, V.V. (2001). *Mixed Jurisdictions Worldwide: The Third Legal Family*. Cambridge: Cambridge University Press.

Pantham, T. (2008). 'Gandhi and the Constitution'. In R. Bhargava (ed.), *Politics and Ethics of the Indian Constitution*. New Delhi: Oxford University Press.

Parmar, Pooja (2012). 'Undoing Historical Wrongs: Law and Indigeneity in India'. *Osgoode Hall Law Journal* 49(3): 491–525.

du Plessis, J. (2006). 'Comparative Law and the Study of Mixed Legal Systems'. In M.R. Zimmermann (ed.), *Oxford Handbook of Comparative Law*. London: Oxford University Press.

Poitevin, G. (2010). 'Folk Culture, the Oral and Traditional Forms of Communication'. In Y. Singh (ed.), *History of Science, Philosophy and Culture in Indian Civilisation* (Vol. XIV). New Delhi: Longman Publishers.

Pool, J. and J. Starr, J. (1974). 'The Impact of a Legal Revolution in Rural Turkey'. *Law & Society Review*, 8(4): 533.

Pound, Roscoe (1921). *The Spirit of the Common Law*. Cambridge, Mass: Marshall Jones Company.

Rajan, R.S. (2000). 'Women between Community and State: Some Implications of the Uniform Civil Code Debates in India'. *Social Text*, 18(4): 55.

Rajput, R. and D. Meghe (1984). *Panchayat Raj in India: Democracy at Grassroots*. New Delhi: Deepa and Deep Publications.

Rankin, G. (1946). *Background to Indian Law*. Cambridge: Cambridge University Press.

Rawls, John (1999). *The Law of Peoples*. Cambridge, Mass: Harvard University Press.

Raz, J. (2012). *The Concept of a Legal System: An Introduction to the Theory of a Legal System*. London: Clarendon Press.

Razi, G.M. (1959). 'Around the World's Legal Systems'. *Howard Law Journal*, 5: 1.

Samal, A. (2003). *Institutional Reforms for Decentralized Governance and the Politics of Control and Management of Local Natural Resources: A Study in the Scheduled Areas of India*. Bangalore: Foundation to Aid Industrial Recovery.

Sarkar, J. (1935). *Mughal Administration*. Calcutta: M.C. Sarkar.

Sarkar, U.C. (1958). *Epochs in Hindu Legal History*. Hoshiarpur: Vishveshvaranand Vedic Research Institute.

Seervai, H. (2003). *Constitutional Law of India*. New Delhi: Universal Law Publishing (4th Edition).

Sen, A. (2009). *The Idea of Justice*. London: Allen Lane.

Setalvad, M.C. (1960). *The Common Law in India, Hamlyn Lectures*. London: Stevens and Sons.

Sharma, K. (1969). 'Civil Law in India'. *Washington University Law Quarterly Review*.

Sharma, R.S. (2015). *Aspects of Political Ideals & Institutions in Ancient India*. New Delhi: Motilal Banarasidass Publishers (7th Reprint).

Shiva Rao, B. (2010). *The Framing of India's Constitution*. New Delhi: Universal Law Publishing.

Siegal, B.J. and A. Beals (1960). 'Pervasive Factionalism'. *American Anthropologist*, 62: 394–417.

Siems, M.M. (2015). 'The Curious Case of Overfitting Legal Transplants'. In M.A. Heirbaut (ed.), *The Method and Culture of Comparative Law*. London: Oxford University Press.

Singh, K.S. (1968). *Outlines of Indian Legal History (Ancient and Medieval Periods)*. Meerut: Western Law House.

———. (1995). *The Scheduled Tribes*. New Delhi: Oxford Univeristy Press.

———. (2002). *People of India: An Introduction* (People of India: National series). New Delhi: Oxford University Press.

——— (2007). *Outlines of Indian Legal and Constitutional History: Including Elements of Indian Legal System*. New Delhi: Universal Law Publishing.

——— (2014). 'Special Editorial Note on Uniform Civil Code, Legal Pluralism & the Constitution of India'. *Journal of Indian Law & Society*, 5: v.

——— (2017). *V.N. Shukla's Constitution of India*. New Delhi: Eastern Book Company (13th Edition).

Singh, U. (2009). *Decentralised Democratic Governance in New Millennium*. New Delhi: Concept Publishers.

Singh, Y. (1973). *Modernisation of the Indian Tradition: A Systemic Study of Social Change*. New Delhi: Thomson Press.

———. (1988). 'Law and Social Change in India: A Sociological Perspective'. In R.F. Meagher (ed.), *Law and Social Change: Indo-American Reflections*. New Delhi: N.M. Tripathi Pvt Ltd.

Singha, R. (1998). *A Despotism of Law, Crime and Justice in Early Colonial India*. New Delhi: Oxford University Press.

Smith, V.A. (1906). *History of India: From the Sixth Century B.C. to the Mohammedan Conquest, Including the Invasion of Alexander the Great*. London: Grolier Society.

Spivak, Gayatri Chakravorty (1988). 'Can the Subaltern Speak?' In *Marxism and the Interpretation of Culture*, edited by Nelson and Grossberg. Urbana: University of Illinois Press, 271–313.

Statutory Commission (1930). *Report of the Indian Statutory Commission* (Vol. 1). Government Of India.

Strawson, John (1995). 'Islamic Law and English Texts'. *Law and Critique*. 6: 21, 22. Cited in Alpana Roy, 'Postcolonial Theory and Law: A Critical Introduction'. *Adel. L. Rev*, 29 (2008): 315.

Sub-Committee, North East Frontier (NE). (1948). *Report of North East Frontier (Assam) Tribal and Excluded Areas*. Government of India.

Sullivan, R.E. (2010). *Macaulay: The Tragedy of Power*. New Delhi: Orient Blackswan.

Sundar, N. (5 October 2006). 'Immoral Economy of Counterinsurgency in India'. Paper presented at the Yale, Agrarian Studies Program, Colloquium Series. 2007–8.

――― (2011). 'The Rule of Law and Citizenship in Central India: Post-Colonial Dilemmas'. *Citizenship Studies*, 15(3–4): 419.

Sunder, M. (2006). IP3. *Stanford Law Review*, 59: 257.

Supreme Court of India. (2007). *http://www.supremecourtofindia.nic.in/speeches/speeches_2007/ctm.pdf*. Retrieved from http://www.supremecourtofindia.nic.in

Tesón, F. (2015). International Human Rights and Cultural Relativism. *Virginia Journal of International Law*, 25(4): 870.

Thapar, R. (2000). 'Towards the Definition of an Empire: The Mauryan State'. In R. Thapar, *Cultural Pasts: Essays in Early Indian History*. New Delhi: Oxford University Press.

Tharoor, S. (2016). *An Era of Darkness*. New Delhi: Aleph Publications.

The World Bank. (2017). *World Development Report: Governance and the Law*. Retrieved from http://www.worldbank.org/en/publication/wdr2017

Thompson, E.P. (1975). *Whigs, and Hunters: The Origins of the Black Act*. New York: Pantheon Books.

Venkatachaliah, M.N. (2013). 'Common Law, Humanism, and Constitutions'. In P.I. Bhat (ed.), *Constitutionalism and Constitutional Pluralism*. New Delhi: LexisNexis.

Viswanathan, G. (1988). 'Currying Favor: The Politics of British Educational and Cultural Policy in India, 1813–1854'. *Social Text*, 19/20: 85–104.

———— (1989). *Masks of Conquest: Literary Study & British Rule in India.* New York: Columbia University Press.

Voell, S., N. Jalabadze, L. Janiashvili, and E. Kamm (2016). 'Introduction'. In S. Voell, N. Jalabadze, L. Janiashvili, and E. Kamm (eds), *Traditional Law as Social Practice and Cultural Narrative.* Unpublished. Retrieved from https://www.researchgate.net/publication/306388391_2016_ Traditional_Law_as_Social_Practice_and_Cultural_Narrative

Wagner, K. (2007). *Thuggee: Banditry and the British in Early Nineteenth-Century India.* New York: Palgrave Macmillan.

Warrington, M. and M.V. Hoeke (1998). 'Legal Cultures & Legal Paradigms: Towards a New Model for Comparative Law'. *International Comparative Law Quarterly*, 47: 495.

Warrington, M.V. (1998). 'Legal Cultures, Legal Paradigms and Legal Doctrine: Towards a New Model for Comparative Law'. *International & Comparative Law Quarterly*, 495.

Watson, A. (2001). *Society & Legal Change.* Philadelphia: Temple University Press.

Weber, M. (1919). *Politics as a Vocation.* Retrieved from http://anthropos-lab.net/wp/wp-content/uploads/2011/12/Weber-Politics-as-a-Vocation.pdf

———— (1968). *Economy and Society* (Vol. 2). New York: Bedminster Press.

Williams, R.V. (2006). *Post-Colonial Politics & Personal Laws: Colonial Legal Legacies & the Indian State.* New Delhi: Oxford University Press.

Winterton, G. (1975). 'Comparative Law Teaching'. *American Journal of Comparative Law*, 23: 69.

Xaxa, V. (1999). 'Tribes as Indigenous People of India'. *Economic and Political Weekly*, 34(51): 3589.

———— (2001). 'Empowerment of Tribes'. In D.K. Singharoy (ed.), *Social Development and the Empowerment of Marginalised Groups: Perspectives and Strategies.* Thousand Oaks: Sage Publications.

———— (2008). *State, Society, and Tribes: Issues in Postcolonial India.* New Delhi: Pearson Education India.

Young, R. (1995). 'Colonialism and the Desiring Machine'. In R. Young (ed.), *Colonial Desire: Hybridity in Theory, Culture, and Race.* New York: Routledge.

Zalaquett. (1983). 'An Interdisciplinary Approach to Development and Human Rights'. *Boston College Third World Law Journal*, 25/3: 28.

Zimmermann, R. (1996). 'Savigny's Legacy'. *Law Quarterly Review*, 112.

Index

About the Authors and Researchers

Authors

Mahendra Pal Singh is professor emeritus, University of Delhi (DU), India, and currently chair professor, Centre for Comparative Law, National Law University, Delhi (NLUD), India. Earlier he was vice-chancellor, West Bengal National University of Juridical Sciences (NUJS), Kolkata, India, chairperson, Delhi Judicial Academy, India, and chancellor, Central University of Haryana, India.

He has published a large number of articles in prestigious legal journals. He has also authored, edited, and co-edited several books including *The Indian Yearbook of Comparative Law* (editor since 2016) and *V.N. Shukla's Constitution of India* (in its 13th edition in 2017).

Niraj Kumar is assistant professor at NLUD, where he is also the project co-director of 'Exploring the Nature of the Indian Legal System' at the Centre for Comparative Law. He is the co-editor of forthcoming volumes such as 'The Indian Yearbook of Comparative Law 2017–2018' and 'Open Markets, Free Trade, and Sustainable Development—Perspectives from the EU and India'. His areas of interest include constitutional law, environmental law, and comparative law.

Researchers

Zainab Lokhandwala pursued BSL LLB from Indian Law Society's Law College, Pune, India, and LLM from NUJS. She is currently pursuing her PhD from SOAS University of London, UK.

Raikamal Roy completed her MA in sociology from DU and MPhil in social sciences from the Centre for the Study of Social Systems, Kolkata, India.

Saika Sabir pursued BA LLB from the University of Calcutta, India, LLM from NUJS, and MRes (Law and Society) from the University of Reading, UK.

Akhilendra Pratap Singh completed B.Com from the University of Allahabad, India, LLB from Banaras Hindu University, Varanasi, India, LLM from NLUD, and is currently pursuing his PhD from Università degli Studi della Campania Luigi Vanvitelli, Italy.